Achieving Excellence
in Guest Service

To my best Aussie mate

Achieving Excellence
in Guest Service

Josephine Ive

Hospitality Press
MELBOURNE

Hospitality Press Pty Ltd
38 Riddell Parade
P.O. Box 426
Elsternwick Victoria 3185
Australia
Telephone (03) 9528 5021 Fax (03) 9528 2645
E-mail hosppress@access.net.au

Achieving Excellence in Guest Service
First published 2000

National Library of Australia Cataloguing-in-publication data:

Ive, Josephine
    Achieving excellence in guest service

    Bibliography
    Includes index.
    ISBN 1 86250 484 9

    1. Customer services - Study and teaching. 2. Hospitality industry -
    Study and teaching. 3. Hotels - Employees - Training of.
    4. Etiquette. I. Title.

647.2071

Designed and typeset by John van Loon
Edited by Frances Wade (Wade's Distractions)
Cartoons by Robin Wade (Wade's Distractions)
Printed in Australia by Ligare Pty Ltd, Riverwood, NSW 2210
Published by Hospitality Press Pty Ltd, Melbourne (ABN 69 935 151 798)

Preface

ACHIEVING EXCELLENCE IN GUEST SERVICE has been written as an inspirational and informed reference and training manual for hospitality managers, staff and students—in fact, for anyone who has a genuine desire to improve their standard of service and its delivery. This book addresses the enormous subject of guest service and offers the reader a valuable opportunity to gain a detailed insight into creating and maintaining service standards and levels, while providing a practical means to achieve excellence.

Regardless of the styles of different establishments, good service is difficult to define, because each environment can offer a different expectation. However, it has been acknowledged throughout this book that an impression of good, unobtrusive service is one that remains long after the service has been received.

Although the book bases most of its text in the hotel environment, its scope is not limited to just this application. Many areas of the hospitality industry, such as motels, bed-and-breakfast establishments, restaurants, cafés, resorts, airlines, function catering businesses, hospital patient services, cruise ships, luxury yachts and casinos will all benefit from the knowledge and techniques covered in *Achieving Excellence in Guest Service*.

My extensive research indicates that guest service staff need exhaustive knowledge and information at their fingertips when it comes to handling guests' requests and meeting their expectations. Those guest service staff who are normally faced with these tasks are identified in the first chapter. In order to improve guest service—with the aim of achieving total guest satisfaction—I believe that a greater understanding of the guest is very important. The best way to gain this understanding is to turn the situation around and put yourself in the guests' shoes.

To that end, this book follows a logical path, chapter by chapter. It offers instructions, advice and inspiration to the newcomer, and a refreshing read to the experienced professional on service. It is also a reference book. It covers such subjects as where the guests come from, communications in a variety of forms, interpersonal skills, techniques for offering basic services, housekeeping skills and food and beverage service skills. It will also inspire the reader to extend that extra special service and help them understand, and become comfortable with, luxury and wealth.

The glossaries contain terms that are often heard in the various kinds of accommodation environments. Although most of them are food and beverage terms, guest service staff, managers and supervisors in all areas—from front office to concierge, from room service to butler—will find them useful.

The chapters contain anecdotes, real-life situations and training exercises. This is not just for the sake of innovation. All of them are designed to inspire the reader to create an individual style of guest service based on traditions, cultural differences, sensitivity and the desire to make a difference to someone else's life through the medium of service.

Assuming that you, the reader, are serious about service, I assure you that, although it can be tough—because service has so many intangible elements—it is a practical ability that can be developed with practice. As you read and study this book, you will not only gain more clarity about service, but you will also become better able to bring positive changes to your professional style. This will be in a way that is sustaining for your environment, your establishment, your colleagues and, most important, for you and the guest.

I want to emphasise that this understanding of guests' needs and expectations is only one tool. If you keep an open mind you will come to realise that service also has to be approached with a careful blend of emotion, logic and, most of all, respectful good-natured humour.

Josephine Ive

www.kingwest.com.au/butlers.html

Acknowledgements

Jean-Philippe Beghin, General Manager, Vice President, Imperial Queens Park Hotel, Bangkok, Thailand

Barbara Browne, The Terraces Miner's Cottage, Maldon, Victoria, Australia

CEIDA, Centre for Education and Information on Drugs and Alcohol, Sydney, Australia

Ric Fletcher, Beachhopper Water Taxis, Sydney, Australia

Jean-Luc Fourrier, General Manager, Hilton Sydney Airport Hotel, Sydney, Australia

Patrick Griffin, Managing Director, Observatory Hotel, Sydney, Australia

Elizabeth Hewlett, Salisbury, England

Hotel Catering and Institutional Management Association, England

Jim Irwin, Head of Department of Hospitality and Tourism Studies, Box Hill Institute of TAFE, Melbourne, Australia

Nick Jeffery, Front Office Manager, Hotel Inter-Continental, Sydney, Australia

Andrew Jessop, General Manager, Westin Hotel, Bangkok, Thailand

Darren de Lacy, Goroka Coffee, Niugini Coffee Importers, Claremont, Tasmania

Kate Lawson, Lecturer, Department of Hospitality and Tourism, Box Hill Institute of TAFE, Melbourne, Australia

Astrid Lewis, Tucker Seabrook Pty Ltd, Sydney, Australia

Francis Loughran, Food Service Retailing Australia, Melbourne, Australia

Greg Maloney, General Manager, Sheraton Sydney Airport Hotel, Sydney, Australia

Glenn Martin, Senior Customer Relations Executive NSW, Qantas Airways Ltd

Andrew Matthews, Wesley Tetuira, Stephen Burt, Jason Ellem, Magnums Butlers, Sydney and Melbourne, Australia

Emanuele Nasi, Resident Manager, Hotel Cala di Volpe, Costa Smeralda, Italy

Anne Parry, Waterford Wedgwood Pty Ltd, Sydney, Australia

Jean van der Puttan, General Manager, Hilton Hotel, Kuala Lumpur, Malaysia

Ritz Carlton Hotel, Kuala Lumpur, Malaysia

Catherine Seydoux, Champagne Krug, Reims, France

Kurt Wachveitl, Managing Director, Oriental Hotel, Bangkok, Thailand

Karen Wares, General Manager, Radisson Kestrel on Manly, Sydney, Australia

Contents

1

The essence of service

IT'S THE ESSENCE OF SERVICE LADIES AND GENTLEMEN. YOU MAY NOT SEE MUCH NOW, BUT IN TIME YOU WILL.

What is service?

Trying to define service is like trying to define love. We could start by expressing it as an equation:

SERVICE = technique + attitude

But that is just the beginning. There is much more to service than that—it is also the unique opportunity to make a difference to someone else's life!

In this book we are not just going to discuss service; we are going to discuss excellent service. Excellent service involves passion. Passion can also be expressed in an equation:

PASSION = energy + commitment

To develop the highest standards of service we need to develop a deep understanding of our guests' needs. This requires the right motivation.

How can we achieve all this? The first factor is willingness. This is a willingness not just to give service, but to really understand the person who is requiring service—the customer—and how and why they need it—our product—in the first place.

The second factor is grooming. This is not just grooming in the physical sense, though looking the best one can all the time is a crucial part of the big picture. It is mental grooming as well. Mental grooming supports both the attitude and the commitment. It not only makes us feel better; it also has a positive effect on our guests.

So how do we recognise that strange blend of realism and idealism which is great service? True service comes from the heart! When we feel excited about the part we are playing in other people's lives, it shows. The ability to make a difference to someone else's life is special, but you have to want to do it. Think about it: if there were no financial benefits, would you still, honestly, like being of service to other people?

Service is about commitment—a form of unwritten contract, if you like. If service is not delivered, not given properly or not up to the required standards, then the agreement has been broken. This contract can take several forms—verbal, non-verbal, implied or telepathic. In most situations, breaking an agreement can have legal implications, but this doesn't happen with service. If it did, lawyers around the world would be clapping their hands and jumping with joy.

Service should be taken seriously, and not just by paying lip service to this much-discussed subject. Such discussions always leave many issues unresolved while more pressing matters, such as the financial bottom line, are attended to. However, in this instance the bottom line is service, and plenty of it. If we blend service with passion it can happen.

If staff are encouraged to indulge customers by giving good service, both parties come away feeling good—it's a two-way street. But how do we make our guests feel really special?

Service is like playing the piano; you don't get any better unless you practise, practise, practise! Actors rehearse. They learn their lines, they pose in front of the mirror and they have numerous dress rehearsals, re-runs and 'takes' until they are sure they have got it right.

Actors take their talent for performance very seriously. Service staff should do the same. The hospitality industry is not so different from show business, if you regard the back offices as the wings and the front door as the curtain. What you have in between is one huge, wonderful stage, and a truly inspired and disciplined artist can create a masterpiece.

Guests, incidentally, don't just wander into your establishment because they want to sleep, have sex, eat and drink. No; they want to be entertained as well. They want to feel important. They want to be made to feel welcome, so that they can relax in the knowledge that they are being cared for in such a way that they will sleep well. When guests sleep well, they wake up feeling better and then they will come back. The showmanship that is genuine service can make this happen.

When a guest walks out of your establishment with a smile, floating on air, that is your product! And that is what makes the service industry such a challenge—putting smiles on faces.

So what is the true purpose of service? Could it simply be the delivery of a product—tangible or intangible—that goes beyond the guest's expectations? The ideas and philosophies that can be set in train when we try to define guest service can be useful when it comes to developing a beneficial, substantial and more personal level of service.

Do guests, in point of fact, know what they want? If they do, it will make our lives slightly easier. If they don't, we have to be one step ahead. Knowing in advance what the customer wants is difficult. However, if you can anticipate a need you won't have to solve a problem, and so you will save yourself a great deal of stress, time and energy.

To a certain extent, service can be construed and offered in many different ways, but the mood of the customer will affect how it is received. The customer's expectations of service can be high or low, but are usually based on the systems or culture that they are most familiar with. Depending on whether the service falls short of, matches or goes beyond these expectations, it will be regarded as poor, good or overdone. We do need to be sure that the service we offer is relevant to the guest's particular needs.

Let's take a look at the word 'service'. The dictionary tells us that it is the act of serving. This defines the physical aspect, but says nothing about attitude. It is the delicate balance of skill and attitude that dictates the level of service.

The attitude of the individual service-giver is influenced by four factors. The first is the desire to put another's needs first. The second is the working environment: for instance, a five-star luxury establishment as compared to one with a lower rating. The third is the need for financial remuneration. The fourth is an understanding of service through product knowledge and skill. We shall take each point on its merits.

The desire to put another's needs first

The desire to put another's needs first is often hard to acquire. It usually depends on individual personality: giving service comes more naturally and easily to some than it does to others. An employer needs to choose self-motivated, sincere, open-minded staff who are genuinely willing to offer a style of service that suits the establishment. Here attitude is all-important. It's hard enough to define service, let alone define the right attitude; however, it appears that ego may have something to do with it! Ego-stroking and attitude-tempering is a delicate area, and many human resources managers will readily admit that they spend a lot of time addressing this aspect. Whatever anyone says, we all have egos. The ability to use our egos effectively has a significant bearing on our attitude. Recognising how to indulge our own feelings should not be regarded as selfish. Instead we should acknowledge how beneficial it is when we set out to approach other people's egos more positively.

The working environment

Many establishments expect staff to be able to offer a great deal based on very little. The backdrop to successful 'attitude-building' has to be the care and welfare of staff behind the scenes. A sub-standard 'back of house' environment does little to engender high self-esteem in the staff. Treating staff with respect—as intelligent, caring and useful human beings—will raise their self-esteem and create a totally different atmosphere. Nurturing staff in this way will not only give them self-respect, confidence and self-esteem, but will also make them show more respect and care for the customers. This includes other staff, who are very important 'internal customers'.

By creating a comfortable working environment, such as providing good staff facilities and raising the levels of staff satisfaction, many establishments have found that they achieve much more in terms of customer satisfaction. The staff feel more important and vital; consequently their attitude reflects how they feel, and this effect ultimately flows on to guests and customers.

Financial remuneration

It is often true that, where no service charge is made, and where individual service-givers are responsible for their own actions, this system still has the edge. On the other hand, a system in which a blanket service charge covers all staff often generates an undesirably lower motivation level among those actually designated to deliver the service.

Product knowledge and skill

Product knowledge and skill almost hold everything else together. If the right personality and attitude are added, the result can be well-near perfect. Without good product knowledge, no service operator can hope to serve successfully. Skill can, of course, overcome this to a certain extent. With skill comes a need for attention to detail. Where does one gain this attention to detail? Is it inherent in one's character or can it be acquired? It can be either.

Many service operators are not in a position to criticise constructively, simply because they have no personal benchmark or experience against which they can make a comparison. They lack skill, product knowledge, attention to detail, quality awareness, and a desire to serve and inspire customers to relax, enjoy, spend money and come back. A lot of this can be gained only by exposure to the right information or the right situations.

Often the staff have never experienced the style of service they are expected to give. It's like asking chefs to serve food without even knowing what it tastes like! Unthinkable! How can they possibly know what they are trying to achieve in their pursuit of perfection? It's largely to do with training—not just skills—and carefully building a basis on which to develop the right attitude.

Understanding service

Some years ago, I was discussing service staff training with the general manager of a five-star hotel in Perth. The waitress in the lobby lounge took orders from us for tea and coffee. When she returned with the order in the space of ten minutes (and with no other customers to attend to), she had forgotten who had ordered the tea and who had ordered the coffee. Without checking with us, she simply placed the order on the table incorrectly. She went on to place the tea strainer straight down on the table without anything under it. The handles of the cups, jugs and pots faced away from us. The GM was embarrassed, to say the least, and apologised on the waitress' behalf, saying that he could not imagine what I was thinking of such service. I replied that he needed, perhaps, to consider how this young waitress perceived five-star service. Had she been exposed to this five-star luxury level of service? I asked. How could she possibly be expected to understand the style or type of service that was expected of her if she had never experienced it for herself?

The interpretation and perception of service should never be at second hand. As with so many things in life, we should resist the urge to form our opinions or make judgements from others' experiences. Many people who have travelled extensively will no doubt agree that there are some places, and some kinds of service, that they would sooner not travel to or experience again. But most would also agree that, given the same chance again, they—like me—would rather find out for themselves than take someone else's word for it. This is not because I am trying to be difficult, or am ungrateful for the benefit of their knowledge, but because their expectations may have been entirely different from mine, and therefore the experience would be different.

In conclusion, service is the unique opportunity to make not just a difference but, like love, to leave an enduring and pleasant memory that lingers on until the next chance comes along to create more good memories.

Who is giving guest service?

Before we look at the way guest service is handled, we should clarify just who is involved in giving this service. Obviously anyone who comes into contact with a guest or customer is responsible for offering and delivering a service. Each individual has a specific role to play in the day-to-day running of an establishment, whether it be a large

Guest service staff include *all* staff who come into contact with guests.

hotel, club, casino or cruise ship. In addition, all guest service staff should be well-trained, customer-oriented people who are attuned to satisfying the needs of customers and guests.

The progress of a guest throughout their stay will probably mean encounters with the following staff, all of whom will be expected to deliver some integral part of the 'total' service.

Doormen and lobby staff

The very first contact the guest has may be with the doorman, so it is important that door staff are aware of the immense responsibility they carry when they are 'passing the guest on'. The doorman is the 'greeter', so he should have a personality that fits with the establishment and its style. This initial interaction has to be as memorable as the final one, when a guest checks out. The doorman is responsible for opening car and cab doors, helping guests get in and out of cars, unloading the luggage and, generally, pointing guests comfortably towards check-in; parking guests' cars; keeping the forecourt clean and tidy; providing information and, of course, selling the establishment.

Chauffeurs and limousine drivers

Some of the large international hotels employ chauffeurs, or drivers, to drive guests to and from the airport to the hotel and on business visits. It is essential that chauffeurs who collect guests from the airport be familiar with the routine of 'meeting and greeting' guests in a warm style. Once they are in the car, chauffeurs have the chance to introduce guests to the new city and the hotel. Duties also include ensuring that guests' luggage is present and correctly stored for travel; driving guests safely to their destination; opening and closing car doors; keeping the car or limousine in near-to-perfect condition at all times and escorting guests to the front door of the hotel.

Front office staff and receptionists

Staff at the front desk have a number of roles: welcoming arriving guests, guest registration, check-in, compiling guests' bills and handling check-out, handling foreign currency exchange, providing information, dealing with complaints, selling the establishment, providing security services, maximising occupancy and generally communicating with guests.

Guest relations assistants

Guest relations assistants, or guest service agents as they are sometimes called, are important liaison staff between a variety of departments, particularly front office and rooms division. They escort guests from reception to their suites or rooms, inform guests of their rooms' facilities and are responsible for co-ordinating a number of options including dealing with guests' requests for room changes, handling complaints, and informing guests of any other facilities available.

Switchboard operators

Switchboard operators or telephonists are usually the first point of contact for guests and other people who may be visiting or contacting in-house guests or management. It is imperative, therefore, that these operators have a good, positive attitude and use all their abilities to impress the guest from the outset of the call. A clear, pleasant voice

and a good understanding of the establishment and its product are essential.

Switchboard operators need to be experts in communication, both internally and externally. The impression given to guests and potential customers is most important. A good working knowledge of the surrounding area is useful, since many guests call the operator first to find out information. Other inquiries from guests may include time zones in other parts of the world, directory assistance and times for various events and happenings. The role of operators depends a great deal on their professionalism. When receiving an inquiry, switchboard operators should be sure that they are passing the caller to the correct department. Like all staff in any hotel or similar establishment, they are very much part of the sales team.

Concierge or head hall porter

Often regarded as one of the management team, the concierge is the 'minder' of the establishment. This involves helping guests with all sorts of requests, from the simple to the seemingly impossible. The concierge offers guidance to guests on all manner of subjects as well as making events and happenings all the more memorable. He or she is also responsible for arranging tours, hiring cars and limousines, checking flight details, making onward reservations and ordering flowers and a myriad of other gifts at the drop of a hat. By necessity, the concierge has to be extremely knowledgeable about the city and the establishment itself.

Luggage porters

Luggage porters collect bags from cars, limousines or cabs and, once they have checked with reception, take the bags to the guest's room. Once in the guest's room, they then place the luggage in the appropriate place for the guest or the butler or valet to unpack, checking with the guest that they have all their pieces of luggage. On departure the porter then collects the bags from the guest's room, takes them to the entrance and is usually mindful that the guest has settled the bill before handing over the luggage.

Pageboys and lift attendants

These two positions are not so common these days. However, there are still some hotels in the world that prefer to offer these services. Pageboys are usually very junior members of staff and their main job is to run messages and 'page' guests either to the telephone or to another person waiting for them. Mostly they use a quaint old system involving a small blackboard and chimes.

When lifts were far less safe than they are now, it was essential to have a lift attendant. Even today, in some large hotels, they are visible and offer extra security for both guests and staff. In these days of dwindling personal services, their presence is often welcomed by guests, particularly in hotels where there may be some confusion over the layout.

Cloakroom attendants

These attendants are also essential, especially in establishments where there are a lot of functions being held. Presiding over the male and female cloakrooms, the cloakroom attendants are responsible for taking and looking after hats, coats and small bags. They sometimes come under the supervision of housekeeping or, depending on the organisation, may report to the banqueting department. On receiving a guest's clothes and other items they issue a ticket with a number; this is required later in return for the items. These staff have a service style of their own, by the very nature of their job, and often become lifetime 'confidants' of guests.

Housekeeping staff

Housekeeping staff include supervisors, room attendants, linen attendants and public area cleaners. Their responsibilities are primarily to clean and service the rooms, suites and public areas. Also, because they are visible, they are constantly asked questions about the establishment, the services and the surrounding area. Although some housekeeping staff are quite shy about their ability to communicate with guests, they are often fountains of knowledge and can be very helpful.

Mini-bar attendants

Mini-bar attendants are responsible for replenishing the in-room mini-bar service, and much of their job involves being in the room at the same time as the guest. Conversational skills and an understanding of interpersonal skills are essential. Part of their job is to document all the 'sales' from the mini-bar, as this affects the revenue of the establishment. The mini-bar attendant must be careful to check the mini-bar correctly.

Room service staff and waiters

Room service staff are responsible for the delivery of pre-ordered food and drink to the guest's room or suite. They should ideally have a flair for creating a 'mini-restaurant' within the guest's room. Their ability to anticipate guests' needs and feelings is crucial.

Club lounge staff

Club lounges have become very popular in international five-star hotels as a separate area away from the main activities of the hotel. Staff in these areas usually have the facilities to check in and cheek out guests and arrange matters normally attended to by other departments of the hotel such as concierge, room service, business centre and front office. They are also responsible for serving breakfast and beverages throughout the day along with mixing and serving cocktails, other alcoholic beverages and light refreshments in the early evening. An unflappable, diplomatic and outgoing personality is a useful attribute for this job, since many of the guests maximise the extra privileges for which they are paying.

Butlers and valets

There are several different levels of service that can be required by guests. Many international five-star hotels offer a butler or valet service. The butler or valet can offer a level of personalised service that exceeds not only the expectations of the guest but can make the difference when the service provided by the hotel is compared to the service in any other establishment. A butler or valet can be either male or female.

Almost always attached to the housekeeping department (although there are areas of crossover into food and beverage) the butler or valet often acts as a 'mini-manager', developing other staff members and offering a style of service that is quietly confident in its delivery. The main role of a butler is that of a personal assistant, anticipating the guest's needs rather than waiting to be asked. In addition to housekeeping and food and beverage service, the butler needs to be well versed in a number of other areas such as concierge work, often combining this with the role of a valet.

A valet, traditionally, is concerned with personal care and valeting. This involves the care and laundering of clothes, packing and unpacking of suitcases and a range of duties that make the personal side of a guest's life easier, such as shoe-cleaning, minor repairs to clothing and so on.

Business centre staff

Business centre staff need to be familiar with as many systems as possible in order to offer a range of office services to the guest. Their ability to handle many different requests is as essential as it is that they remain calm, personable and professional. Guests expect business centre staff to be able to manage a range of activities with the same sense of urgency that they are used to in their own offices. This sometimes makes the role of a business centre a very busy one.

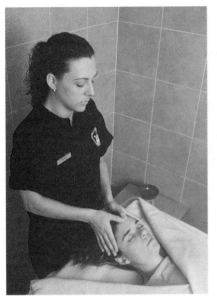

Fitness centre and health club staff

Fitness centre and health club staff are usually—and need to be—very fit. The image they present to the guests and members must be confident and professional. Most of these staff are also registered first aid providers, with a knowledge of sports medicine and other subjects related to healthy living. Their manner with guests, because of the more personal nature of the job, needs to be understanding as well as firm; sometimes guests do not realise their limitations with respect to health clubs. It is the role of the fitness and health club staff to advise guests on the use (and frequency or duration of use) of the equipment in the gymnasium.

Engineering staff

The engineering staff may seem a strange addition to the list of staff expected to give guest service, but very often they are requested to attend guests' rooms or suites. They need the special skills of handling guests in situations that may be uncomfortable, for instance if a piece of equipment or a system has failed and needs urgent attention.

Restaurant and waiting staff

All the food and beverage staff in the restaurants, night clubs, bars, lounges and coffee shops that are part of most large establishments are an important part of the sales team. Whether they are bar staff, hostesses, order-takers, waiters, waitresses, busboys, chefs, captains, supervisors or managers, the way they interact with guests contributes enormously towards the success of the establishment. Their performance becomes part of the overall concept of the particular food and beverage outlet.

Lobby shop personnel

Frequently the staff in the lobby shop are not employed by the establishment directly. However, since most guests are not aware of this fact, it is important that the staff in the lobby or concession shop give a good impression in their day-to-day dealings with guests.

In a small establishment

In motels, smaller hotels and bed-and-breakfast operations it often falls to owner-managers to fulfil many of the above function themselves,

with the help of family members or other casual staff. Fulfilling a guest's anticipated level of service involves wearing many hats! This can result in a great deal of pressure. However, for the dedicated operator, occupying many positions can have its own reward. There is a lot of truth in the old maxim 'If you want a job done properly, do it yourself!'

At least in bed-and-breakfast operations there is a certain amount of flexibility in as much as business can be paced to suit the needs of the owner, and owner-operators have much more freedom to decide whether to be open or closed.

In smaller establishments, dealings with guests are obviously much more casual in style, but the spirit in which service is given remains the same.

Service at a
bed-and-breakfast

First impressions are lasting impressions

A good 'first impression' is vital to the guest and the business. It is easy to forget that a guest has chosen (or the choice was made for them) to make your hotel, motel or bed-and-breakfast their home for the duration of their stay. This being done, they may be excused for feeling entitled to the same courtesy and treatment that they would normally expect in the comfort of their own home or cultural surroundings. In other words guests, from their point of view, are spending a considerable amount of money on the understanding that they will receive, at the very least, good service. They should not be disappointed!

In many cases, at the time they make the booking they have never actually seen your establishment. They may well have referred to a hotel or accommodation guide, booked through a travel agent, or simply phoned around until they found a place that fitted most of their requirements. That important first impression, therefore, may not be made face-to-face; it may well be conveyed through correspondence or by telephone.

Telephone courtesies will be covered in a later chapter (see pages 87-91). For the moment we shall deal with the first impression that a guest receives on arrival at a hotel. At this point the guest has just walked into a large and probably unfamiliar foyer and may well be over-excited, nervous and tired after a long flight. They may even have misgivings, brought about by some past bad experience with hotels—such as not having been expected, or having had a booking recorded inaccurately. It is up to the guest service staff to put the guest at ease as soon as possible and extend a real welcome to the hotel, thereby reflecting their own and the hotel's personalities. A 'tourist' guest may even start subconsciously evaluating the hotel on a value-for-money basis; business travellers, on the other hand, will be less likely to pay so much attention to this aspect—until they are leaving the hotel and review the account!

The same applies to smaller establishments—give or take the large foyer! Your personality will be even more intimately connected with the personality of the bed-and-breakfast or motel where you work. Many of your guests will be local holiday-makers, weary from the road. Their needs, however, will be much the same as those of international travellers checking into a hotel. Some guests may be from overseas, and unfamiliar with the ways of your country. A warm, welcoming reception will go a long way towards allaying their fears. Again, a positive impression made on your guests when they first arrive will be a powerful factor in whether they choose to come back.

Training exercise: step out of your shoes!

It's worthwhile, at this stage, stepping out of your shoes and into the guest's shoes. For the purposes of this exercise, use a hotel. It will obviously be impossible to do the same thing in a motel or bed-and-breakfast without looking like a very suspicious character indeed!

Select a hotel in your town or area that you are preferably not too familiar with. Arrive at the front door dressed and thinking like a guest. Take a note of your first impressions of the hotel: the entrance, the door, the staff and so on. Enter the hotel and imagine what it must feel like to be a guest doing this for the first time. Look around you and briefly take note of the surroundings remembering, of course, all the attendant emotions that guests feel on entering a hotel: tired, emotional, expectant or curious. Public areas of a hotel, particularly the lobby, are often grand and sometimes awesome; this can have quite an effect on an individual, and they can react with some surprising mood shifts.

This exercise should demonstrate to you how it feels to be on the receiving end, and should help you think about how you can position yourself more effectively to create a good first impression. See what the guest feels, not what you see from the other side. Record your feelings as accurately as possible and then indicate how you would like to be 'handled' through the various stages of the transition to a registered hotel guest.

Everyone should aim to give the establishment a 'guest-pleasing' personality right from the outset, so that a guest approaching a staff member will gain an immediate impression of friendly competence.

Remember that the guest who is mishandled at this stage is less likely to return. A satisfied guest, on the other hand, is a mobile advertisement and may well become a regular who will recommend your place to friends and colleagues.

You can see from all this that it is not enough for guest service staff just to impress a guest with their competency. A warm welcome is as essential a part of this first impression as it is a part of good manners.

There are a number of issues, therefore, that should be addressed at this stage: in particular, what constitutes a good first impression and, secondly, what form this first impression is likely to take.

Group discussion points

When people come into contact with you, either personally or by telephone, how soon do they form an impression of you? Turn the question around. How quickly do you form perceptions and feelings about people from whom you buy? And here is another question. What are the factors that influence these feelings and perceptions?

What does the guest see first?

The truth of the matter is that most of us quickly form our first impressions of people from their initial appearance. We often decide subliminally whether we like people, feel good about them, or want to do business with them in the first few seconds of contact. It all takes place on a subconscious, intuitive level.

It happens very quickly. Incredibly, people form eleven impressions of you in the first seven seconds of contact! When they are asked what the first of these eleven impressions in seven seconds may be, the answer is usually 'A smile'. Well, that may be partly true, but the real answers deal with more basic details.

Consider, if you can, the moment you saw a particular person for the first time. Did you really see their smile first? I think not. It is more likely that you observed whether they were male or female, the colour of their skin, their height, their build or size, whether they had two legs, two arms, a nose and two eyes, the colour of their eyes, the style of their dress, whether they were wearing glasses and so on. This swift assessment having been made, a mental note would then have been taken of posture and attitude.

How can we influence this first impression?

Attitude

To generate a good impression, the right attitude must be adopted. If a positive and excited attitude is conveyed, the response will be immediately apparent. This may be shown simply by the expression on the recipient's face or by the words they use. An enthusiastic approach to any situation appears to net the best response. Put simply, you can only hope to gain from a situation what you are willing to put into it.

The ability to tune the world out and tune the guest in is achievable with practice. Admittedly, when you are standing or sitting at a desk you have to concentrate with your head down. (How else can you see what you are doing?)

But when a guest approaches, if you are able to bring your head up with a smile—no 'cut and paste'—you promote several good impressions. The first is that you are pleased to see the guest and the second is that you are enjoying your job. This offers a two-way boost of confidence. How well you have communicated a good first impression will be measured by the response you receive. Further to this, you have to be able to gauge that response and assimilate the information quickly so that you can ensure that the impression you are making continues to be a positive one.

Often one of these impressions—attitude—is overlooked, though it is the underlying behaviour to a positive intention. A positive attitude will achieve success. In the same way that donning a uniform affects how you apply yourself, attitudes are often subjected to the same process. Attitude was touched on briefly at the beginning of this chapter as being an important component of good service. Adopting the right attitude is essential, because guests are very sensitive to the underlying emotions that can cause your attitude to shift. Just by look-

ing at another person we tend, rightly or wrongly, to make an instant assessment of their wealth or their status in life, and can inadvertently and swiftly change our attitude accordingly. By carefully monitoring our reactions we can reduce the risk of offending other people.

Experts in neuro-linguistic development suggest that 'pacing' be engaged as a useful tool to help us enter another person's world (see pages 16-17). Put simply, this means that we must seek first to understand before we can be understood. The first training exercise in this chapter should have helped you substantially towards achieving this level of understanding. We have to establish a connection. The next chapter, 'Where do our guests come from?' will help you move closer to this goal by developing the necessary skills to gracefully enter the other person's world, thus making it more comfortable for both yourself and the guest.

Posture

Attitude can be linked to posture. Words like 'graceful' and 'elegant' are often the first words that come to mind when we set out to describe good posture.

Poor posture not only affects our work by causing health problems; it also conveys a lack of approachability. If someone is standing facing away from you or with their back to you, it is harder to approach them effectively (apart from the protocol involved) and create a good impression at the same time. Facing another person with full and good posture shows a willingness to offer service. The manner in which you walk towards them will influence and affect their immediate impression of you.

Training exercise: 'dropped coins'

Good deportment is as essential to good attitude as it is to good health. Too many people walk with their heads down, apparently looking for dropped coins. It's probably better to assume that there is more likelihood of money growing on trees and to look up instead! Practise good deportment by walking with a book placed squarely on your head. If you find this difficult to begin with, perhaps your deportment and posture do need some revision. Although it may seem a slightly old-fashioned notion, if you take this exercise seriously it will help to reconfigure your body so that it gives a more acceptable impression. Practise walking straight and upright with your head up (but not too much), your arms moving gracefully at your sides, your shoulders relaxed and your hips in line with your head. Eventually you will find it quite easy to adopt a comfortable posture that will increase your confidence enormously and create what may be termed as a 'presence'.

If you watch successful people closely, you will usually notice that they exude a distinct aura—a presence or charisma. Although it is hard to define, this plays a large part in creating the setting for the scene that will follow. Acquiring such an attribute involves increasing one's poise, self-assurance and confidence. 'Walk tall' may sound like an over-used cliché, but in this sense it refers not only to the physical state, but also to the state of mind or attitude.

Pacing and rapport

The two words 'graceful' and 'elegant' emerge again when we discuss techniques for building rapport. When we meet someone for the first time, we naturally look at their overall appearance. From this we can develop the ability to pace them. Pacing another person should not be confused with imitation; it would be better to describe it as trying subtly to influence their next move.

We see and hear examples of pacing all around us. Look at a group of friends walking together. Their postures will often be virtually identical, their voices will adopt similar tones, and their gestures will be similar.

There are two types of pacing: mirroring and unconscious mirroring. All of us mirror unconsciously in the company of people we are comfortable with, or people we want to get to know well.

Adopting a similar posture to that of the person with whom we want to communicate, apart from being a form of pacing, is another component in building rapport. In a later chapter we shall deal with body language and how we can improve our level of rapport with others (see pages 60–63). When we learn to pace successfully, the other person relaxes and becomes more comfortable and the channels of communication open for a much easier flow.

Backdrop

I was sitting in a hotel lobby bar with a training colleague in Phuket, Thailand. Happily chatting about work, of course, we became increasingly aware of a 'backdrop' that quickly began to irritate us. All the floors had ceramic tiles, so noise levels were higher than normal. But above this we noticed that several members of staff who passed through the area did not realise that, rather than just walking, they were scuffing and dragging their shoes at the same time. This very action gave an impression of low spirits and a tired attitude to their work. Although staff may consider this normal, many people (including guests) don't. Partly because of their own cultural norms, guests can interpret it as an indication of low energy levels and self-esteem and find it quite frustrating.

So you can see there is very little time to ensure that our greeting is understood and well received! Additionally, good posture or pacing can lead others to follow suit and make the whole process of greeting and setting people at ease a lot simpler.

Non-verbal expression

Eye contact, attitude, posture, the ability to break preoccupation and good presentation will all make an immediately favourable impact on people. It can't be explained with logic; it all happens on an emotional level. Non-verbal gestures, body language and facial expression will also make quick subliminal impressions on people.

Your initial greeting or impression should not just be verbal. It should, even when you are taken by surprise, also illustrate your sincerity, genuine interest and excitement about who you are and what you do. These are the factors that put people at ease and make them feel welcome. Good customer service isn't just about painting a smile on your face and performing certain actions because you are expected to do so. People—guests and customers alike—can quickly see through these thinly-veiled attempts at 'niceness'.

Verbal expression

However good a first impression may be visually, it can be quickly destroyed the moment you open your mouth. When you open your mouth people don't always hear what you say (as you will learn in Chapter 4); they see your teeth or your smile. Please make sure they are both in good condition! Once you start to speak, ensure that the 'volume control' is at the correct level—some people are embarrassed if the whole area can hear what is being said, while others will find it frustrating if you speak too softly as though you are frightened of what you are saying. A guest who has just walked in from a noisy street will have their hearing attuned differently from that of a guest who has just come from their quiet guest room.

Take steps to practise speaking clearly; this pays dividends. Otherwise you will spend half your time repeating yourself. You should also be sure of the correct pronunciation of certain words.

Once you have the volume sorted out, the next step is to regulate the tone of your voice. However much you are aware of the volume and clarity levels of your speech, the tone you use for certain sentences or comments can change the meaning beyond retrieval. Even the simplest questions, such as 'How may I help you?' can be coloured by your tone. Sarcasm and disdain are two styles of 'tone misuse' that immediately spring to mind. On the positive side, though, it should become easier with practice to convey caring and cheerfulness through the tone of your voice.

Training exercise: the four Cs

Consider the four Cs that can be applied to speech: Control, Clarity, Caring and Cheerfulness. Write a script for a new guest service staff member that will offer an appropriate greeting for a regular guest or convey the basic facts about a guest room, for instance. Practise your script and those of others in a role-play situation if possible. Test out some of your 'lines' in different formats, using a different tone of voice to imply a different meaning. Take note of the reaction to some of these tones. In addition, list some of the more difficult words to pronounce and test yourself and others in your group.

This exercise will make you more aware of how it feels when common courtesies are offered to you.

What is it about the way people speak that sometimes makes you feel great? It will be at least one of the four Cs. This is a form of pacing. They are pacing you. Notice how you feel when people say, not just with their words but with their actions: 'Welcome to the Hotel ... Mr/Mrs ... We are so pleased to see you again, and looking so well!' (In fact, what they are really saying is 'Hey, you are the guest and you are paying my salary! Thank you!') With sensitively chosen vocabulary— in other words using tact—and the correct volume and tone you can become really professional at handling people and achieving an outcome that will leave everyone feeling better.

So if you want to stand out from the crowd—practise, practise, practise! It is the only way in which you will eventually be able to do these things unconsciously. You will then have the most positive impact on others. You will consistently put them at their ease and make them feel comfortable.

The way we dress is an indicator of our professionalism.

UNIT

THHBH06A

Personal presentation

One all-important aspect of professionalism in guest service staff, whatever their job title, is the attention they give to personal presentation. The first and most obvious sign that staff are professional in their approach to their work is, oddly enough, what they wear to work. In fact, whether in or out of uniform, or whether or not they are at work, the real professional will have more than sufficient self-respect to dress well at all times. Guest service staff need to be keenly aware that they are perfectly likely to bump into guests in a shopping mall, in a restaurant, in the local supermarket, or even just on the way to the hotel or establishment—thus creating yet another impression!

Good grooming and meticulous attention to personal hygiene not only express a positive attitude to guests but also build poise and self-confidence in the individual. High standards of personal hygiene are essential for all guest service staff members.

A note about name badges

These are a very important part of your identity—so much so that, if you lose your own name badge, you should resist the temptation to wear someone else's. If an emergency or other situation occurs in which the name of the person involved has to be identified, it is

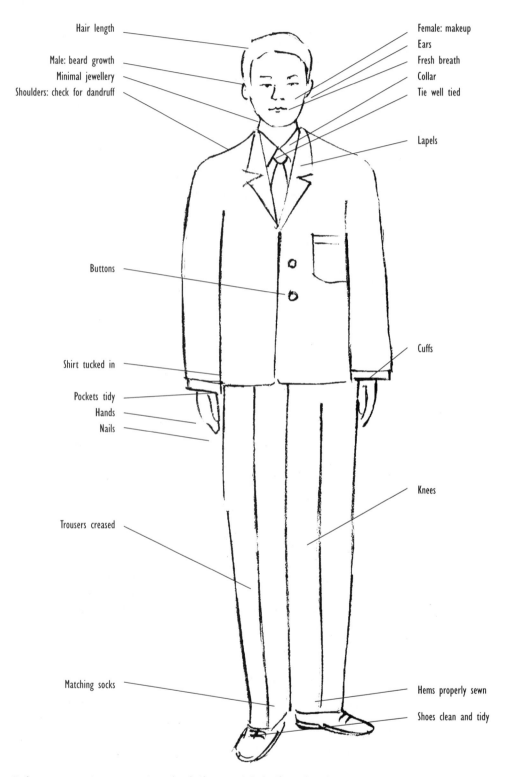

Hair length

Male: beard growth
Minimal jewellery
Shoulders: check for dandruff

Female: makeup
Ears
Fresh breath
Collar
Tie well tied

Lapels

Buttons

Cuffs

Shirt tucked in

Pockets tidy
Hands
Nails

Knees

Trousers creased

Matching socks

Hems properly sewn
Shoes clean and tidy

Before you meet your guests—check these points in the mirror!

essential that you are wearing the correct badge. This will reduce both confusion and the risk of being incorrectly identified. Also, guests may become curious if you do not answer instantly to the name that is printed on the badge you are wearing. You may have forgotten, but they can see it quite plainly!

The overall professional manner

Maintaining a professional manner is a natural follow-on from creating that good first impression. Establishing and maintaining rapport is essentially a preventative mechanism: it prevents the discomforts, ill feelings and misunderstandings that can arise from seemingly simple situations.

Guest service staff should endeavour to conduct themselves in a professional manner while giving friendly and consistent service at all times, regardless of the endless frustrations that may be present. It is not always an easy task to rise above these frustrations, particularly if they are not of your making. Guests are not there because they want to share your frustrations. They are there because they were led to believe that you, as 'host', would make them feel comfortable.

Guest service staff will, more often than not, be the first and last members of staff that the guest will encounter. It is important that this experience is a pleasant one for the guest. The overall impression should be one of quiet confidence, professionalism, style and excellence.

Smile!

In spite of what was said earlier about the eleven impressions that are formed in the first seven seconds, a smile is still everyone's best asset. It shows not only sincerity, genuine interest and care but also a good, positive attitude. A smile should be used frequently for all guests and other members of staff. It will reassure guests that they have made the right decision to stay at your establishment in the first place and encourage them to come back in the future.

Remember: first impressions are lasting impressions!

2
Where do our guests come from?

Anywhere and everywhere!

In Ian Fleming's *From Russia with Love* a Russian agent tries to pass himself off as an English gentleman. He looks the part except that his tie has a wide knot. Since no gentleman uses such a knot, James Bond immediately knows him for the fraud he is.

If you meet a lady from India she may be wearing a beautiful sari. On closer inspection you may notice that she styles her sari in a particular way; this will indicate her position in her society. It is by such minute details that people from different cultures reveal whether they belong to one social group or another.

In the hospitality industry we need to take a good look not only at different social groups, but at where our guests come from geographically. Equipped with this knowledge, we are able to deal with people from diverse backgrounds in a more informed and sensitive manner.

It seems odd that, although we meet people from all over the world, we bury our heads in the sand when it comes to knowing anything about their backgrounds and why they think the way they do. Understanding a variety of guests should be an important part of all training programs—not just for new guest service staff, but also as an opportunity for existing staff who are in contact with guests to exchange and share their knowledge with one another. In the previous chapter it was suggested that we as guest service staff should really step out of our own shoes and into the guests' shoes. This chapter is about doing just that. In fact, you could treat this chapter as an opportunity for an armchair whistle-stop tour of the world!

'How was your trip?'

When I asked a group of twenty-five students in Thailand how many of them had travelled overseas, I was surprised that so few in the group had done so. On further questioning, I found that not many more had even been to the local airport. This prompted me to ask them what was on their minds when they asked an arriving guest, 'How was your trip?' Before I gave them a chance to answer, I asked them to consider this real-life story of a pair of guests who had travelled from Germany to Thailand.

The German couple in question left their home to drive to the airport at 6.30 on a chilly October morning. On the way to the airport their car broke down and they were forced to walk to a callbox and telephone for a taxi cab. This meant a wait of forty-five minutes. They stood by the roadside feeling very uncomfortable, since they were dressed for travel to a warmer climate, not for standing on the autobahn at this cold, unearthly hour. The cab arrived and they reached the airport. In a rush they checked in for their 9.30 a.m. direct flight to Singapore. After they had checked in and passed through customs, they were appalled to learn that their flight was to be delayed by four hours and had to be rescheduled as a 'two sector' flight via Bahrain! There was little they could do but sit and wait—leaving the airport at this stage was prohibited for security reasons. They waited.

Finally they were in the air on their way to Bahrain. In Bahrain they had a further delay of one-and-a-half hours due to unexpected heavy local air traffic. Singapore-bound, they settled back to enjoy the rest of their flight. In spite of a screaming baby two rows in front of them, they did manage a couple of hours' sleep. By the time they touched down in Singapore, it was 12.30 a.m. in their home country but 7.30 a.m. locally—a new day! Well, the new day started badly. One piece of their luggage had gone missing. They had to report this and then rush to another end of the airport terminal to catch their newly rescheduled connecting flight to Thailand. They hoped that their missing luggage would reappear and be redirected to their destination.

Now they were at last in Thailand. Remember that they had left their home in late autumn, and by this time jet lag had set in. Imagine the shock of walking out of the terminal into thirty-eight degrees! And they were not only bowled over by the temperature. In front of them was a huge crowd of airport hotel representatives all jostling and all anxious to meet their respective guests and transport them to their 'holiday of a lifetime'.

Confusion reigned. In situations like this nobody recognises anyone unless, of course, they are return guests, so it is always a bit bewildering. On top of this, our travellers were busy enough peeling off layers of clothing and trying to cope with their new surroundings. They finally made it to their limousine and prepared to sit back and enjoy the passing scene in peace. But now it was the airport representative's turn to put them through a chatty interchange. He seemed oblivious of their reluctance to take any part in this conversation. He had his job to do. They arrived at the front entrance of the hotel. The guest service staff member stepped forward, ready and willing to help them out of the car and asking brightly, 'Did you have a good trip?'

From this story you can see just how a little 'inside' knowledge could have helped the welcoming staff member meet the tired guests with a more appropriate greeting.

Training exercise: greetings!

Look at the anecdote again and then list the instances, in your opinion, where more knowledge would have been useful in creating a more sensitive and appropriate greeting.

Expanding your knowledge

Expanding your knowledge is and should always be a joy. It not only feeds your mind; it also trains it to be constantly on the lookout for more information. If you enjoy meeting people in your job, imagine how much more impact you will have if your conversation shows some depth of understanding—not just a general overview—of the individual guest.

It would be a mammoth task to thoroughly research every kind of background that guests can have. However, we can at least learn some salient points of interest about their origins. Even developing a repertoire of trivia will enable you to talk more confidently. This is especially useful in situations where you find yourself alone with a guest in a lift, or waiting for another guest or staff member, when all the usual comments or clichés rapidly become irrelevant or even tedious to the listener. You can fill the silence more entertainingly than by inquiring about the weather, whether the guest has had lunch, how long are they staying or when they are leaving. You may be able to provoke interest by offering some snippet of information or trivia. A colleague of mine will no doubt be amused to recall the following piece of trivia I dropped into the conversation on learning that he was going to travel to the Victoria Falls in Africa.

21 Olympic swimming pools!

Did you know that the amount of water that falls in one minute down the Victoria Falls is exactly the same amount required to fill 121 Olympic-sized swimming pools?

Whichever way you look at this information, you can't fail to be amazed. Wow! What a memory! Whether you believe it or not at this stage is immaterial. What is important is that this sort of information depends on your style of delivery and timing. By all means check it out; while you are doing that you may even come across another snippet of trivia. But if you ever travel to the Victoria Falls armed with this knowledge you may, like my colleague, suddenly realise with awe the immensity of nature and ... there is always a chance to pass on that bit of trivia!

It's harmless fun and certainly thought-provoking.

Different countries

For any information to be of value, you have to be sure of your facts and figures—no guesswork! There are a number of ways you can

See training exercise: country research, on the next page.

acquire knowledge about other countries: the Internet, specific CD-ROM programs, television programs, encyclopaedic textbooks and world gazetteers all offer substantial opportunities to broaden your world view. If you are a reader of any sort you will know that you can also pick up a lot of information just by reading good works of fiction whose authors have extensively researched their subjects. Start with the basic information that can easily be researched on those countries that most of your guests come from. Find out the following details about each country:

- name of country (including correct pronunciation)
- continent and hemisphere
- capital city (including correct pronunciation)
- main international airports
- population
- currency (plus rough exchange rate)
- official languages
- current head of state
- main political party
- current prime minister
- main religions
- climate
- time zone in relation to GMT (also called UCT, see page 27)
- main imports
- main exports
- main newspaper

- local greeting
- main cultural difference (if appropriate)
- trivia
- points of interest (this could be a famous monument, person, tourist attraction or current news topic).

Once you start on this journey of discovery you will be surprised how much you remember and how much more you will want to know about some countries, particularly how they have evolved to their current status. It will certainly give you an insight into the people of each country and possibly why they think along the lines that they do.

Training exercise: country research

Using the above list as a guide, research one or two countries of your choice. As part of the exercise, prepare a short presentation of five to seven minutes on one country. Overhead slides and visual aids will greatly support your presentation. You should aim to make it as interesting and informative as possible, but don't forget a little humour.

Some particularly useful points

One of the most useful insights you can gain when you find out about a guest's country is that country's *population*. If the land mass of a country is large and the population small, the general demeanour of its people will be affected by the amount of space they have. They will usually be more willing to use all the space available to them. Conversely, in a country with little space and a dense population, the people will tailor their body language and demeanour accordingly. They will not mind being crowded together in smaller areas; it will come quite naturally to them.

Official languages can often be confusing—for obvious reasons!— particularly in those countries where there is more than one language spoken, such as in Switzerland or the Philippines. Even checking the luggage tags may not be much help. In Switzerland, for instance, there is only one main international airport and three languages are spoken there. If Switzerland had more airports, you might have been able to guess which language-speaking region the guest came from.

In general conversation it is useful to be aware of such points as *political parties*, *prime minister* or *president*, and *religions*, and to have some background history. However, unless you are forced to do otherwise, it may be best to avoid mentioning these subjects, in case you offend the listener.

Knowledge about *climate* is certainly worthwhile. In the anecdote above, an October morning in Germany may not seem to have much importance unless you know about the vast difference between the temperatures in Germany and a country like Singapore or Thailand, which is enough to have quite a staggering effect on a traveller.

Acclimatising is an individual thing. Some people find it easy to enjoy warmer weather and very quickly adapt, while others find it more difficult to cope. It helps to understand this when you are greeting a guest. If you lived in a hot country, how would you feel if the temperature suddenly dropped by thirty degrees Celsius? I suspect it would be quite a shock to the system!

Another issue is *time zone difference*. This is often a source of confusion to both guests and staff. You can see from the above anecdote how difficult 'catching up' with the time difference can be. Some guests will not know whether they should be sleeping or eating! This is also important information when guests ask about making telephone calls at the appropriate time in their home country. Note that GMT (Greenwich Mean Time; that is, the time at Greenwich Observatory at zero degrees longitude) is also referred to as UCT (Universally Co-ordinated Time).

A brief overview of the *imports and exports* of other countries will help you understand not only the types of industries that a guest may represent, but to a certain extent how their economy works; this will be reflected in their attitude. When you consider a specific country, there is usually one element that will spring to mind. For instance, both France and Italy have fantastic fashion designers and perfume houses. France also produces many wines, including champagne, and cheeses. Italy manufactures cars and, like Germany, is heavily into engineering, electronics and technology. China exports vast quantities of textiles around the world; Thailand is famous for its exquisite silk.

These points should be noted well so that, as guest service staff, we can make informed suggestions when we are asked about business matters or shopping trips.

Guests, like everyone, need to feel at home. A *newspaper* from their own country can help them do just that, particularly if they have been travelling for some time or are long-stay guests, anxious to keep abreast of events at home. Many of the major international newspapers are available around the world, but many of the other, not so well-known, newspapers can be sourced or ordered. If you get the chance to read some of these newspapers, take it! You will gain an interesting insight into the people who read them every day. From newspapers you gain an update on current affairs and find out which people are making the headlines, which sports are currently of interest and what the local community issues are. The main cartoon in a newspaper often illustrates the style of humour enjoyed by the people of that country. Cartoonists like Lat in Malaysia, Giles in England and Leunig in Australia give a humorous perspective on how individuals cope with the more serious current political and social issues.

Greeting a guest in their own language has an enormous impact. Knowing the cultural boundaries with regard to physical contact on greeting is essential. Many times we see people, particularly celebrities,

kissing and hugging and shaking hands, but some or all of these gestures are not always welcome to people from other cultures.

Points of interest, although placed at the end of this list, are important in demonstrating your interest in another country or culture. Just
because you may not be able to travel as frequently as a guest, it should
not stop you wanting to find out more. Besides which, you may just get
there one day! Imagine how impressed you would be if a person talked
to you knowledgeably about your own country. Believe me, whether it's
general conversation or trivia it certainly leaves a lasting impression; it
creates empathy and a sense of comfort and ease.

Training exercise: research and presentation on your own country

Research your own country and prepare a three-minute talk and presentation (bearing in
mind that you are 'selling' your country), with ten questions to ask your audience. Present
this and identify both the information you learned from your audience and that which
you were able to teach them about their own country.

The saying 'Different strokes for different folks' is apt at this stage. To
understand what works for different people, you need not only the sort
of information we have been discussing but also a knowledge of the different manners, codes of etiquette and behavioural patterns common
in other cultures. As well as language differences, you need to consider many other aspects, such as non-verbal communication, forms of
greeting and cultural values and attitudes.

To cover the subject of different cultures more fully, I suggest that you
obtain a copy of *Cross-cultural Communication* by Helen Fitzgerald (see
bibliography, page 259). In this fascinating book you will find a wealth
of interesting current information that will serve you well when you set

out to learn the essential components for successful communication with international travellers.

International language

Because people of English-speaking nations have travelled so much, many English words have spread around the globe and this will continue as the world gets smaller. There are many words from other languages too, including French, German and Greek. To help make it easier for you, I have compiled a short list of 'international' words that have now assumed common usage around the world. Most people will understand these terms, particularly if they are pronounced slowly. Be aware, though, that these terms can also differ according to the country in which they are used. The Japanese, for example, have adopted numerous English words, but they can be difficult to recognise because Japanese syllables have been added to them to indicate their function and because some of the letters are pronounced differently. For instance, the English *l* is pronounced as *r* in Japanese.

airport	express	police
alphabet	fax	program
atom	golf	radio
ballet	hello	reservation
bank	hotel	restaurant
bar	license/licence	salad
beer	magazine	sandwich
bus	mathematics	sport
business	medicine	(movie) star
camera	menu	studio
chocolate	message	supermarket
cigarette	Miss	taxi
cinema	Mister	telephone
Coca-Cola	motorcycle	television
coffee	music	temperature
communications	okay	tennis
computer	opera	theatre
dance	orchestra	traveller's cheque/check
doctor	passport	violin
dollar	piano	whisky/whiskey

Whenever you speak to a person from a foreign country use their language first, if possible. If they speak English so much the better, but you will still have made an important and rewarding step in international relations. Chapter 3 (page 40) gives some of the most commonly-used expressions in various languages that you are likely to encounter in your work. And don't stop there! A collection of phrase-books in various languages will not only be an excellent addition to your library—it will also enrich your knowledge and enhance your skill in making guests feel at home.

Training exercise: pronunciation

Go through one or more of the glossaries. Make a list of 20 words you can't pronounce and find out their correct pronunciation, either by asking people of the appropriate nationalities or by consulting language dictionaries.

Training exercise: information gathering

Now perhaps you can start developing other areas of information that may be relevant. You might even consider expanding this amount of information to cover extra topics such as:

- What makes these people laugh?

- Do different parts of the country have different dialects? If so, how do they differ?

- Do they have a national costume?

- When is their national day?

- What other national or religious holidays are important to them?

- Are there any easily-recognised physical features pertinent to individual countries?

- Do they have special preferences when it comes to being 'handled' by service staff? (This last topic could be the subject for a group discussion to establish how much is known about another culture.)

These topics are often related to current affairs, which is one more area of awareness that can lead to a broader understanding not just of international guests, but of local guests as well. An apparent lack of interest in world events makes a poor impression. Also, knowing something about how the world works helps you understand why certain people have more money to spend, why some tourists prefer to be in a large group and why others are more reluctant to join in crowd situations. You will also know why certain nationalities don't travel at particular times of the year (for instance, very few Muslims travel during the festival of Ramadan), or why there is an influx of guests as a result of school or national holidays.

If it's possible, read a good newspaper every day. This will enable you to at least converse about local topics. Oddly enough guests, particularly tourists, would be surprised if you knew very little about your own country, because they as travellers are constantly learning and assimilating knowledge and different viewpoints. They are also inclined to believe that everyone is as interested as they are. The impression you give at this stage is crucial.

Another benefit from reading about local news topics is that you will also become more familiar with some of the companies and activities in your own area. You will find out more about what these businesses do. It is not enough to just know a company's name; to understand more about a guest's activities you will need to know what the business does and where, for instance, its headquarters are.

Training exercise: country dossiers

On the basis of the information in this chapter, construct a relevant dossier on as many countries that, at this stage, you believe to be necessary for you to achieve a better understanding of guests within your area of interest.

When you have finished the exercises in this chapter you should feel confident about providing service to a foreign guest, mainly because you now have so much more information to work with, and you have created a whole new world of interest for your own pleasure as well. You should now know where your guests come from.

3
Etiquette and manners

Good manners: weapon or tool?

Like the air we breathe, good manners cost nothing. It was William of Wykeham, Bishop of Winchester from 1367 to 1404, who said 'Manners maketh man' and this has been the motto of one of England's most famous public schools—Winchester—from that time on.

But what of manners? What can be gained by possessing and using good manners? Are manners just a good way to get what we want, how and when we want it? Should manners be used as a weapon, or as a tool?

The terms 'etiquette' and 'manners' tend to be used interchangeably. In essence, etiquette concerns the letter of the law, whereas manners are governed by the spirit of the law. The truly well-mannered are aware that their ways are not necessarily the 'right' or only ways in every situation. They will go into another person's home, office or country with their antennae out to sense what behaviour would be most fitting in that environment and will treat people accordingly, regardless of their relative social standing.

A great deal of social life—and we in the accommodation industry are a vital part of this social life—is not necessarily pleasant. When it is carried on for business or other special reasons, it can strain affability. Also, it is not the nature of the human species to be fully at ease in unfamiliar surroundings or among strangers; we need to feel a sense of security before we can relax. It's up to guest service staff (or any staff member in the front line) to understand these points. This is where custom and courtesy play an important role: custom gives us confidence and reduces the risk of misunderstandings; courteous behaviour reassures us that our associates mean to be friendly.

This recipe for social or professional success can rarely be improved, as it means that everyone is charmed, nobody is slighted, and inappropriate behaviour is kept to the barest minimum. Good manners cannot be donned like a uniform or a suit, just to impress everyone around you. Nobody will be fooled for very long by someone whose outward behaviour is correct but whose inner attitude is cynical or manipulative.

One of the principles of good manners is that they should make life easier for everyone. There are rules of etiquette that are generally accepted as the benchmark of good form, even though they don't always apply in every region or social group and may only apply to a particular time. Normally the standard etiquette in a particular society is that which appears to be the most successful for that society. Sometimes an apparently trivial point of etiquette may be an expression of some aspect of a nation's history or culture, and will therefore be a part of its people's identity. Infringing on or ignoring such points of difference may offend some quite deeply-held attitudes and values.

This chapter isn't here simply to tell you how to behave; rather, it should give you a choice—whether to follow your accustomed rules or to adapt to other people's standards. Although our social behaviour is only the tip of the iceberg, it is the part of our personalities by which most people will judge us. Once that first impression has been made (see pages 12-21) it is up to each of us to choose the behaviour that will make us appear larger or smaller in the eyes of others.

Good manners are both creative and flexible. They allow change and adaptation; they create better relationships and a better atmosphere. The attitudes that underlie these good manners will offer gentleness and calm in an otherwise hectic world. Some people dismiss good manners and regard them as a merely petty aspect of social and professional life. But manners are about the enjoyment of life. They are an expression of feeling. They ensure warmth, appreciation and understanding. They should be a pleasure, not a chore, and should combine respect for the self and respect for the other person.

Sarcastic or pointed comments are frowned upon; they rarely get a good response from the person to whom they are directed. However, deliberate rudeness from a normally courteous person can have quite an impact. It seems that the well-mannered have all the aces!

Most of us at some time show our fellow human beings some form of respect or consideration; it is a sort of 'do as you would be done by' situation. It often happens from force of habit. But maybe, on the cusp of the twenty-first century, some of the old values that have been the basis for etiquette and good manners need to be taken off the wire coat-hanger in the wardrobe of life and placed on a more comfortable, padded hanger that will suit future corporate and personal needs.

Training exercise: the benefits of good manners

'Good manners are the enlightened means to selfish ends.' What are the main benefits? Use this statement and the question that follows it as group discussion points. List the benefits discussed in order of priority.

An instant impression of respect

Etiquette and good manners give an instant impression of respect and this has always been a crucial basis for good human relations. It has been said that good manners are the enlightened means to selfish ends. On consideration this is probably true; recognising the importance of knowing how to behave in the appropriate way at the right time does actually help us in our endeavours.

The expressions 'Please' and 'Thank you' are only the first steps towards expressing due appreciation and not making unreasonable demands on others. It is practically useless to utter these words in a graceless manner, as they then run the risk of being really insulting. If these words are to be said, make sure that they are said with conviction. The essence of good manners is in the underlying attitude. Really well-mannered people don't just say the right words—they say them with total honesty.

Unfortunately, there are many words and expressions that are used unnecessarily. We all know them. They include: 'you know', 'No problem', 'I know', 'No worries', 'Sure', 'OK', 'Have a nice day !' and 'How are you?' These should be used only when they are relevant. Some of them convey an approach that is far too casual; others are simply unnecessary—they are often said out of force of habit and have little impact.

One real purpose of etiquette and manners is to enable people to come together with ease, stay together for a time without friction or discord, and part from one another amicably. This is the essence of all civilised behaviour. On the face of it, it hardly sounds difficult. However, although thoughtfulness and kindliness are a part of our nature, so too are irascibility, selfishness, intolerance and suspicion.

Shaking hands

Displaying an open palm was an ancient greeting ritual, which developed into the interlocking of palms that eventually became the handshake that we know today. Originally, an exposed palm showed that no weapons were being concealed; it conveyed honesty and goodwill.

However, these days handshaking itself can become fraught with anxiety and suspicion. Many people, particularly females, feel very self-conscious about this very personal physical contact. Judgements

A normal hand-shake. The hands are shaken or pumped five to seven times.

are made, rightly or wrongly, on the way you offer or return a hand-shake.

For people in some non-Western cultures handshaking and other types of physical contact are not a part of everyday etiquette; howev-er, they will often quite readily use the handshake when greeting people from other parts of the world.

These days the question of who should offer the handshake first is not so tricky as it once was. Years ago, the lady was advised to offer her hand and the gentleman would take up the offer. It was never the other way round. However, today all parties should take it upon themselves to proffer their hands. The only exception occurs when you are greet-

The 'glove' handshake—not recommended!

ing royalty (see pages 36-39). Royal personages of all nations still pre-fer to initiate the handshake.

A handshake is a part of good etiquette, whether or not gloves are being worn. It would be clumsy to take off your gloves before shaking hands.

There are many different styles of handshaking. The basic hand-shake should be made with the palms meeting in a vertical position.

The hands are then pumped or shaken five to seven times. Oddly enough, just holding the hand can put some people off.

Avoid grasping the other person's hand so tightly that it hurts (and jewellery can pinch!) or, at the other extreme, proffering a hand so limp that it feels like a dead fish. The 'dead fish' handshake will make the receiver feel quite uncomfortable. The 'glove' style of handshake (see the illustration) may be intended to give an impression of trust-worthiness, but can have quite the reverse effect. Styles of handshake, and the subtle messages they convey, will be dealt with more fully in Chapter 4 (pages 65-67).

Addressing royalty and VIP guests

Jean-Philippe Beghin, General Manager of The Imperial, Queen's Park, Bangkok, greeting a VIP guest with a traditional Thai offering of flowers.

What is the correct procedure for meeting a member of a royal family? Who should start the conversation and what should it be about? Most people become very flustered and nervous when they meet a member of a royal family or a titled person for the first time. They are unsure of what to say or do. They often find themselves babbling nervously or unable to utter a sensible or coherent word.

Bowing and curtsying

Confusion abounds on this subject. Americans seldom bow or curtsy and are not expected to; but the British and most citizens of the Commonwealth are expected to do so as a mark of respect to the Crown. Other sovereign countries have their own forms of protocol.

Greeting members of a royal family is far easier if you know the ground rules of etiquette. However, few of us are given many opportu-nities to practise, so the chance of this skill becoming second nature is often remote. Since you generally know in advance if you are to meet with royalty, some practice or rehearsal is advisable.

When you are formally introduced, you should wait until a royal hand is proffered to shake yours, and when this happens you should then curtsy (if female) or bow (if male or a female wearing trousers).

The curtsy should not be a quick jerk but should be a slow, graceful movement with the head slightly lowered. Put the right foot forward and the ball of the left foot roughly sixteen to eighteen centimetres behind the right heel with both knees bent. With a straight back lower yourself to about twenty-five centimetres from the ground. This is not

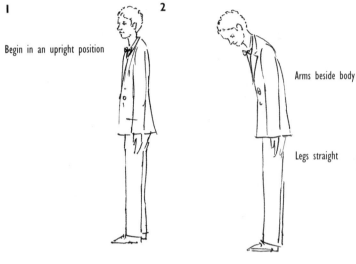

1 Begin in an upright position

2 Arms beside body / Legs straight

Men bow; so do women in trousers. A bow from the neck is usually enough, but you can bow from the waist if you prefer or if it is appropriate to the culture.

1 Standing upright, place right foot about a foot's length behind left foot

2 Bow head slightly forward

Hold arms slightly out from body to create balance

Lower right knee to about 25 cm (10 inches) from floor. Left knee bends with right knee and body weight goes down

How to curtsy.

always easy; if you are likely to wobble, don't attempt to lower yourself so much.

A man shakes hands and bows by lowering his chest with a definable jerk of the head. In some instances (or cultures) it is incorrect to bow from the waist. However, when dealing with the Japanese, a bow from the waist is appropriate for both sexes.

Royal families around the world do not consider it stupid to curtsy or bow in this way; they appreciate it as a mark of respect. However, they are quite used to people making mistakes and will not be offended if the curtsy is not perfect.

Forms of address and conversation

The correct forms of address for royalty can also cause confusion. Female members should be addressed as 'ma'am' to rhyme with 'lamb', not 'marm' to rhyme with 'farm'. When you are presented to a king or queen you first say 'Good evening/good morning/good afternoon, your Majesty', and then in continuing conversation say 'sir' or 'ma'am', unless you are an employee of the royal family or a tradesperson involved in some occupation within their domain, in which case it is correct to use 'your Majesty' all the time.

The British royal family always seem to have the right techniques to put people to whom they are talking at ease. In return, you should steer clear of any contentious or awkward subjects. They do not like being asked personal questions and certainly will not discuss other members of their family.

After you have greeted and addressed a royal or VIP guest in the correct manner, it is best to keep the conversation to generalities. It is quite acceptable to ask a member of the royal family what they have been doing recently or which places they have visited. The old rule of letting them ask all the questions is now a bit dated, but for the first few minutes it is better to allow them to speak and set the pace.

All guests are entitled to be addressed according to the correct protocol, although this may differ with each nationality. If you are unsure, it is best to check first with the relevant embassy or consulate. Never use guesswork; this can cause extreme embarrassment, not just to you but to those around you as well.

Be prepared to do some homework. There are volumes of the annually-published *Who's Who* in libraries or at the local embassy office. Sometimes hotel front offices hold copies of *Who's Who* as a source of reference. Also, most embassies have a protocol department and will happily give answers to your questions. Listed opposite are a few guidelines for addressing people with titles. For more information refer to the bibliography at the end of this book.

Rank	Method of address
King	First time 'your Majesty'; subsequently 'sir'
Queen	First time 'your Majesty'; subsequently 'ma'am'
Prince	First time 'your Royal Highness'; subsequently 'sir'
Princess	First time 'your Royal Highness'; subsequently 'ma'am'
Royal duke	First time 'your Royal Highness'; subsequently 'sir'
Duchess	First time 'your Royal Highness'; subsequently 'ma'am'
Countess	First time 'Lady (last name)'; subsequently 'ma'am'
President	'Mr/Madam President'
Senator	'Senator ... (last name),
Ambassador	First time 'Ambassador ... (last name)'; subsequently 'your Excellency'
Prime minister	'Prime Minister'

When in doubt, address the person as 'sir' or 'ma'am'. Never call a guest by their first name, even if you are asked to do so; it does not sound very professional or respectful. Remember that the needs of a guest with a title are just the same as those of everyone else. Always behave in a friendly but not familiar manner, and do your best to make the guest feel at home.

UNIT

THHCORO2A

Addressing people from different cultures

UNIT

THHCORO2A

All guest service staff should try to address guests as much as possible in their own language to help them feel a little more at home. A few basic phrases are included on the next page.

These few examples will cover most eventualities. There are some really good books that offer just enough of the basics to get you through the formalities in most languages without the pressure of trying to become completely fluent. Three are suggested in the bibliography.

Business cards

The offer of a business card should be treated as a gesture of recognition. Unless you do not wish for further contact with a guest, you should always proffer your card. Here are some points to remember.

- When handing out business cards, avoid just dealing them out like a pack of playing cards! Also, if you are in a large hotel, be mindful that the guest may already have received cards from other departments. Perhaps it would be better to wait until the end of the conversation and then ask the guest politely if they already have a card with the relevant information. If they have, then simply ask them if they would like one of yours as well. Unless there is a specific reason why they may need to make

American/Australian/British English

Until noon (12 midday)	Good morning
Any time	G'day (Australian, informal)
Afternoon (12 midday to 5 p.m.)	Good afternoon
Evening (after 5 p.m.)	Good evening
After meeting and greeting in the evening	Good night

Cantonese

Good morning (7 a.m. to 10 a.m.)	Chou san
Good day (10 a.m. to 5 p.m.)	Lei hou
How are you?	Lei hou ma?
Please or thank you	M'goi (for a favour)
Thank you	Tou sjai (e.g. for a gift)

French

Good morning/ good day	Bon jour
Good evening	Bon soir
Good night	Bon nuit
See you again	Au revoir
How are you?	Comment allez-vous?
Please	S'il vous plait
Thank you very much	Merci beaucoup

German

Good morning	Guten Morgen
Good afternoon/day	Guten Tag
Good evening	Guten Abend
Good night	Gute Nacht
See you again	Auf wiedersehen
Please	Bitte
Thank you	Danke
How are you?	Wie geht es Ihnen?

Indonesian

Good day	Selamat pagi
How are you?	Apa kabar?
Good evening	Selamat malam
Please	Tjoba
Excuse me	Waf
Thank you	Terima kasi
You're welcome	Kembali
Very well	Baik

Some commonly-used phrases.

Happy to meet you	Selamat bertemu
Goodbye	Selamat tinggal (said by person leaving)
Goodbye	Selamat djalan (said by person staying)

Italian

Good morning (morning until late afternoon/4 p.m.)	Buon giorno
Good evening (late afternoon/ 4 p.m/evening)	Buona sera
Good night	Buona notte
See you again (formal)	Arrivederci
Goodbye (friendly)	Ciao
Thank you	Grazie
How are you?	Come va?/Come sta?
Are you well?	Sta bene?
I am well	Sto bene

Japanese

Good morning (after getting up until 10 a.m.)	Ohayo gozaimasu
Good afternoon (10 a. m. to 5 p. m.)	Konnichiwa
Good evening (after 5 p.m., meeting guests during the evening)	Konbanwa
Good night	Oyasuminasai (mase)
Please	Dozo
Thank you	Ari gato zai masu
How are you?	O gengi desu ka

Malaysian

Mostly Malaysian expressions are the same as for Indonesian.

Spanish

Good morning	Buenos dias
Good afternoon	Buenas tardes
Good night	Buenas noches
See you again	Hasta la vista
How are you?	Como estas?/Que tal?
Well	Bien
Please	Por favor
Thank you	Gracias
You are welcome	De nada

direct contact with you, it is wise not to press your cards on people.

- Business cards are for business. It is incorrect and inappropriate to pressure other people into giving you their private or home telephone details or, on the other hand, to offer yours, as this could potentially become a security issue.
- When it comes to receiving a card, be sure that you fully appreciate the privilege and read it. Always turn the card over. This is not just to check for more information—sometimes people make notes on the reverse side of a business card and then forget to store the information elsewhere. It is also worth remembering that many business people have their vital information printed in two languages and may use both sides of the card for this purpose.
- Never just take a business card from another person and pocket it straightaway without studying it: this is considered rude and insensitive. If possible, make some appropriate comment. This may help you develop a memory for connecting names, faces and business cards.

Making introductions

Introducing guests or staff to each other is an important part of good manners; no one likes to feel left out. When you introduce people you are giving them the opportunity to take part in a situation. It is then their choice whether they continue to chat after the introduction, though it would be considered rude if they did not. When it is appropriate, or if you see a need to put guests at ease or help them get to know each other, offer an introduction. You shouldn't suggest this in front of everybody; just find a tactful way. For instance you may say to one set of guests, 'Would you like me to introduce you to some guests who have travelled from your part of the world?' while you indicate with your body language the direction you want to lead them; or 'Mr and Mrs ... from Switzerland are interested in golf; let me introduce you to them'; or 'Miss ... has just travelled from India. Perhaps you would like to meet her?'

Getting names right

It is essential to do your homework and check the other person's full and proper name, and maybe the name of their home town. When you make an introduction it is important to speak clearly so that those being introduced can understand you. It is also important to concentrate and listen carefully to those names if you are being introduced. Some names, for instance Muslim names, can be very long and difficult to remember and pronounce. If this is the case, you can always ask the person to repeat their name and, if it is easy to do so, write it down so that you can recognise the pronunciation in print. This will help not only your memory but also your understanding of the name.

Introductions should always be spoken clearly, so that all concerned can hear and are able to remember names and any other information you give. If you are uncertain about a name, however, it is better to establish it accurately with the person in question. You could say 'I'm sorry, but with all the background noise I could not quite hear your name. Is it ... or ... ?' It is much better to do this than to have to guess when you eventually try to introduce the other person. It is quite acceptable to read a person's name from a notebook or a piece of paper; this will show your willingness to get all the details right.

If you abbreviate a person's name, please make sure you get their acknowledgement or approval to do so as part of the introduction. Also, if you find yourself in a situation where you are making an intro-duction and a name has completely left your mind, try this:

'I'm so sorry; I've forgotten your name.'

Then, when the other person replies with their first name, say

'No, no, Robert, not your first name, your last name.'

They will almost certainly reply with their last name and you will then have the full name without losing too much face!

To make guests feel more comfortable, always introduce them by name and add a little more information, but nothing too personal. Simply introducing Mr and Mrs Black to Mr and Mrs White will prob-ably only create grey! Without any additional information guests may have an embarrassing time stumbling over possible topics for conver-sation. By giving them more to work with you will give them an immediate opening. So you may be able to offer the following: 'Mr and Mrs White are in town from Beijing (indicating them to Mr and Mrs Black with your hand). Mr and Mrs Black are here on their second visit to ... from Perth, Western Australia.'

More experience in doing this will increase your confidence, so long as you speak clearly and have all the correct information about names, home towns and some point of note. If you can imagine being the host in your own home, where you want your guests to feel comfortable and where you would never dream of not introducing guests to each other, then it will be easier to make a sincere introduction.

While this responsibility may not always fall on the shoulders of guest service staff (managers usually get this job), the ability to make correct introductions is part of the very subtle skill of handling guests. Guests will not only be impressed, but will be grateful for your respect, care and understanding. It is the attention to these details that marks the true professional.

Order of introductions

People often get flustered and confused about introductions. Despite the modern emphasis on equality, with introductions the old rules still apply. In principle you move and introduce a less important, or younger, person to a more important one. And for once—unless the man is royal or exceptionally distinguished, or the two meet on business terms and the man is senior—women rank higher than men! Introductions should therefore be male to female and junior to senior as a matter of respect for everyone.

People often get confused about whose name should be spoken first. The names can in fact be in any order, provided the wording shows that you are introducing the junior to the senior. For instance, here are three ways you can say the same thing:

'Your Highness/Sir/Mr . . . , may I/allow me to introduce Robert Moneybags, our financial controller?' or

'May I/Allow me to introduce Robert Moneybags, our financial controller, your Highness/Sir/Mr. . . . , or

'Your Highness/Sir/Mr . . . , may I/allow me to introduce Robert Moneybags, our financial controller, Your Highness/Sir/Mr . . . ?'

Although this seems very formal, it is essential to get all the facts across clearly and concisely. So long as the people are introduced by name in the right order, the only other consideration is that the names be remembered.

A less formal introduction might run like this:

'David, I'd like you to meet Elizabeth Able, the Managing Director's wife. Elizabeth, David Inpaper is the local newspaper Business Editor.'

If you are in doubt, it is always best to ask fellow business associates or guests how they prefer to be introduced, particularly if they are foreign guests.

A good introduction can alert people or fellow guests to potential areas of conflict. If, for instance, you know that one guest may be related to another guest you can avert certain remarks that may be made accidentally or tactlessly. If fellow business associates or guests are

connected with sensitive areas—say political, religious or trade union—it is better to let everyone know so that they can all still enjoy the occasion or event fully.

How to respond

The correct response to an introduction is 'How do you do?' or simply 'Hello'. The expression 'Pleased to meet you' can, at times, seem insincere and inappropriate. It is also a rhetorical (requiring no answer) remark.

Once introductions have been made, ignoring someone is not only bad manners, but is also very hurtful. If by chance you meet someone to whom you have just been introduced but you feel you do not want to have a conversation, a kind smile is sufficient recognition and will be appreciated.

Helping guests with coats and jackets

Throughout this book impeccable etiquette and manners, good first impressions and genuine service are treated as priorities for building that special rapport with guests. Whenever you see a guest or another person putting on or removing their jacket, it is good manners to offer some help.

With a jacket (or coat), hold the garment by the collar at the midpoint of each shoulder. As you hold it, make sure it is positioned so that the person can easily slip the first arm into the appropriate sleeve—not too high or to one side or the other—and then offer the other sleeve to the other arm.

If you observe people you will notice whether they are left- or right-handed, depending on which arm they offer first. Adjust the way you hold the jacket accordingly. Allow the guest to slip their arms into the sleeves comfortably, one at a time. Once both arms are in the correct sleeves, gently pull the jacket up over the person's body, holding the upper part high on their shoulders so that, as you fit it onto the shoulders, it will feel comfortable for the guest. As you do this, check that the shoulder pads and collar are in place.

Once you have lifted the jacket onto the person's shoulders, lift it again immediately to settle it over the clothes underneath. This gives a more comfortable feel to the jacket. If you observe body language, you will know in advance if a guest is likely to need assistance in removing their jacket. Help by gently taking the jacket by the collar as it slips from their shoulders. Avoid rushing them; they often have to check their pockets, or adjust another item of clothing, or remove a scarf. Ask them if there is anything valuable in the pockets that they would like to take out.

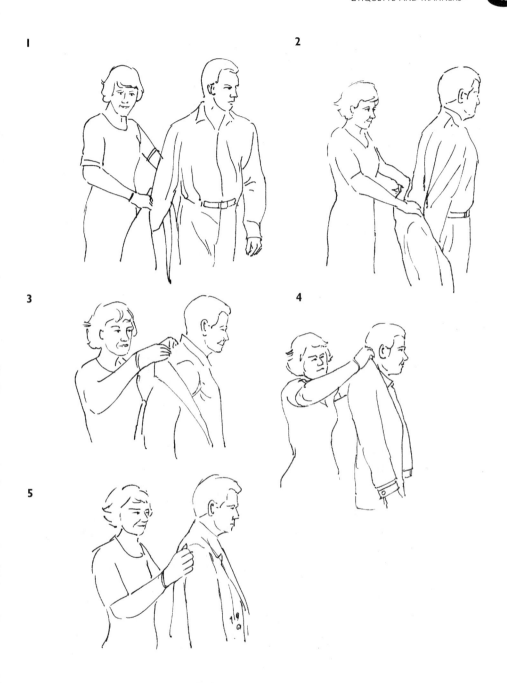

1

2

3

4

5

Helping a guest with a coat or jacket.

Once the jacket is removed, offer to hang it or place it around the back of a chair. Sometimes a guest needs to be reassured that they will actually get their jacket back, particularly if a large number of people are present. Your workplace will have guidelines that will dictate whether you use duplicate number slips that you can present to the guest in return for caring for their jacket.

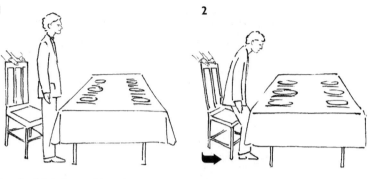

1 Move the chair back at a slight angle (30-35') so that the guest can get in

2 Slide the chair forward so that the guest becomes aware of the chair and bends their knees

3 Ensure that the guest is seated. Watch the guest's arms and hands; they may want the chair moved forward

4 The guest should now be seated close enough to the table for comfort

Seating a guest

Seating guests

However good your intentions may be, helping a guest with a chair can be more annoying to them than helpful, particularly if you are not paying careful attention to their actions and reactions. If the chair is at a table, it should be placed at a reasonable distance from the edge of the table—say 40 to 60 centimetres. This will make room for the guest to stand between the table and the chair.

As you begin to push the chair towards the back of the guest, try to avoid tilting it, although you may need to lift it slightly if the floor is carpeted. As you continue to push the chair towards the guest, they will feel the front of the chair seat against the backs of their knees and will automatically bend and sit.

Once the guest is seated, watch the body language. Most people will indicate if they are too far from the table by automatically reaching down each side of the chair to pull it in closer. Make sure the chair is 'in' sufficiently for their comfort—but do this carefully. The whole process should be effortless, effective and discreet. In this situation a quiet approach is often more appreciated than a chatty one.

Etiquette in guest suites or rooms

Guest rooms and suites require a different approach from that used in the more public areas. Occupied guest rooms require even more reverence and respect. In-room etiquette is very much based on the maxim, 'Imagine how you would feel in the same situation', so act accordingly. Show a combination of sympathy, consideration and care—sympathy because you may be genuinely sorry for interrupting the guest; consideration for their feelings; and care in delivering your service in an appropriate manner and as effectively as possible.

Even ringing the doorbell or knocking on the door takes a special skill. Knock too urgently and the guest will think there is an emergency. Ring the doorbell too many times in quick succession and the guest will be irritated. Once the door is opened, introduce yourself and inform the guest of the reason why you are there. Then wait for the guest to invite you into the room, bearing in mind that it is their 'home' now, not yours. Whenever possible, carry out the job quickly and efficiently. This will save making the guest feel any more uncomfortable than necessary. For more information about this procedure, see pages 78 and 79.

Try to avoid just standing and staring. Guests become quite nervous if they feel they are being scrutinised. Be aware of what you may be interrupting. Guests may be talking on the telephone, working at the desk, showering, bathing, shaving, resting, sleeping or reading. Any form of interruption or break in a chain of thought can be irritating for them.

In the next chapter the subject of personal space will be covered. It is important when you are in a guest room to remain in the correct 'personal space zone'. This will ensure that, everyone feels comfortable. Pause briefly to remember your own body language as well as to quickly take in the guest's body language, which will give you some indication of how they are feeling.

If a guest is in bed or sitting down, do not stand too close when you are speaking to them. This can be very intimidating. Guests will usually feel impatient while you are in the room, so do not overstay your welcome. Besides, this action may seem to indicate that you are expecting a tip or that you do not have enough work to do!

On leaving the guest's room, ask them if there is anything else you can do, wish them a pleasant day and remind them to call on you if there is anything further they require. Always close the door behind you as gently as possible.

Let us now look at some other aspects of etiquette and manners that are relevant to our daily lives.

Personal conduct

Punctuality

Although there seems to be a growing trend to be more relaxed about times, it is still not only bad manners to be late for work, meetings, workshops or seminars, but also extremely annoying to the person or people whom you are keeping waiting. It is particularly rude to be late for appointments. If you are delayed, ring ahead and always apologise on arrival.

Apologising

A useful tool in any situation is the ability to apologise. Learning to apologise effectively means first having enough self-confidence to admit to being wrong. Apologies, far from being a sign of weakness, help to defuse anger. When they are made warmly and immediately (and not profusely!) they are seen as a sign of strength. Never mumble an apology, as this may appear grudging; a well-spoken, clear apology will show good character.

'White lies' and untruths

Lying is more a matter of morality than manners. However, if none of us lied we'd all know what other people thought of us: interesting, but hardly comfortable! So the issue is not whether to lie, but whether it's permissible or acceptable to do so. Lying is despicable, particularly if it is done to serve our own ends, but 'white', or minor, untruths that make other people feel better can be allowable, provided no long-term harm is likely to be done. A better alternative to lying may be to with-hold the truth—that is, if you can't tell the truth, don't say anything at all.

Always keep social untruths understated; elaboration makes them far less believable! And remember, if the rocky path of fibbing is the one you choose, you will need a good memory.

Giving praise

Most of us need praise at some stage in our lives. Human nature dic-tates that our egos need stroking from time to time. This is also a harmless pastime; done carefully it can be very effective.

We have established in this book, so far, that our entire role in the hospitality industry is centred around making a difference to someone else's life. We can do this in a number of ways. If our guests are tired we give them a bed to sleep on. If they are hungry we feed them; if they are thirsty we give them a drink; and so on. If a guest or fellow staff member can be made to feel better about themselves through your giving them praise, do it!

It's always good manners to give praise where praise is due. People often neglect to do so out of self-consciousness and resentment, but overcoming this will clearly give pleasure and make both parties feel better. A part of building deeper rapport, as discussed in earlier chapters, involves leaving the other person in a better state or feeling much better.

There are appropriate times and places for praise. Actors and writers need praise because it represents reassurance which, after any stage show, actors crave. Just praising for praising's sake, however, shows a lack of social skill. If a guest is in a hurry, it's definitely not the right time to delay them just to offer some praise.

It would be considered inappropriate to offer praise or compliments to guests, particularly in front of their visitors. This praise may be misunderstood. If a guest asks your opinion, you may feel obliged to answer. However, if you cannot say a good word, don't say anything without considering the other person's feelings first. This is probably a good time for that little white lie!

Criticism

Criticism is a dangerous weapon—for the critic, that is. Taking criticism is an entirely different matter. If people have a criticism against you, the best and most successful reaction is thoughtful and silent attention to what they are saying. It is better to let them get it off their chest. Don't fall into the trap of thinking the criticism is a total condemnation of you. If the point they are making is good—however personal—say so and apologise graciously.

Part of the pacing process mentioned in Chapter 1 involves realising that people often criticise one thing when a trickier subject is really troubling them. So simply dismissing a guest's complaint may be dismissing some deeply-felt hurt, emotion or grievance. Be sure to pursue the comment carefully so that you get the full picture before you make your next move or comment.

Pointing

Pointing with the finger is for monuments and landscapes. It is a habit that is hard to break. It comes so naturally, but it embarrasses others since it makes them think they may be the subject of your conversation. You can use your hand more effectively by showing an obvious 'open palm' gesture, which clearly registers in other people's minds that you are sincere and that there is no threat in your action.

Grooming in public

Civilised behaviour tries to avoid doing that which comes naturally to monkeys, so any form of public grooming or readjusting of our image or presentation is out. All combing and preening should be kept for the bathroom or cloakroom. Resist the urge to run your hands or fingers through your hair, or touch your face or other parts of your head or body. These are habits that are unfortunately very hard to break, because they often stem from nervousness. If you watch yourself on videotape you will notice those little traits that keep recurring habitually.

If you imagine that there is a video camera (not a security camera!) trained on you at all times, you will find it easier to break some of these habits. Remembering that someone may be noticing you from afar is a certain motivation to improve your image!

If you have to do anything to your body, do it in private. This includes anything to do with your nose and cars. When it comes to sneezing or blowing your nose, do so quietly and as much out of the view of others as possible. Nothing is quite so off-putting to guests than to hear these bodily functions being carried out in their earshot. Yawning in public suggests boredom rather than tiredness; not only is it impolite, but it does not serve to make others feel very comfortable.

Loyalty

Loyalty to the 'boss' and the company you work for remains a funda-mental behavioural necessity in the hospitality and accommodation industry. This does not mean that you should not question policies or work modes, but it does mean that as long as you are employed you should remain, at least in public, totally loyal to your company.

Comments to colleagues about the company or other staff members in front of guests should be avoided at all times. Failure to do this may instil some unsettling feelings in guests and convey an inappropriate impression.

Guest and staff politics

Good manners and management guidelines should be combined with simple procedures that can case tension, aid communication and lessen feelings of isolation and victimisation. For instance, it is bad manners to spread rumours, to gossip incessantly about others, to form small groups or cliques, to sneak on a workmate or to generally malign your colleagues and your employer.

It is good manners, however, to be polite, civil and positive with everybody at all times, unless special circumstances require you to be otherwise. Resist the temptation to get involved in the politics of your workplace unless it is absolutely necessary.

Mobile telephones and bleepers

However much these innovations have made our lives easier, they can also be a nuisance and very intrusive at times. However, they are definitely here to stay, so we have to make them an integral part of our business and social lives with care. This can be difficult when a person with whom you are speaking face-to-face is continually taking calls and apparently ignoring you. If you are being ignored, the best action is to pick up a newspaper, use the time effectively, and read. However, if there are so many calls that it looks as if you are not going to be able to finish the meeting in peace, suggest that you reconvene the meeting for a later time. Most people will get the hint, and will either switch off their telephone or allow incoming calls to go through to the voice mail facility.

Bleepers can be very distracting to guests. The vibrating variety are far less intrusive but have created a new wave in body language: when the bleeper is activated, the receiver automatically reaches inside their jacket or to the top of their trousers or skirt to glance at the message. This is amusing, but it is worthwhile developing a more acceptable style of reaction if you want to look more professional.

Memos

Memos should be treated with respect by both the sender and the receiver. Memos are a very good tool for communication, but should only be used to give thoughts, information and directions a permanent form that a spoken communication would not give. Memos can be stored for future reference; they should not be used for very personal communications such as complaints or praise about job performances. Typed and dated, they require no introduction or signature—just the relevant information with the time, date, subject, sender and recipient. Email is now the preferred alternative to memos where this is practicable: the same guidelines still apply.

Meetings

Meetings should only be necessary when there is a reason to have one. Clever time-managers will set an agenda rather than just the starting time and closing time of the meeting. Punctuality is essential. So too is allowing other people to finish their statements without interruption.

Interrupting other people is very frustrating, as it often breaks a line of thought. It is bad manners not to turn up to a meeting where your presence has been requested. Once at the meeting you should appear interested in the topics and offer clear input without interrupting, monopolising the conversation or becoming in any way aggressive. The best outcomes are achieved with calm and constructive discussion. Meetings should be kept as short as possible.

Personal questions

When it comes to conversation, there are several subjects that are definitely taboo. These will be discussed in more detail in the next chapter on communication. Direct and indirect questions designed to discover other people's income, parentage, education or the cost of a possession are unacceptable.

So too are questions about personal matters, for instance if the other person—particularly if they are a guest—says that they have been ill or in hospital. It is inappropriate to say anything more than 'I do hope it was nothing serious' and leave the other person to elaborate if they wish to do so.

Younger people, however, are becoming more open about these questions, and in certain cultures they may be acceptable. Etiquette suggests that you should be sure which cultures are not keen on such personal questions before you embark on such a line of questioning.

Swearing

Nowadays, very few of the traditionally 'taboo' words offend people so much. However, that does not mean that they acceptable to everyone. The interpretation of swearing, like beauty, is in the eye (or ear!) of the beholder. It is better to avoid swearing or using bad language in other people's company. Although some words are accepted as exclamations of frustration, irritation or pain, adopting a substitute word has the benefit of allowing you to get the wrath out of your system without losing control.

Gifts and presents

Guests from time to time love to give presents to staff as a mark of their appreciation. It not only gives them pleasure, but they want to give pleasure as well. Accepting gifts graciously is important; offence given at this stage will be hard to retract. Thank the giver sincerely, assuring them that you appreciate their thoughtfulness. Don't feel obliged to open such gifts immediately; however, givers of gifts generally like to see reactions (but see the next paragraph).

If you are giving a gift to a guest, be sure that it is appropriate. Consider the weight for a start, which is a very important consideration for travellers. Make sure the value of the gift will not embarrass them, and don't press or expect the guest to open the gift straightaway. Some people are very shy about receiving gifts and consider it inappropriate to their culture or background to rush into opening the gift like a child at a birthday party!

Treatment of airline crews

Airline crews should be treated exactly like other guests: as VIPs. Try to make them feel special. Often it is very difficult for crews, since they are usually very tired. Realise that the short time they are going to spend at your hotel is crucial to how well they are going to cope with the next leg of their travel. Every effort should be made to ensure that they have a smooth and comfortable stay. Any form of complacency in providing such a service to airline crews is unacceptable.

Good relationships can be created by offering extra hospitality such as a room set aside for airline crews to meet and relax in during their stay or prior to their check-out. A special area could be set aside for regular visiting crew members who require storage for surfboards, sports gear, sewing machines and hobby items, or even summer and winter clothes.

Although airline crews may indicate that they want the same service, that's not necessarily true; it is important to give them their own space. At all times maintain a pleasant, interested and positive attitude. Like all guests, they are also potential 'salespeople' for your hotel!

In summary

All the aspects of manners covered in this chapter are essential to becoming, and giving the impression of, a true professional. This form of self-discipline can actually make you feel better about the image you are conveying. Despite the fact that, in the hospitality industry, we all have to 'act' from time to time, these 'image improvers' should not just be part of an act—they should come naturally.

4
Communication: the basics

Although the subject of etiquette and manners was well covered in Chapter 3, it is important to look more closely now at one of the most obvious manifestations of manners, both good and bad: the way in which we communicate with one another. Much of what we do in the hospitality and accommodation industry involves conversational communication, and the most successful professionals have gained a high degree of confidence in talking to others.

Sometimes we may feel that this form of communication—conversation—is not going anywhere. However, everyone has a story to tell and you may be amazed at what you can learn from the most unexpected sources. There are certainly plenty of occasions when, in the course of your work, good conversation may not only prove interesting but may well defuse a potentially awkward or difficult situation by creating a more relaxed atmosphere.

In this chapter we shall cover basic conversational skills and how to read and convey body language. We shall also explain the value of listening—a powerful tool that assists in increasing confidence in conversation for both social and business purposes.

The art of good conversation

Well-mannered speakers seek to put those around them at ease. They are as good at listening as they are at talking, and have the ability to come up with easy, appropriate and sometimes amusing conversation.

Ill-mannered speakers, on the other hand, sadly have none of these qualities. Some fortunate people seem naturally to possess good conversational skills, while others have to learn them over a period of time.

The essence of making good conversation is to give someone your total attention and ask them about themselves. The ability to make conversation is one of the most charming arts, since it not only involves self-expression but also creates spaces in which others can express themselves.

Every time you meet someone and strike up a conversation you are unconsciously revealing all sorts of things about yourself. At the same time, you are able to assess certain points about them without making hasty judgements.

Conversation openers

Opening a conversation is often the most difficult part. The best 'starter' questions aren't over-personal but still allow the other people to reveal something about themselves. It requires a great deal of tact and a certain knowledge of the world to decide just how you do this successfully.

A good opening move is the invitation, 'Tell me.' Pause, look attentive and then follow up with a suitable question, preferably one that is an implied compliment. Listen to the answer carefully and attentively, maintain eye contact, pick out some point in the answer and say, 'That's very interesting; so you...' and repeat the point. This not only flatters the speaker but makes them feel understood and appreciated. So naturally they will expand on the subject.

To bring more people into the conversation, turn to them and tell them that the other person has been saying something interesting (use any appropriate adjective that fits) about X, Y or Z and politely encourage that person to repeat it. Amazingly, instant group conversation will result and you—who set it in motion—will be seen as a great conversationalist and host.

As a student or guest service staff member you may well think good conversation is a waste of time. However, as you progress through your career you will find the benefits of such skills invaluable in achieving rapport with guests, other staff members and business associates, not to mention the benefits gained from conversational networking.

Training exercise: party talk

Write some ideas for conversation openers for various situations in the hospitality industry such as the General Manager's cocktail party, riding in the elevator with a guest or waiting for another staff member or guest to join you. Then try out these suggestions in a group session.

The jargon of leisure activities

Jargon is often derided as a device to exclude those who aren't part of the 'in' group. However, when total strangers meet, they look for common ground in the sports, games or cultural activities that they all enjoy. It is now that jargon comes into its own! It is actually a very useful form of verbal 'shorthand' for a group who understand the topic they are discussing.

Four forms of recreation that are enjoyed everywhere are horseracing, tennis, golf and sailing, and it will often be possible to initiate a conversation, or keep one going, if you understand the jargon that goes with each one. Of course, there are countless other leisure pastimes that people like to talk about, and you are advised to gain as wide a knowledge as you can about them. As a start, turn to the glossary at the back of this book, where you will find some useful jargon that will help you when guests want to discuss any of the four sporting activities mentioned above.

Popular card games and casino games

Although you may not play any of these games or go to a casino, again it is always useful to know what other people are talking about.

- **Roulette** Roulette is one of the oldest and most famous casino games. A small ball is rolled around a shallow bowl with numbered sections. The object of the game is for players to guess correctly which number the ball will come to rest on. In addition, alternative bets can be made by betting on the winning number's colour, and whether it is even or odd.
- **Blackjack** (also known as **Vingt-et-un** or **Pontoon**) This is a card game in which each player's aim is to obtain from the dealer cards totalling 21 points, or more than the dealer's total without exceeding 21.
- **Mini baccarat** (also known as **Chemin de fer**) Baccarat is generally considered to be a more glamorous game with high limits, played in elegant surroundings. The object of the game is for the player to choose which side—the player or the banker—will finish closest to nine when all the cards have been drawn. Even with nominal stakes this game is exciting.
- **Stud poker** (originally known as **Brag**) This is a form of poker in which each player is dealt some cards face down and some face up. In casinos it is usually played against the 'house'.
- **Craps** Craps is a fast action game. The object is to bet on or against the numbers, or dice, that will be thrown by the shooter. Each player has a chance to be the shooter. Often the first throw of seven or eleven wins.
- **Two up** Two up is a traditional Australian game and a national favourite. The object of the game is for the player to select either

heads or tails, and just wait to see where the two pennies come to rest after they have been tossed in the air.

- **Pai gow** Pai gow, which translates as 'make nine', originated in China several thousand years ago. Steeped in the traditions of ancient gaming, it is the oldest game played in today's casinos. Each player receives two hands of tiles or dominos and plays against the banker's hands to win.

Training exercise: jargon

Using the above text and the 'sporting jargon' glossary (page 255) as a guide, develop your own vocabulary of specific areas of interest to guests such as opera, literature, other sports and music (both contemporary and classical). In a discussion group, discuss the merits of this information and how it can be incorporated into both your styles of service and your conversation.

Points and pitfalls in conversation

Drifting eyes

There are a few 'dos' and 'don'ts' in the art of conversation. It has already been mentioned that you should give your undivided attention; this applies not only to your conversation but also to your body language. 'Cocktail party eyes'—that is, glancing over your companion's shoulder, quite obviously to spy on who else is present—can be offensive, rude and hurtful. Although you may need to be aware of what is going on around you, you have to be diplomatic. It is far better to excuse your behaviour by being honest about checking to see if a particular person is in sight. Likewise, if your feet are pointing away from the other person or group, it will give the impression that you would rather be going in that direction.

Group conversations

In a group nobody should dominate the conversation; at the same time, nobody should be left out. This can be quite a complex task. Although there are many people who would prefer to listen rather than take part, they should be encouraged to join in. For instance, if the topic is controversial you can bring a shy person into the conversation by saying 'Well, what do you think about this?' Most people will be pleased to venture an opinion.

Taboo topics

Certain areas may be sensitive. While there are fewer taboo topics these days, it is still tactful to respect the other person's privacy in regard to certain subjects such as income, religion, sexual preferences

or even political preferences. With guests, it is important not to say anything that may upset or offend them in any way, so these subjects need careful handling and an awareness of the cultural background of the guest. Discussions about ailments, allergies and therapies are now commonplace, but your own anxieties and troubles are best kept to yourself; otherwise they can give a negative impression.

Sex, like money, can be a compulsive subject for some, but many people are more reticent about such matters, believing them to be very private areas of interest.

Valuable opportunities

Some time ago it was considered inappropriate or tacky to comment on the décor or the food and wine; but now, because it is such a common interest among people, it is good value as a topic of conversation. This is particularly the case for anyone involved in the hospitality industry, as it may represent a good opportunity to upsell one of the outlets or the next grade of room or suite.

Name-dropping

A common pitfall is name dropping, in the mistaken belief that this will impress. The socially insecure will sometimes subscribe to this line of conversation. It can be irritating and besides, you do not know whether anyone in the group or party is acquainted with the person in question. Title- or name-dropping to show that you know or deal with eminent people or guests implies that you feel superior by association. This is not just bad manners and bad politics; it also creates jealousy and dislike. If you have to mention a name in the course of a conversation, take the simplest line and use the most formal name possible so that you do not appear to be over-familiar. Here is one helpful technique: rather than say 'the Company President and I worked on that . . . ', you could say 'I had the good fortune to be able to help the Company President on that . . . '

Social silences

A pause in conversation should not be allowed to go on for too long. It is far better to start another topic as soon as possible; otherwise these social silences can seem like an eternity. Try making a light remark to someone across the group so that all are aware of the new line, or ask a general question such as 'What does everybody think about ... (suggest a movie title)?' This sort of remark usually gets some response, and the conversation will flow again.

Title formalities

The use of first names is becoming more widespread in our industry as a result of our attempts to be more friendly and approachable. However, there are still a lot of people who would for the time being prefer to be more formal. Usually older people still expect to be addressed by their full names. If this sounds a little old-fashioned, it may be worth thinking about this quotation from the movie *Twelve Angry Men*. One of the jurors asks: 'Why are you so polite?' The other juror replies: 'For the same reasons you are not. I was brought up like that. This rather sharp remark illustrates why some people adhere to their traditions and cultures. The use of 'sir' or 'ma'am' is nearly always safe, even when dealing with younger people.

Interrupting

Interrupting other people's conversations is a bad habit. It often happens out of excitement over what is being said. As a guest service staff member you are unlikely to interrupt to disagree; however, this is permissible if someone is misquoting you or misinterpreting something you have said. Many people use another person's remarks as an excuse to launch into their own favourite topic, which is usually about themselves. Apart from being irritating, this is just another form of bad manners and distracts the speaker from the subject. If someone interrupts a conversation you are involved in, simply smile and go back to the original speaker and suggest that he or she continue. If you are interrupted, perhaps by another staff member, just hold up your hand to indicate that they should wait and keep talking. Guests will appreciate your undivided attention.

Training exercise: handling tricky questions

Discuss the following situations and suggest how you would deal with them.

- You are explaining some points to a guest, and another staff member interrupts with a comment that is incorrect.
- Someone asks you to guess their age or the price of something they have bought.
- A guest or another staff member makes an offensive sexual joke.
- A guest asks you an embarrassing personal question.
- A staff member starts gossiping about one of your friends.

'Something to say'

Never miss an opportunity to ask if a guest is enjoying his or her stay. If the guest does not look too busy, you can continue the conversation by asking a sensible question, but at all times be sincere and show that you are interested in the answer. However, if other people are engrossed in a conversation and you need to talk to them, stand back and wait until they have noticed your presence before launching into your speech.

Body language: a framework for understanding

As we settle into this new century, we are beginning to recognise the value of studying non-verbal communication. It is an essential component of understanding more about our guests and customers in both the travel and the hospitality industries. Professor Albert Mehrabian, a well-respected expert in the field of communication, found in his studies that the total impact of a message was about 7 per cent verbal, 38 per cent vocal (including tone of voice) and 55 per cent non-verbal.

Regardless of culture, certain words and movements occur together with such predictability that someone who is well trained should be able to tell what movement the other person is making just by listening to their voice. Conversely, what they are saying can be assessed by simply watching their gestures.

Body language recognition

We all have the ability to understand non-verbal language. Shortly after birth we all began to recognise body language. It usually signalled what was going to happen next. As babies we cried and our parents, more often than not, stretched out their arms to pick us up and comfort or feed us.

Most of us are much better attuned to the interpretation of body language than we think, but for the most part we have become very lazy! Just look at the way babies or children use body language to get what they need. And babies don't just use body language; they can also instinctively recognise what another person is seeking to convey. Of course, once our vocabulary increases and we learn the need for tact and diplomacy, we subconsciously begin to control the movements that go with our verbal communication.

Some body language gestures are clear. If a guest fiddles with their teeth they may require a toothpick; if they shade their eyes when they are sitting next to a window you may need to shut out the sun by closing the curtains. If you interpret these gestures correctly, you will not need to ask so many questions.

Some of the signs
of weariness.

Throughout the course of a day in the hospitality industry we see many emotions. We could give even better service if we paused for a few moments to study the accompanying body language. This would enable us to anticipate a guest's needs without asking if they needed help, when it is quite obvious that they do! This less obvious approach will clearly pay dividends.

For example, when guests arrive, more often than not they are tired from travelling. They may convey this by wearing a more serious facial expression, rubbing their eyes, easing their neck with their hands, stretching, putting their fingers through their hair frequently, moving more slowly and, of course, yawning.

Similarly, in new surroundings, guests may be a little confused. There will be some shaking or scratching of the head and frowning. This should not to be mistaken for disbelief in which, along with the head-shaking, the eyes are usually wide open. Turn the situation around and ask yourself how you, in this situation, would like to be treated. Consider your reactions if you feel and look exhausted and someone walks up to you and brightly asks if you are tired! Instead, it may be better to say 'You look tired; is there anything I can help you with?'

Since most guests are likely to be feeling exhausted, they will probably show some signs of impatience when they cheek in. Tapping the fingers, sighing, shaking the head, walking back and forth or moving around a lot will all be good indicators of this. The obvious, and best, course of action here will be to help with the luggage. Many hotels now offer hot and cold refresher towels at this stage—absolute bliss for the weary traveller (see pages 133-4). If it is at all possible, offer the guest a seat and perhaps a refreshing drink while you speed up the check-in process as much as possible. Showing sympathy and an interest in the guest's journey helps tremendously.

The whole object of understanding body language is to reduce the number of questions and answers necessary to find out the guest's needs and not prolong their discomfort. The key is in your ability to anticipate their needs by quickly studying their body language and then deciding on the best way to distract and reassure them.

Cultural versus genetic gestures

All cultures use much the same facial gestures to show emotion, which indicates that these gestures may well be inborn or inherited. When you cross your arms on your chest, do you cross left over right or right over left? Most people cannot confidently tell you which way until they try to do it! While one way feels comfortable the other way feels completely wrong. Evidence suggests that this may well be a genetic gesture that cannot be easily changed.

We do all sorts of things without giving them a second thought. Some of these gestures are part of our personality, such as running our fingers through our hair in a particular way or expressing certain emotions such as thoughtful concentration when we are interested, or shaking our heads furiously when we disagree. We often find ourselves copying our parents' style of non-verbal communication.

Most basic communication gestures are the same all over the world. When people are happy they smile; when they are sad or angry they frown or scowl. Nodding the head is almost universally used for 'yes', while shaking it usually means 'no'.

The shoulder shrug is another good example of a universal gesture that is used to show that a person does not know what you are talking about. It is a multiple gesture with three main components: exposed palms, hunched shoulders and raised brow.

Gesture clusters

A combination of gestures is often referred to as a cluster. One of the most serious mistakes a novice in body language can make is to interpret a solitary gesture in isolation from other accompanying gestures and the surrounding circumstances. For instance, folding the arms across the body should not be interpreted on its own; there are several reasons why people may use this gesture. Scratching the head is another example. It can mean a number of things: dandruff, fleas, sweating, uncertainty, forgetfulness or lying, depending on the other gestures that occur with it. So it is important to check out these other gestures before making any assessments of the person's mood.

A common 'critical evaluation' cluster is the hand-to-face gesture with the index finger pointing up the cheek while another finger covers the mouth and the thumb supports the chin. Further evidence that this listener is critical of the speaker may be tightly crossed legs, which usually means 'I don't like what you are saying and what's more, I disagree with you.' In 'body language lingo' this group of gestures is a cluster. Here two, three or more gestures need to be assessed together in order to come to some reasonable conclusion.

Gestures should be interpreted according to the accompanying body language. Folded arms do not always convey negative emotions.

One of the best and most effective ways to learn more about this area of non-verbal communication is to either sit in a park or public place and just watch, or turn down the volume on the television or video and see just how much you can learn by studying other people's body movements and what you are able to read from them.

As you become more perceptive, these gestures will begin to form 'sentences' and will invariably give some indication about the other person's true feelings and attitudes. Some gestures are open, expansive and positive; some show interest and acceptance; others send negative messages of defensiveness, indifference, anger and rejection.

A classic example of the importance of reading these clusters is the above mentioned one of the folded arms. A stance with the arms folded, shoulders almost rigidly square, face set in a serious expression and feet set apart could indicate that the person is not happy—in fact, more likely angry. However, a slight change in the shoulders to a hunched position may show that the person is feeling cold. Or the same person could relax their shoulders, sink into a chair, cross their legs and fold their arms just for comfort. The interpretation of the other movements is what will lead you to the right conclusion.

Personal space

Another important aspect of body language is personal space. When you want people to feel comfortable in your presence, there is a golden rule: keep your distance. The more intimate our relationship is with another person, the closer we are permitted to move.

Most animals have a certain air space around their bodies that they

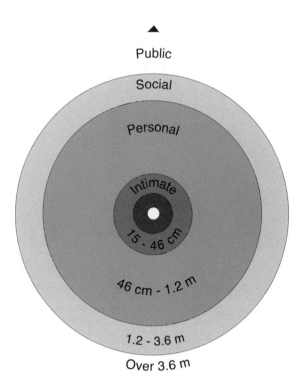

▲

Public

Social

Personal

Intimate

15 - 46 cm

46 cm - 1.2 m

1.2 - 3.6 m

Over 3.6 m

The four personal zones.

claim for their personal space. Human beings are no exception. They, too, have their own personal 'air bubbles' that they carry around with them. The size of the 'bubble' is dependent on the environment in which the individual has been raised—it is culturally determined. People from some cultures, like the Japanese, are more accustomed to crowding. Others prefer wide open spaces and like to keep their distance. In the hospitality industry we need to be very aware of any intrusion we may make into a guest's personal space. Although some people may regard this as friendliness, others may feel awkward and uncomfortable if you are too close to them. Personal space can be divided into four distinct zones:

- When we find ourselves addressing a large group of people, we are in the *public zone*. This is usually over 3.5 metres and seems a comfortable distance to choose in these situations.
- The *social zone* is about 1 to 3.5 metres—a step or two closer, but still keeping at a distance from strangers. This zone is normally reserved for people whom we do not know very well. It applies to the new employee at work, people involved in doing repairs and sales assistants in shops.
- The closer *personal zone*, about 0.5 to just over 1 metre, is the distance we usually stand at friendly gatherings and parties. It is also a comfortable distance to be able to talk and hear other people clearly.
- Of all the zones, the *intimate zone*, between 15 and 45 centimetres, is probably by far the most important, as it is the zone that

each individual is entitled to guard as their own property. Only those who are emotionally close are allowed to enter this zone comfortably—that is, lovers, parents, partners, children, close friends and relatives.

While we may tolerate strangers moving within our personal and social zones, the intrusion of a stranger into our intimate zone causes certain physiological changes to take place within our bodies. The heart begins to pump faster and adrenalin pours into the bloodstream as blood is pumped to the brain and muscles. It is the sort of fear response we have when we feel threatened.

Simply put, this means that standing too close or placing your arm in what you may consider to be a friendly manner on or around someone you have only just met may just result in making that person feel uncomfortable and, in turn, a little negative towards you, although they may not readily show it. You may think that this is just a friendly gesture, but many cultures regard such actions as offensive. Additionally, standing or moving too close to another person will naturally make them step back or retreat in order to retain their own personal space.

One of the many benefits of observing personal space is that you can easily identify the relationship between two people by assessing the distance between them. The closeness of the hips indicates the depth of the relationship, although when two people are kissing it should not be assumed that they are close! It could indicate that they are just good friends.

Small spaces often alter people's facial expressions, giving the impression that they are miserable or unhappy. This is not necessarily the case. In a lift or on public transport, for instance, where people are forced to stand close together, their faces may simply show a dislike of having their personal or intimate zone invaded.

Although you will want guests to feel welcome, remember that you should not stand too close when you greet them. Likewise, when guests are seated consider their personal space. Try to avoid standing too near or towering over them. This will intimidate them and force them to look up at too great an angle, reversing your roles with regard to who should be receiving the respect and attention.

Handshaking styles

The etiquette aspect of shaking hands was covered in Chapter 3 (pages 34-36). However, there is much more to handshaking than that! Handshaking offers the participants a valuable opportunity to do a quick character or personality assessment by observing the overall body language.

Several factors influence handshaking styles. One of these is profession. Musicians, surgeons and others whose jobs require fine work will have a softer handshake. Other people, because of their cultural back-

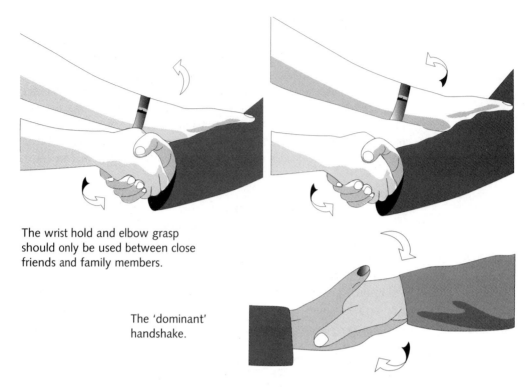

The wrist hold and elbow grasp should only be used between close friends and family members.

The 'dominant' handshake.

ground, may feel very nervous about such a personal greeting and may hold back, unsure of what they should be doing. If you stand back and observe different handshakes, it can be both amusing and illuminating. It will tell you much about people's day-to-day lives. City folk will keep their arms close to their bodies, while their country cousins will go into a handshake with the arm outstretched, showing their familiarity with wide open spaces.

If you continue to watch, you may notice that the left hand is often introduced to create another effect—the 'glove' handshake (see page 35). This, like the wrist hold and the elbow grasp, shows a desire to communicate an extra feeling of security and trust and should generally only be used between close friends and relatives. Sometimes clever salespeople and those wishing to emphasise their sincerity will resort to this tactic. Placing the left hand on the upper arm or shoulder usually signifies an even closer emotional bond and, unless the feeling is mutual, the recipient will become suspicious and distrustful.

Observing handshaking styles can teach you a lot about other people. For instance, watch the way the hand is offered: this will tell you something about the person initiating the handshake. One of three basic attitudes is transmitted through a handshake. The three attitudes are equality, dominance and submission. Often they are transmitted unconsciously. Dominance is conveyed by presenting the hand with the palm down; submission is demonstrated by presenting the palm upwards. Equality is, naturally, shown by the hand in an 'equal' position between the other two styles.

If you spot a 'dominant' handshake coming your way you can, with a little practice, reverse it. Most people, when shaking hands, have their right foot forward. As you take the offered dominant hand, bring your left foot forward so that you enter the other person's intimate zone. This tactic will distract them, thus allowing you to alter or straighten the handshake to that of submission or, better still, equality. Technically no one should be either dominant or submissive; however, each situation can offer a challenge. We in guest service have to exercise our discretion and 'behave' appropriately according to the situation.

In-room body language

Once the guest is installed in their suite or room, in-room etiquette is not only a part of good manners but is also essential to the wellbeing and comfort of the guest. Guests will not appreciate their personal space being invaded. Learn to recognise 'in-room' body language. Many guests may feel quite nervous when staff enter their rooms.

These feelings can be easily recognised; signs will be wandering eyes and little eye contact. Usually the guest will walk slowly about in a distracted fashion and convey a general mood of impatience to see you gone from their suite or room.

If, however, you have posed a question to a guest and they begin rubbing their chin with their hand or fingers, wait until the thought process that this gesture indicates is complete before you continue or interrupt, otherwise you will distract the guest from their answer. The first answer they were considering could well have been more positive.

Some 'negative' body language pointers

Nervousness

Some guests show nervousness at various times during their stay. This can often be indicated by their making little eye contact, looking around, fiddling with clothes or bags and sometimes sitting right on the edge of the chair. Putting people at their ease is a special skill, but most nervous people appreciate an inquiry as to their welfare. You can anticipate this and act accordingly.

Anger

None of us relish an angry guest, since we are in the business of creating calm and comfort. Generally, angry people seem to have a greater effect on others. It's fairly easy to spot anger; it often manifests itself in a serious face with eyebrows furrowed or frowning, clenched fists or closed hands, teeth set together, shaking head, tense shoulders, perhaps a defensive arm-fold and up-and-down pacing. It's more difficult to reverse anger. Anger is often coupled with a complaint, and should be handled carefully. Chapter 6 covers this in detail.

When an angry or complaining guest finds a good listener, who uses their own body language to help—nodding their head to show that they understand the problem, looking at the guest and giving good eye contact—the story they relate often sounds less important than it seemed at first. The powerful tool of listening is covered in the next chapter.

Hand-to-mouth gestures

Hand-to-mouth gestures often signal other emotions such as a feeling of dishonesty. It's important not to see these gestures in isolation, though, because you could misinterpret a very crucial aspect of the other person's body language. Often described as the 'mouth guard', a hand-over-the-mouth gesture could be an unconscious attempt to suppress the deceitful words being said. It works both ways, though, just to confuse the issue! Sometimes a person who is speaking to you will cover their mouth because they are telling a lie; however, if they cover their mouth while you are speaking it indicates that they feel you could be lying—or they may simply be considering what you are saying.

The hand-to-mouth gesture or 'mouth-guard'.

Also, be aware of other gestures that may indicate that the speaker is simply nervous rather than dishonest. Judgements should be made wisely.

Boredom

Boredom can also be identified. It is usually indicated by a blank look on the face, rubbing the eyes or face, raising the shoulders and sighing, letting the eyes wander and tapping the foot.

Bored people showing these signs could be offered some distraction to take their minds away from their boredom. A magazine or a newspaper can be a good distraction; alternatively, a suggestion of some activity that may be available, such as a swimming pool or sauna, may be helpful.

Boredom.

Worry

Worry puts a preoccupied expression on the person's face; accompanying signs can be perspiration, tense shoulders and rubbing of the face with the hands. Without even asking, your first step should be to try and reassure. If you see someone who is worried, offer some kind words (such as 'Is there anything/something I can do to help you?' or 'How can I help you?') but resist the urge to pry into their private life. This approach usually results in the other person 'opening up' with their concerns, some of which you may be able to help sort out.

'Positive' body language pointers

A relaxed manner is a noticeable part of a confident person's body language.

Positive body language includes an expression of delight and excitement on the face, smiles, wide eyes and rubbing the hands together. Surprise can be recognised by an open mouth or raised eyebrows. A relaxed person drops their shoulders, crosses their legs, leans back in the chair and generally has a happy facial expression.

Confidence

Confidence manifests itself in a variety of gestures: straight body, upright head, relaxed shoulders, swinging hair, sometimes an exaggerated walk, plenty of eye contact, hands in pockets, a smile and perhaps one hand holding the wrist of the other arm behind the back. Confident people need to be handled in a quietly confident manner; they respond well to a professional and informed approach.

When to wait

Guests conversing with each other

Guests in conversation often give pointers such as hands moving for emphasis, preening and stroking. Steepling the hands upwards indicates that an opinion is being given. Steepling downwards indicates listening, sometimes with a slight smugness. If two guests in a lounge or restaurant are engaged in a deep conversation with their heads together and eye contact with each other, you should reconsider interrupting them at that moment. If this is the case, it is far better to wait at a suitable distance from the guests until they become aware of your presence. They will then naturally make a break in their conversation, allowing a polite interruption.

If guests are deep in conversation, do not break in and interrupt; stand a little way off.

Concentration

Concentration has many styles. Usually it is shown by the head or chin resting on the hand and a frown. Again, you should ask yourself whether you should be interrupting this guest. A quick assessment is very worthwhile.

Concentration.

Recognising when guests need assistance

In restaurants, guests' needs can be interpreted quite easily; a guest in need of assistance may be looking around and perhaps using a hand wave. Looking at a watch will indicate impatience or annoyance. Head-shaking may mean exasperation.

When to go

And by the way—if you are standing with a guest, don't forget to notice the direction of their feet. When someone feels the conversation has run its course, very often one of their feet will unconsciously move in the direction they wish to go. When people disagree they may unconsciously turn their bodies away from each other, indicating their displeasure.

Some more indicators

There are many factors in body language that may inspire and help you in your interpretation.

One is status and power. Royal personages, politicians and entrepreneurs often display their status with far more confident gestures than the people they regard as being on a different social level. Likewise age, culture and background are pointers. It's well worth bearing in mind that certain cultures have a low tolerance of some of the more casual forms of Western body language.

Children and teenagers have far more innocent body language than adults; they have no inhibitions about flinging their arms around. However, by the mid to late teens they tend to become conscious of their bodies and begin to rein in their more extroverted gestures and make them subtler. As adults we are very aware of ourselves and seek to control our emotions and any hints that these may communicate through our body movements.

Continual awareness of body language in your workplace will make your job a lot easier and, most of the time, more enjoyable. It offers a valuable insight into human nature.

So how should we look?

It's subtlety that we need to cultivate in our industry. Whatever our role in the hospitality industry and regardless of where we work in the world, our own personal body language will set the scene and help to create the right atmosphere. The following points are noteworthy.

The professional look

Even with just an upright standing position we are letting the guests know that we are professional. Slouched shoulders, a hanging head, bent neck and scuffing feet are all very negative pointers. We need to show we are ready for action, alert to our role within our place of work. If you have difficulty in achieving this demeanour, try pretending you are on stage or playing to a video camera. This will give you the motivation to be aware of your own body language, and thereby achieve a better result. Traditionally actors were always advised not to turn their backs to the audience. Since in this industry we are always on show, this is a good first step.

The smile

To keep a smile on your face continually is hard work, but it should never be far from the surface. The minute a guest walks in, tune the guest in and the world out. Give total attention wherever possible. Your smile must be genuine; use not just your facial muscles but also your eyes to convey this sincerity. A good smile is one of your most important assets.

Well-mannered personal body language

Good personal body language means giving full attention through your body language. In other words, try to avoid having your body turned slightly away from the guest; this will suggest some lack of interest. In order to indicate full attention, your feet should be pointing towards the guest. Your head should be up and your shoulders should be relaxed. If it is appropriate, your hands should be clasped behind your back illustrating a readiness for action. (If your hands are clasped in front of you, you are betraying a slight defensiveness.)

Eye contact

Eye contact is very important in showing recognition and establishing a sense of sincerity. However, this may not be appropriate if the guest is from another culture. In Chapter 5 (pages 77-8) we will look at this question as regards people who, because of their religion or culture, prefer not to make eye contact, for instance Muslims and the Japanese.

Deportment

When you walk, walk with an air of quiet confidence: not too fast, but at the right pace to maintain an attitude of professionalism. Avoid touching guests except to help or guide them in awkward places, such as on steps. Remember that too much familiarity may offend the guest. Resist the temptation to run your fingers through your hair. Don't tidy your hair, don't touch your nose or ears and don't pick your nose. If you have to give some attention to your personal appearance, do it in private. Even if you think that no one is watching, this is no excuse—besides, you may find you've been captured on the security camera! Unless you have something in your eye try not to rub it; this will indicate frustration or tiredness and thus portray a negative attitude.

Positive attitude

With practice your own body language can become a useful tool. Skilful use of good body language will not only make just the right impression, but will also send a powerful message to the guest that will most probably influence their reaction—we hope that this will always be positive.

Your positive body language should include the points we have covered, such as facing the guest properly and maintaining eye contact (where appropriate) to assure the guest that your attention is directed to them. Other gestures should include inclining your head to one side to indicate that you are listening intently and, of course, having a smile on your face.

The resulting positive response from guests will make them much easier to deal with, and when it comes to giving good service we need all the help we can get!

Training exercise: anticipating guests' needs

Now you have this knowledge, put it to work effectively. List the different ways by which you can recognise and anticipate guests' needs and prepare several role-play situations to work with in your group. These role-plays should illustrate as many different tasks that involve contact with the guest as possible. One good way to do this is to divide your group into several smaller teams, prepare and present the first role-play, and then ask each team to create a second 'surprise' role-play that can be circulated to the other teams. Listed below are a few general indications, for your guidance, of some of the more common moods and emotions.

Negative signs

Tiredness or exhaustion	Eyes closed or half-closed; slow movements; head down; putting hand through hair; touching face; easing back or neck
Nervousness or fear	Wide-eyed; restless; no eye contact; moving hands a lot
Anger or frustration	Eyebrows down; staring eyes; straight mouth; fast walk, pacing up and down; use of fist or clenched hand
Impatience	Sighing; nodding head; walking back and forth; tapping fingers or feet
Sadness or seriousness	Crying; frowning; shoulders hunched; turning body away from subject
Confusion	Scratching head; frowning; shaking head
Lying	No eye contact; hand over mouth or near mouth
Disbelief	Shaking head; wide eyes
Worry	Tense shoulders; sweating; frightened face; shaking hands
Absent-mindedness	No eye contact; walking slowly; looking all around

continued

Negative signs

Boredom	Sighing; moving head all around; similar to impatience
Sickness	Expression on face; arms across body; shoulders tense
Embarrassment	No eye contact; biting lips or fingers; moving body from side to side; picking at clothes

Positive signs

Happiness or delight	Open mouth; eyes wide; hands open; smile
Excitement or surprise	Head back in a more relaxed position; mouth slightly open; eyebrows raised
Relaxation or comfort	Happy look on face; shoulders relaxed; legs crossed; open gestures
Thought	Hand-to-face gestures; stroking chin; frowning
Confidence	Straight body; eye contact; head up; faster walk; relaxed shoulders; smile

Training exercise: guest/customer relations

How well do you communicate with guests and other staff? How do you react when things are busy and you are under pressure? Can improving your body language techniques, conversation and communication skills and the powerful tool of listening work?

Test your people skills by deciding what you would do in each of the following situations; then produce a 'personal format' or your own set of guidelines for handling these and other such situations.

1   A small group of tourists carrying suitcases is standing ahead of you in the bus queue. They are studying a map with puzzled looks on their faces. You overhear one of them saying 'But do you think we can get to where we want to go from here?' What would you do?

2   A gentleman arrives for a 10.00 a.m. appointment with Mr Walshe, the hotel Sales Manager. After he has waited half an hour, becoming steadily more impatient, he complains in a loud voice: 'This is intolerable! Why is your hotel always so disorganised? Don't you care about your other customers at all?' What do you say?

3   A guest says in a loud voice: 'Hey you! Do you think you could stop talking long enough to give me some service over here?' You are currently dealing with another guest. How would you handle this?

5
Communication: putting the basics to work

Meeting and greeting guests

Every time you see a guest, you should smile and make an appropriate comment. But be aware that there are some expressions that become increasingly annoying and sound trite. Questions like 'How are you?', 'Have you had a good day?', 'Have you had your lunch yet?' and 'Are you on holiday?' should periodically be re-examined and the scripts edited. A courteous staff member says the right words; a warm staff member uses the right tone. Oddly enough, guests expect all staff to be pleasant and well-mannered at all times, regardless of any hassles or frustrations they may be experiencing.

Speak to the guest in a friendly, enthusiastic, courteous tone and manner. Inquire if they are enjoying their holiday, if they are having a good day or whether they need some ideas for other things to do in your city, but be ready for their answers. If you do not think you can handle the answer, don't ask the question. In other words, be prepared for a negative reply. That way, you can tailor your next comment to provide a distraction. Answer the guest's questions or requests as quickly and efficiently as possible, or take personal responsibility to get the answers for them.

Watch the guest's body language. This will help you anticipate their needs and resolve any immediate problems. If by looking at the guest

UNIT

THHGCSO2A

and reading their body language you sense that they have a purpose or are on a mission, don't hinder them any more than necessary.

Differences between cultures

It is appropriate at this stage to offer some advice about different nationalities. Each nation has its own code of conduct, which to people from other cultures may seem quite bewildering. Much has been written regarding the differing behavioural norms of individual countries. The following information, though brief, should help you find ways to approach and deal with people of these nationalities. The nationalities are listed alphabetically for the sake of impartiality.

UNIT

THHCORO2A

- **American** Americans love friendliness and a show of interest in what they are doing, and expect good service. Be prepared for a detailed order or set of instructions. These should be carried out with efficiency and not haste. Americans expect clear answers to their questions. Anticipate language problems—some words do not have the same meaning as they do in other English-speaking countries.

- **Australian** Australians are often described as being overfamiliar and friendly. This is borne out in their tendency to shorten expressions—'brekky' for breakfast, 'stubby' for a small glass bottle of beer and 'g'day' for 'good day'—and abbreviate names to nicknames or diminutives. They can be very direct and forthright; but this is often mitigated by a tendency to be casual or 'laid back', and they do joke a lot.
- **Chinese** The Chinese appreciate a tidy appearance and it is essential know your products. A sensitivity to Asian religions is important, and too much eye contact should be avoided. The Chinese are dedicated and sophisticated shoppers and will ask many questions about merchandise, menu items and products in general.
- **English** The English can be impatient, awkward, sarcastic, formal and sometimes a little pedantic. Like all guests they need to be respected; they ask a lot of questions and expect good service. However, they won't always complain when they don't get it—they simply won't come again. But they do have a highly-developed, and often subtle, sense of humour.
- **French** The French are usually well dressed, though not always when they are on holiday, when they really relax and sometimes even appear untidy. Their manner is often misunderstood for unfriendliness. They are, however, demanding and discerning. They are very careful with money but do enjoy good food and wine, take their time over dining and sometimes become very noisy and excitable.
- **German** Germans expect fast, efficient service. They tend to speak in a very formal manner. Be prepared for abrupt requests; these demands are not intended to be rude. They are very precise in their requests. It is wise to be careful with humour, because it can easily be misinterpreted. In a working situation a tidy appearance is important. Good service is considered to be efficient service.
- **Italian** The Italians who travel are usually quite wealthy; they enjoy and expect good quality and good service. They can be quite demanding and are sometimes concerned about their privacy. They are often considered a bit snobbish, but they do not mean to be rude. They can be very noisy and exuberant. They particularly enjoy strong coffee, good wines and, like the French, smoke strong cigarettes.
- **Japanese** The Japanese should always be addressed as 'sir' or 'ma'am', or by their last name followed by '-san'. They appreciate

it if you do not introduce yourself by your first name; this is generally considered too familiar. Rather than shaking hands, many of the older Japanese prefer a return bow from the waist. However, many of the more 'western-travelled' Japanese now give handshakes as a matter of form. Apart from avoiding eye contact, always be pleasant in your manner and careful with humour. Respond to their questions as clearly as possible. Speak clearly, using no slang if possible. If a misunderstanding arises, a sincere apology is the best remedy.

- **Russian** Russians are now travelling more frequently. They can be very noisy and are unlikely to speak English, or any language other than their own. They do, however, spend a lot of money, often without asking the price. Because of language problems, this can create some difficulties that need careful handling.

Entering a guest room or suite: the 'open door four-step'.

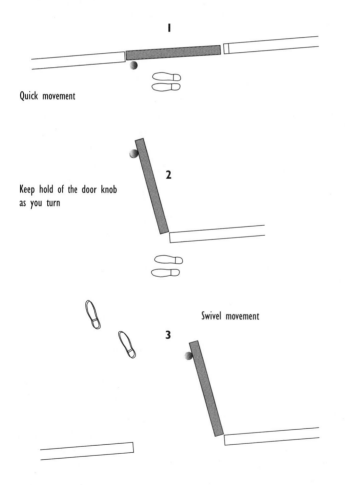

I

Quick movement

Keep hold of the door knob as you turn

2

Swivel movement

3

Entering a guest room or suite

Before you even contemplate knocking on a guest's door, check to see if the 'Do not disturb' sign is displayed. Double check the exterior of the suite or room for any other signal that may warn you, such as a red or green light. Another indicator may be the presence of a morning newspaper that has not yet been pulled under the door. For further instructions, contact housekeeping if necessary. However, if all is clear, knock on the door and announce yourself. Your introductory greeting should be clear, polite and friendly.

Wait eight to twelve seconds and listen for room noises, or the guest's reply, before knocking again.

- If the guest answers, allow them to open the door, introduce yourself and address them by name if possible. Then offer the service or

4

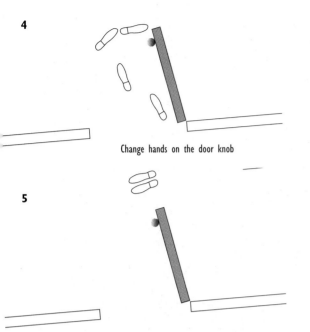

Change hands on the door knob

5

explain your reason for being there. Enter the room and place the item or continue the service with the door open.

- If there is no answer, the guest may still be in the room. Knock again. Open the door slowly and make some noise, such as a polite cough, so as to avoid startling the guest, introducing yourself at the same time: 'Good morning. . .' Enter the room and place the item or continue the service with the door open.

After completing your task, excuse yourself and walk out quietly, closing the door behind you in a discreet manner.

How to become good at listening

Before we start discussing the powerful tool of listening, check out your own listening skills. Just after contact with one or more other people, assess yourself. Ask yourself these questions and see if you can answer them fifteen minutes later:

- What colour were the person's eyes?
- What did they do with their hands?
- How comfortable were they with you?
- How effective were your questions in drawing them out?
- How well did you understand what they were wanting or looking for?
- What distinctive or unique features do you remember about them?
- Do you remember their names?
- Could you call them by their names and recognise them again?
- If they called you on the telephone would you remember them?
- If they described you to another person, how would you want them to do it?

Since this exercise concentrated on testing your visual observation of others, you are probably wondering what it has to do with listening. Listening is not just about listening to a voice; it is also about becoming aware of other factors that can help you establish a future rapport. How would you feel if someone you spoke to fifteen minutes ago had promptly forgotten all about you? Not very good, I suspect. The key to listening is to observe not just the voice but the features as well. This is especially important when you are conversing with someone from another country. Ask any foreign-language student what they find hardest about another language—they will nearly always say it is the tone or the inflection of the spoken word, apart from the obvious difficulty they may have with slang.

Remember to:
• listen to people's words
• listen to their tone of voice
• listen to their body language
• listen to their features

All these pointers will help you give service with extra empathy.

Pay attention

After you have carefully asked a guest how you can help them, it's time to do something that very few people do well—listen! When you become good at listening to people you'll tower above others who may try to take your guests away from you.

Don't just listen casually; tune in to each person and cut out your own distractions. Really listen to what they tell you, but more importantly listen to their tone of voice and observe their body language.

Listening isn't just hearing, it's also understanding. It's understanding feelings and emotions. It's picking up subtle voice inflections and meanings. It's observing what people do with their hands and eyes—the congruence of their body language with their words.

A lot is said about interpersonal skills. The word 'interpersonal' is a term used to describe a set of social skills that help us succeed in dealing with other people. When it comes to interpersonal communication—specifically listening—remember that each person we meet has a common need: for us to listen to how they feel through what they have to say. Be sure to listen to people's emotions, not just their words. To do this successfully we have to break our preoccupation with whatever we were thinking about when we were interrupted. Unfortunately our preoccupations get in the way of effective listening. Preoccupation is thinking about something else when we are supposed to be listening to the customer! It's allowing our own feelings, biases or problems to occupy our thoughts, and screening out what people are saying to us.

Our own emotions can also get in the way. We may want to put forward our suggestions without properly listening, or interrupt before the other person has finished speaking, or tune out from the conversation in order to plan our reply in advance. Even anger, happiness or enthusiasm gets in the way of our listening. It quickly becomes clear that when we don't listen properly we are unable to respond effectively. While this is quite normal behaviour for most of us, our guests and customers feel they have a certain right to our undivided attention, since they are paying for it.

In the previous chapter I spoke of drifting or 'cocktail party' eyes (page 57). When you buy something from someone, just watch what they do with their eyes and hands. People often say the right words, but their eyes lack congruence and betray their real feelings or focus of attention. People who are really listening to you look into your eyes. In other words, when people aren't looking into your eyes, it's virtually impossible for them to hear everything you are trying to tell them. However, this does not necessarily apply to people from an Asian background, who may have different feelings about eye contact, as we shall discuss in more depth in the next chapter.

You can train yourself to make eye contact. Constantly do it with each guest for 21 days and you'll develop a habit so strong that you will then do it unconsciously. It will just be a natural part of your communication skills.

Looking into just one of the other person's eyes while you are listening to them will make a much stronger impact on them. When you have focused eye contact you concentrate all your emotional energy upon them. Doing this automatically helps break any preoccupation that you might have had before you started interacting.

Not only will this focused eye contact make a stronger impact upon people; it will also help you communicate your sincere desire to understand their needs and serve them better. They'll know it too! Another benefit of concentrated eye contact is that it helps you listen to guests much more closely. It enables you to understand them better and assure them that you want to help them. Guests, and people in general, intuitively respect people, including staff, who look them in the eye. All this happens on deep, emotional, unconscious levels. One word of caution, however: do not stare or glare fixedly into another's eyes, as this may be interpreted as anger or hostility.

Mirroring body language often works, although it seems an unlikely aspect of listening. You can very often get more positive responses by modelling the same positive body language or behaviour that the guest is using. Conversely, your own 'open' body language will often encourage guests to follow your lead.

Listening isn't just hearing the words people say; it's also understanding how they feel. It's sensing how open they are to you. It's understanding their tone of voice and body language. It's emotionally plugging into them! We are in a very emotional business: we experience people at their best and at their worst.

Listening is also the highest form of persuasion. There is probably no better way to persuade your guests and to get them to believe you, have confidence in you and buy from you, than to truly listen to them—to show you really care. When you listen, you silently say to guests, 'I want to understand you; I want to understand your needs and wants; I want to solve your problems, because you're important, and I know that when you are happy and satisfied, you'll come back and tell others. Then I'll be more successful.'

Few people listen well. Check this next time you go to buy some-thing or have a problem to solve. You'll make strong, positive impressions on people when you truly listen to them. The secret is lis-ten totally—to break your own preoccupation by tuning your world out and tuning the other person in. Refrain from interrupting people and try to remove biases that filter out what they are saying to you. Your own opinions are simply that—your own—and no one else really needs to know them at this stage.

Finally, notice where guests direct their eyes when they talk and when they listen. This will help you understand their feelings and emo-tions and establish a rapport.

Training exercise: operation recall!

In a group discussion, ask each member of the group to describe a person they met on the way to work or college. Next, ask each member to recall a person or guest they dealt with over the last forty-eight hours. After these sessions ask the group members how easy it was and, if it was difficult, why? List the features that proved to be the main tools in remembering through effective listening.

Approaching guests

In Chapter 1 we discussed first impressions (pages 12-21). We learned that eleven different impressions are made in the first seven seconds of meeting. Approaching a guest or anyone else can be difficult, but you can make it easier if you take a quick mental note of the guest's body language. Then check your own attitude, presentation and body lan-guage as well.

Next you have to decide: do they need to be interrupted? We have already discussed the fact that service is the unique oppor-tunity to make a difference to someone else's life. Before approaching a guest, ask yourself.

- Are they happy?
- Are they relaxed?
- Are they angry?
- Are they nervous?

Once you have assessed all these points, ask yourself again: do they need to be interrupted?

What is the next course of action? ... Think! Ask yourself: is the change you are about to make a positive one? Are you about to convert that positive emotion to a negative emotion?

Having made sure that you do need to approach the guest, what is the best way to do it? Remember the importance of personal space; consider you own body language. Make eye contact and smile. (Your best asset, remember, is your smile.)

A script could run like this: 'Excuse me sir, I know you are busy, but when would be a good time to talk to you about ... ?' Give the guest the choice. Do not assume that other people always want to discuss certain subjects when you do. Mostly guests will concede and answer you, but really sensitive service is about giving them the choice.

When you do ask questions, consider those that are open-ended: in other words, those that begin with 'when', 'why', 'how', 'where', 'what', 'who' and 'which'. Questions that, for instance, simply ask a question like 'Would you like a drink?' will only bring a 'yes' or 'no' response. If the question is rephrased to 'What would you like to drink?' or 'Which cocktail would you like?' it is harder for the guest to reply with a 'yes' or 'no'.

Training exercise: open versus closed questions

Rephrasing a question by putting 'when', 'why', 'how', 'where', 'what', 'who' or 'which' in front not only makes the question more interesting, but also ensures that the reply is not just 'yes' or 'no'. Thus you get the opportunity to upsell as well as get the answer you require. Construct questions that will ensure that you get answers other than 'yes' or 'no' and practise them within your group.

How to remember people's names

Most people will admit that from time to time they have a memory lapse and forget a name. If this happens only occasionally it's not so bad, but if it happens more regularly you stand the chance of giving offence. The section on making introductions in Chapter 3 (pages 41-42) gives some advice about obtaining a personal name that you may have forgotten without anyone losing face.

Over the years lots of techniques have been suggested to help people 'store' names in their minds by noticing something about their appearance and 'storing the connection' as well. Another suggestion is to write the name down. A name that is written down can be more easily remembered. This will give you the opportunity to ask whether you have the correct spelling as well as the correct pronunciation of the name (assuming that the name is not so simple that you should not have forgotten it in the first place).

Getting into the habit of remembering guests' names will be easier if you have a strong desire to do so. In other words, if you take a real—not superficial—interest in the other person it is more likely that you will remember their name in the future. Actually, there is no such thing as a bad memory, as you will see from the following story, which is culled from a fascinating book by Harvey Mackay titled *Swim with the Sharks*.

There is no such thing as a bad memory

Little Johnny, in sixth grade, came home with a report card that was all Ds and Fs. His father asked why. 'I can never remember anything,' answered Johnny. The old man said, 'Well, you're not going to any more baseball games until you get your grades up. And to begin with you can forget tonight's game.'

'Now, wait a minute,' said the kid. 'You can't do that to me. The Dodgers are in town. Valenzuela is pitching. He was 21-11 last year with a 3.14 earned run average, led the league in complete games and victories and was second in innings pitched with 269 and strikeouts with 242.'

Can't remember?

Basically, you can remember anything if you are interested. There are so many people who can't remember names, but they know the words to every song a particular singer has sung, or they can tell a string of amazing jokes or remember all sorts of pieces of trivia. Why? Perhaps at some stage they wrote all the lyrics down or really liked the song; they almost certainly were amused by the jokes or found the trivia interesting.

There is no need to remember everything, though. The brain is like a computer disk; when it gets too full it can store no more information, however hard we try to make it do so. So it makes sense to commit valuable information to the written word. Beryl Pfizer, an American writer, once said 'I write down everything I want to remember. That way, instead of spending a lot of time trying to remember what it is I wrote down, I spend the time looking for the paper I wrote it down on.'

Don't try to rely on your memory for all the information you think you may need. No one expects you to remember all the names of a guest's children, but that doesn't mean that you can't write them down. When you know that the guest is due back in-house, you can quickly check your memory jogger. Before you know it, the guest will think you are a genius! If it's written down you can look it up. Likewise, you don't need to memorise everyone's telephone numbers if you can look them up in a telephone directory.

You can also cultivate a better memory by listening attentively to guests and absorbing their conversation, noticing some detail about their appearance that will jog your memory and writing down notes (not necessarily in front of them) that you can refer to later. If you are in doubt simply apologise, ask the guest for their name and then continue the conversation without letting yourself be intimidated by your temporary lapse. With some practice you can only improve—if you really want to!

Training exercises: shopping lists and art galleries

1   Make a list of 12 items that you might buy from the supermarket. Put it to one side. About two hours later, write the same list in the same order without referring to the original list. You can make this task easier if you are able to picture your local

supermarket and list the items in the order in which you normally find them when you go there.

2   If you are in a group, produce a 'gallery' of photographs of people with real or fictitious names on removable labels. Allow, say, ten photographs for a group of five. After each member has viewed the gallery, remove the names from the photographs, shuffle them and then distribute an equal number of names to each participant. They then have to place the names they have been given under the correct photographs. This exercise should be done without consultation among the participants.

Correct pronunciation

In addition to all that has been discussed in the previous chapter, serious service professionals will want to be sure that they pronounce their words correctly when they communicate with others. This is particularly important when you are talking to people from other countries; incorrect pronunciation may lead to misunderstanding. If you are at all unsure of the right way to pronounce a word, refer to a dictionary. Directly after the word listing in the dictionary you will find a telephonetic breakdown of the word that will help with the pronunciation. At the beginning of the dictionary there is usually a brief guide explaining how the pronunciation is shown. Foreign words that have become part of another language often present difficulty, especially if the language is not your own.

Given the choice between appearing knowledgeable or appearing foolish, wise people do their homework and practise those words that can cause difficulty or confusion. I have compiled a list of some of the more frequently mispronounced words to help you focus on their correct pronunciation and incorporate them in conversations. If you have any doubts about a word from another language and you know someone who speaks that language or comes from the country in question, they will be flattered, to be asked for the correct pronunciation.

Simply battling on and hoping you are right is not recommended. Guests will not only be annoyed but may question an establishment that allows its staff to demonstrate such inadequate knowledge.

croissant	Nuits St Georges	fête
Chardonnay	à tout à l'heure	fromage
Sauvignon	cliente	Moselblümchen
blanc	hôtellerie	Pommery et Greno
rouge	chinois	Gewurztraminer
Launceston (Tas.)	jeudi	Châteauneuf du Pape
Launceston (UK)	Angleterre	entreés
Leicester	au revoir	Côtes du Rhône
brioche	moulin vent	mousse au chocolat

Oustau de Baumanière   Küche   saumon fume
Melbourne (Aust.)   Perrier-Jouet   jus de fruit
Melbourne (UK)   Carrefour   Côtes de Nuit
trompe l'oeiul   Lanson Père et Fils   Camembert
Moët et Chandon

Training exercise: testing talk

Selecting some of the words in the list, or compiling your own list, refer to dictionaries and find the correct pronunciations. Practise these words. This exercise is more successful when you work with a partner or a group. A small tape recorder can be useful; you can use it to play back and listen to your pronunciation and correct it when necessary.

The phonetic alphabet

To relay words successfully, you need to not only pronounce them correctly but spell them correctly as well. Unfortunately, the hospitality industry has a lot of people who can't spell; often they choose to bluff and guess rather than get the words right.

Fortunately, there is a method for conveying correct spellings that is recognised universally. This is the phonetic alphabet. It is used globally by travel companies, airline emergency services and other organisations that rely on accuracy in spelling and terminology.

Knowing this alphabet by heart is essential to smooth, correct and efficient communication. It will also avoid any problems with different accents. The alphabet is particularly useful when you are speaking on the telephone, since it eliminates the number of times words have to be repeated and thus reduces the risk of annoying people.

The phonetic alphabet words in the table below have been carefully and specifically chosen for their clarity in reaching another person's ears without causing confusion.

Phonetic word	Pronunciation	Phonetic word	Pronunciation
Alpha	alfa	November	nohvembuh
Bravo	brahvoh	Oscar	osskuh
Charlie	chahlee	Papa	puhpuh
Delta	delltuh	Quebec	kwuhbek
Echo	eckoh	Romeo	rohmeeyoh
Foxtrot	foxtrot	Sierra	seeyerruh
Golf	golf	Tango	tanggoh
Hotel	hohtell	Uniform	yoonifawm
India	indeeuh	Victor	viktuh
Juliet	jooleeyet	Whisky	wisskee
Kilo	keeloh	X-ray	ecksray
Lima	leemuh	Yankee	yangkee
Mike	mike (to rhyme with 'bike')	Zulu	zooloo

Training exercise: India, Victor, Echo!

Since your own name is likely to contain letters and syllables you will have to spell out frequently, practise communicating it by this method. My surname is easy enough to remember—India Victor Echo—but yours may need some extra practice. After you have your own name in your mind phonetically, try communicating other information in the same way: for example, instructions for getting to another part of the city.

Telephone manners

YEAH, WHAT NOW?

It is essential that all staff, especially guest service staff, answer the telephone in a professional manner that illustrates their understanding, care and genuine desire to be helpful. Guests should always experience polite, friendly, clear and professional attention when conversing with staff on the telephone. Often the telephone is the first point of contact for a guest, so you should create the best impression from the beginning.

First, make sure that the telephone is answered within three rings. Answer all incoming calls according to the standards of your establishment. One common way to answer the telephone is this: 'Good morning/afternoon/evening ... Alan speaking. How may I help you?' Beware of creating a 'script' that is unnecessary, too long or annoying to the caller, particularly to guests who are calling long distance or are in a hurry. State the simple facts, allow the caller to say their piece and then offer appropriate additional information as the call continues. For internal calls, address the guest by name as indicated on the telephone display. After the initial greeting, however, do not overuse the name to the point of irritation.

Extra care should be taken when speaking to a guest on the telephone, because you cannot see each other and misunderstandings can occur more easily. It is worth noting here that many people, including you, use their hands and arms to emphasise a description. Remember that the caller cannot see this extra 'body talk'. Telephone conversations by necessity should be professional; a good use of vocabulary should save any need for unseen gestures.

When making telephone calls it is important to remember that you have no idea whether your call is coming at an inconvenient moment for the other person. Unless you are geographically close to the person you are calling, it is inadvisable to ring before 8.30 a.m. or after 10.30 p.m. Be aware of other people's timings with regard to meal times and be particularly careful about ringing overseas numbers without first checking their local time.

If you have to make a telephone call to a guest or another staff member, remember that it is a business call, not a social chat. If the matter about which you are calling is not urgent, you should ask whether it is a good time to talk. This allows the other person the opportunity to suggest a better time.

If you find that you have to leave a message on an answering machine or voice mail system, be both brief and concise. In practice we sometimes feel a little awkward about leaving a message, because we are usually caught unprepared and do not have a 'script'. The message you leave should contain first your full name and position in the organisation, then the time of the call and then the return telephone number. Leave your message, ensuring that the subject matter is appropriate to be left on a voice mail system. The content of your message should always be relevant and never upsetting or distressing—a potentially distressing message may be better conveyed in person. Speak clearly and, if instructions or directions are being given, spell out some of the more difficult words. Once the message is completed, repeat your name and return telephone number. You may add a time when it would be convenient for you to receive a return call, particularly if you are finishing your shift or are leaving for an appointment.

If you dial a wrong number, simply say 'I am so sorry, but I have dialled the wrong number' and then gently hang up. Just hanging up on the other person without a word is very rude. If you receive a call from someone who has dialled a wrong number, be gracious and reassure the caller that it is all right.

Always smile, even though you are on the telephone. Amazingly, this changes the tone of your voice. Your tone of voice is much more evident on the telephone than it is when you are speaking face-to-face. You will find, too, that with perception you can detect moods and emotions from another person's tone of voice. This will help you deal with the conversation in the appropriate manner. For instance, if an impatient caller comes on the line, talking slowly or distractedly may well incite the caller to be rude. However, if you pace the speed of your conversation to match that of the caller's, the outcome will be more successful.

If for some reason you have to put the caller on hold—perhaps in order to retrieve some information for them—be mindful of how irritating this can be. If what you have to do is taking longer that you expected, check with the caller and courteously ask if they would prefer you to call them back. Do not put a caller on hold and then continue to help other people while they are on the line. This will be even worse if they can hear what is going on in the background; they will feel insulted by your lack of consideration for their feelings.

If you are the one making the call, make sure that you have allowed enough time for the conversation and will not need to put the recipient on hold.

Telephone etiquette is rather like playing tennis. Each player has alternate turns at the ball. This is the same for the run of a conversation as it is for returning calls. It is bad manners not to return calls as soon as possible, even if you do not wish to speak to the person. Unless you are genuinely rushed off your feet, the only polite time to return a call is on the same day as the person called. If you take a call for another person, it is impolite to ask the caller to ring back later. The correct thing to do is to offer to take a message so that their call can be returned.

During the telephone conversation, make sure you have all the relevant information you need from the other person. If they appear vague, ask questions and offer specific examples. Reconfirm the request at the end of the conversation. The person will then feel more confident and reassured that their request is being handled efficiently.

Always remember that communication is far more difficult on the telephone, especially when you are dealing with different languages, nationalities, dialects and accents. In England alone there are seventeen different regional dialects; it is difficult for some English people to understand a dialect from a different part of the country. It is even harder to understand some of these regional dialects if you are from a different country altogether.

It is interesting to study this aspect of language; in time you can detect these different regional accents. Some travellers are very happy to tell you the difference in people's accents, whether they are from Tasmania and Queensland in Australia or Newcastle in the north of England and Cornwall in the south-west of England. In America it is often easy to detect a mid-western accent, which is very much stronger than its softer coastal counterparts. If possible, become more aware of regional ways of speaking. It is very impressive to be able to 'spot' these accents and include some complimentary reference to them in your conversation.

Do not rush a guest's questions or requests. Give them all the time they need. Even if you do not have a lot of time, try to give the impression that you have. Focus on the guest and never interrupt them—this is very rude! Listen carefully to what they are saying. Avoid, if possible, saying 'no' to a guest. There is always a solution. If you are unable to fulfil a request, find the person who can and ask them to handle it. Always notify the guest of the situation and always follow up with a courtesy call to check that they are satisfied.

Take care with your choice of words:

- Use expressions like 'Certainly, sir/ma'am' or 'With pleasure, sir/ma'am'. Try not to use 'sure' or 'OK'—this is too casual and should be avoided at all costs.
- The expression 'no problem' suggests that there may have been a problem. The word 'problem' is negative, so try not to use it.

Our subconscious minds tend to screen out minor words like
'no' and seize on the main word spoken.

- Resist the urge to use the slang term 'phone' instead of the full
word 'telephone', as this can be confusing. Although 'phone' is
listed in current dictionaries, like so many words the use of the
full term has greater effect.

Ending a telephone call can sometimes be difficult. Even though you
may do your best to avoid being too abrupt or rude, you will find that
in trying to extricate yourself from the conversation you may give the
wrong impression. If there is a time limit on the call, it is probably a
good idea to indicate this at the beginning of the call. However, by now
it may be too late, so you could simply say 'I am so sorry, but it's already
10.30 and I shall be late for an appointment; I really must go.'

At the end of the call, having reconfirmed the guest's needs, allow
them to put the telephone down first. This will give the guest the
impression that you were in no hurry to end the conversation.

Don't forget that all establishments have 'internal customers' the other
staff—and they deserve to be accorded the same polite and courteous
treatment as do the guests.

Mobile telephones, pagers and bleepers

Dealing with guests when they are using their mobile telephones
requires sensitivity, especially when they are taking a call that is important to them. Most of the time, people step aside so that they can
conduct their conversation more privately; generally they are aware of
the intrusion that such calls make on others' lives.

If someone takes a mobile telephone call in your presence, simply
stand to one side or find a small job to do and make yourself busy while
they continue with their call. At all times give the impression that you
are not tuning in to their conversation. This involves not showing any
form of response or emotion at any comments made by the other person, and by assuming a facial expression that is neither angry-looking
nor amused but is just pleasant. Once the call is over, quickly resume
the original conversation without making any reference to the interruption.

Pagers and bleepers can cause minor irritation, particularly to guests
when you are in conversation with them. It is interesting to note how
quickly body language behaviour has caught up with the times.
Immediately a bleep sounds, most recipients dive for their pagers and
often have to delve under layers of clothes. However entertaining this
can be to others, it is not very professional imagewise.

When you realise that you need to check your pager, do so discreetly
without upsetting the balance of the situation. You could do this by
turning to one side, reading the pager quickly, absorbing the informa-

tion and then deciding how best to deal with it without offending the people with whom you have been talking. It is a tricky area, since it is another distraction, like a mobile telephone, which can make others feel that they are intruding on your time or being a hindrance to you.

Act sensitively unless it is an emergency, in which case you should gently end the conversation or reschedule the meeting for a later time but on the same day. This will leave both parties feeling better about this potentially awkward situation than they otherwise would.

Explaining telephone systems to guests

The system for using telephones in guest rooms may be explained by the receptionist or manager checking the guest in, by the butler who greets the guest in their room, or by the porter who is 'rooming' the guest. Hotel compendiums usually also offer information and instructions on how to use the telephone.

There is usually a list of extension numbers located beside, or on, the telephone so that the guest can direct dial whatever department they want, for instance room service. Alternatively, the guest can call the operator, request the desired area or department and be transferred.

A guest may dial outside telephone numbers directly from their room. Usually the guest does this by simply dialling a number (usually zero) to gain an outside line; upon hearing the dial tone, they can dial the number they require. If they have any difficulty, they can call the switchboard operator who can make the connection for them while they remain in the comfort of their room.

Taking guests' messages

Garbled or muddled messages are a guest's nightmare. Messages are very important to them. Imagine if someone left a message for you at 10.30 a.m. telling you that if you managed to sprint over to the other side of the city, pick up a certain item and return immediately collecting a dozen red roses on the way, all in an hour, you could win ten thousand dollars! You would be pretty annoyed if half the message was lost and you did not receive it until after lunch. Unbelievable as this sort of scenario may appear, such things do happen—and all too frequently.

When a person calls to leave a message for a guest, the first step is to make sure that there is actually someone registered, or with a reservation, under the name supplied by the caller. *It is important that you never reveal a guest's room number*—only the guest has the right to disclose their room number to someone else.

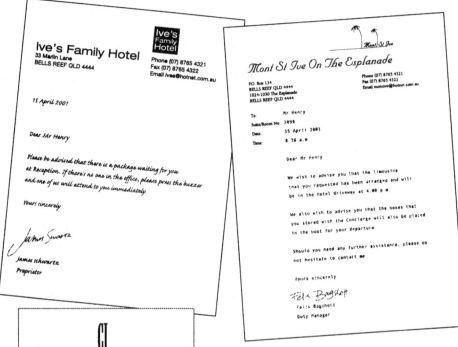

Messages for guests can come in a variety of forms.

Check that the guest for whom the message is intended is in-house. If the guest is not inhouse, check the reservation system for a future booking under that name. A message for a future guest can be made and attached to the reservation.

A large hotel will almost certainly have its reservations entered on a computer system. Once you have located the guest's name in the computer system, you will be able to record a typed message. This method supersedes the old one of taking a handwritten message. If your establishment still uses the old system, all handwritten messages should be taken on the correct message pad, recorded and filed to ensure that the correct message is given to the guest.

When typing a message into a computer system, you will often follow a preconfigured format. For example, you may have to ask for the caller's name first and type this in before you can take down the actual message the caller wishes to leave. It is most important that, on conclusion of the call, you read back the details (especially the caller's name, who the message is for, and the contact number) and confirm any spelling that you are not sure of.

> **Date**   15 April 2001   **Taken by**   Alec Lee
>
> **Time message taken**   8.00 a.m.
>
> **To**   Mr Henry   **From**   Robert Cox
>
> **Suite/Room no**   2042   **Duty Manager**
>
> I wish to advise that the limousine you requested has been arranged and will be in the hotel driveway at 4.00 p.m. Should you need any further assistance please do not hesitate to contact me.

A typical hotel system message.

Whether the information is taken over the telephone or in person, you must obtain:

- who the message is for
- the caller's name and room number
- the name of the company (if relevant)
- the time of the call
- the date of the call
- a contact number
- the best time to return the call and any other follow-up action
- a brief message
- your own name or signature as message-taker.

To ensure that all information is accurately recorded, repeat back all the details to the caller for verification. If you are taking a message for a guest from overseas who uses a different writing system—a Japanese, for example—try to take that message in their language, if you are able, and manually as opposed to typed, if possible.

If the message is for a registered guest, once you have entered the message check that the information is correct. Before saving it in the appropriate system, be sure to check the spelling, punctuation and grammar. This is not done just to avoid confusion. To some people it is very insulting to have their name spelt incorrectly, and if there are any mistakes this will reflect poorly on your operation's professionalism.

Many systems will automatically date the message and record the time when it was typed in. The best practice here is to directly input the message, so that the guest has an accurate indication of when the caller rang. The printed message should then be delivered to the guest by whichever method is most effective. The staff member responsible for delivering these printed messages should make sure that, when messages are slipped under the guest's door, they are pushed under far enough to be secure. From a guest's point of view this is an important issue.

If a guest has already checked out, make sure you have the correct forwarding telephone or fax number or address so that any late messages can be dealt with immediately. However, in most cases you will need to advise the caller that you are unable to take a message. Another tip for utmost professionalism is to avoid abbreviations such as 'ASAP'. Such a term can be replaced with 'at your earliest convenience', which sounds more polite and ultimately communicates the same message.

Bad news

There will be some occasions when the delivery of a guest message is inappropriate to the content of the message itself. Circumstances such as the notice of a death in the guest's family, or news of a serious illness, should be handled with the utmost care, tact and sympathy. In fact, the better course of action may be to inform the manager on duty, who can take the message to the guest in person and ensure the guest's welfare when they receive the message.

Alternatively, a message may be relayed to the guest to contact the manager on duty on his or her return. If the message is received early in the working day, it may be prudent to try to contact the guest's business destination. This can be tricky, but very often staff who work closely with guests are aware of their activities. This 'detective' work may help the guest handle this sensitive situation sooner.

When delivering such a message the manager should offer as much sympathy as possible without overdoing it. In these situations practical assistance is often far more appreciated than words. Any sympathy offered should be heartfelt and sincere. If it is appropriate the manager could, in anticipation of the guest's needs, contact the airline the guest is travelling with, if this is known, to see if a seat is available on the next flight out. Alternatively, a seat could be reserved with any available airline pending later confirmation and payment.

Once the bad news has been delivered, the manager should recognise the guest's need for time to absorb the information. Quietly ask the guest if there is anything they would like in the way of tea or coffee, or perhaps a stronger drink, but don't press your sympathy. Every individual has their own way of handling these situations, and some coping mechanisms can be quite surprising. If another person's reaction does not coincide with the way you would react, it does not mean that they are not going through shock and grief. Contact at this stage is similar to first aid; it has to be effective without hindering the healing processes.

Another kind of message that requires special handling is news of the cancellation of a guest's flight. In this case a reservation for an alternative flight can be booked and held provisionally, pending the guest's decision about what they wish to do. Much the same action should be taken as in the above paragraph, in that practical help is far more valuable to a guest than repeated apologies from the management and staff for the inconvenience. A sympathetic and practical approach will create a good impression and will, without a doubt, stay in the guest's mind.

Handwritten notes

In hotels these days handwritten letters and notes are almost a thing of the past. This is sad in a way, since nowadays people get little chance to practise their handwriting and create a style of their own.

Letters, notes and messages written to guests should always be neat, concise and unobtrusive. If your establishment is large enough, it will have appropriately-headed stationery for this purpose. If so, use only this stationery, whether it be headed 'From your Butler', 'From the office of . . .', 'From the Housekeeping Department' or 'From the Laundry/Valet'. Avoid just writing on your business card. If there is no special stationery for messages, use a fresh clean sheet of paper and head it appropriately.

Make sure the paper or card is clean. Generally, cards that are already printed (requesting service time of laundry delivery, menus and so on) should not be written on. This is not only expensive and wasteful, but also looks very unprofessional. Handwriting should be neat. Check that your spelling and grammar are correct. If your handwriting is not very neat, ask a colleague to write for you. But take some time to practise.

The note should be written in a formal style for the first-time guest. For example, it should begin 'Please be informed that . . .' Naturally, if your establishment is a motel or a bed-and-breakfast your writing style will be less formal, but a courteous tone will still show a professional approach.

Avoid writing too many notes, as this can get very confusing for the guest. Service should be unobtrusive at all times. In a large hotel you can also leave a note for a guest through the Fidelio, or similar front

An example of a handwritten note.

> From the Duty Manager
>
> *15 April 2001*
>
> *Dear Mr Henry*
>
> *We wish to advise that the limousine that you requested has been arranged and will be in the hotel driveway at 4.00 p.m.*
>
> *Yours sincerely*
>
> *Robert Cox*
>
> *Duty Manager*

office reservation system—with this system the telephone will have the message light showing and a printed message will be delivered to the room. This can be arranged through the butler or housekeeping co-ordinator. This method should be used for important messages.

Well-constructed handwritten messages, however, will be appreciated by guests. The handwritten note should be put into an envelope and then placed on the bedside table with the lamp switched on to draw the guest's attention to it.

Accessing messages from a hotel system

Guests can access their messages in a number of ways. These will depend on the establishment and what systems and technology it has in place. Some examples are:

- Access to messages through the switchboard operator or reception. When a front office employee records a message on the guest's computer file, a light on the telephone in the guest's room automatically switches on. When the guest returns to their room they will notice the light and can call the operator, or anyone at the front desk, and ask for the message to be repeated to them over the telephone.
- The front office staff member can access the guest's message by first looking up the guest's name and room number in the computer system. Usually there is something on the guest's file within the system that indicates that they have a message, such as a flashing M. The front office employee can then access the message and read it out over the telephone. After the guest has received the message, it is important to delete the message so that the light on the guest's telephone switches off. Deleted messages can usually be accessed again through the system at a later stage if necessary. In some hotels, after a message has been recorded for a guest it is possible to print it. A porter or butler will then deliver the printed messages to the guest room, thereby providing the guest with an additional, printed copy of the message.
- A third method is one in which the message is typed into the computer and appears on the television screen in the guest's room. When the guest returns to the room or suite an infra-red light shows on the screen, indicating that there is a message to be accessed. The guest uses the remote control unit to turn on the television and read the message.
- There is now a new method being used by hotels. If someone calls for a guest, the operator transfers the call to the guest's room as usual. If there is no response in the room, instead of the call being automatically diverted back to the switchboard operator's console, the caller is given a pre-programmed option to leave a voice message. This leaves the onus for accuracy with

the caller and reduces the work load for the front office staff. When a guest returns to the room they can access their voice mail message in the same way as they do at home. This sort of technology is easy for most people to handle.

If you are using any of the first three methods, where the guest has so many opportunities to access their messages through the medium of print, you will appreciate the importance of spelling, grammar and accuracy!

Checking in same-sex couples

It is important not to make assumptions about the relationship between two guests checking into the same room. When an inquiry is made regarding the check-in, you should monitor your reactions and response. Watch your response in terms of body language, facial expression and tone of voice. All these reactions should be nonjudgemental and pleasant.

If possible, ascertain and confirm early in the conversation the room type and bed requirements of the guests. The question, if the information is not available from the records, should be asked regarding king-size or twin beds, rather than assuming the guest's needs. If necessary, use the word 'partner' rather 'husband', 'wife', 'spouse', 'boyfriend' or 'girlfriend'. Any overt public display of emotions on the guests' part should be overlooked and the situation should be moved on as quickly as possible. Resist being confronted, amused or intrigued; treat it simply as a normal occurrence.

About gratuities

Another matter that relates to communication is gratuities. Gratuities should always be handled in a discreet and professional manner. Staff should not see themselves in a gratuitous position, expecting guests to tip. However, guests may try to tip staff. The best way to handle this is to say to the guest 'Sir, it is not necessary,' or 'Ma'am, it is not expected.'

If the guest persists, accept the tip graciously, smile and respond with eye contact and a sincere 'thank you'. Try to resist the urge to look at your hand when a gratuity or tip is handed to you; simply, and quietly, put it in your pocket. Never fumble with a bill payment in front of guests; you may give the impression that you are 'money hungry' and eager to see how much you received! Always continue to provide the same attentive service, whether you have been tipped or not, or whether the tip was large or small. Tipping is really about thanking; if you focus on that, it's easier to put tips into perspective. If a guest tips very little it often indicates that they were either unsure of the amount they should tip or they were not pleased. If the latter is the case and tips are important to you, then lower tips probably mean that you need to get your act together and read this book again!

T.I.P.S.

Tips have an interesting origin. In the seventeenth and eighteenth centuries, gentlemen's clubs were flourishing in London. As gentlemen entered these well-respected establishments, they would drop coins into a large wooden box with a slot carved in the top. On hearing these coins drop into the box, stewards and their assistants would come running to be of service to the gentlemen. On the side of this wooden box was printed 'T.I.P.S.'—an acronym for 'To Insure Prompt Service'. (The spelling 'insure' hadn't yet gained its specialised meaning—'insure against damage'—and was used interchangeably with 'ensure'—'make sure'.)

It is improper to discuss the tips you receive and you should never carry them in your outside breast pocket, or anywhere visible. Tips are a bonus and not a guarantee. Waiting for a guest to 'cough up' with a tip is considered very bad manners and will only make the guest feel uncomfortable, which is definitely not how they should feel at the end of their stay. Some hotels and other establishments include a percentage surcharge on all their transactions to cover tips and gratuities. A guest who is aware of this (and most are) will certainly view any 'cough' style of reminder as impertinent and may even, justifiably, complain to the management.

The need for a smooth departure

Every guest is entitled to as warm a departure as, hopefully, the welcome was when they arrived, whether it is a five-star hotel, a resort, a motel or a bed-and-breakfast. Remember: in as much as the first impression is important, so is the final one. It is, in fact, the last chance you have to impress a guest until next time, if there is a next time!

Asking a guests about their stay is appropriate at this stage. You, like everyone else in your establishment, need to know if guests enjoyed themselves.

A smooth, unhassled check-out is essential. Most guests are on a mission by this time and may be anxious about their onward trip. They may be running late, in which case everything should be done to expedite their arrangements. If they are catching a flight, confirm the airport transfer and reassure the guest, who may be quite nervous at this stage.

Check that all pieces of luggage have been retrieved from the room. It is a guest's nightmare to have left something behind.

In-room guest check-out

More hotels are starting to offer the more personalised service of an in-room check out. This, along with delivering the interim account the night before, speeds up what might otherwise be a very irritating and tedious chore for the guest. The interim account saves time for both the guest and the establishment and allows the guest to check their account carefully and in their own time. A guest information form will have been filled in by hotel staff previously to check-out. (Credit card details will be on the registration card.)

Twenty-four hours ahead of check-out, make an appointment with the guest either by telephone (leaving a message if appropriate) or by letter. This letter will confirm onward flight particulars and details of the airport transfer. It can also be used to alert the guest to other facilities and services such as a packing service by a butler or valet, an early breakfast delivered to the room, last-minute business preparations, or anything else that will smooth the guest's way to their next destination. These last few hours are most likely to be the ones that will influence a guest's overall impression of the hotel and whether they will come back. So you can see just how important this service can be.

The final bill should be accurate. Do not forget to include late charges (see below). Care should be taken when asking the guest any questions about the mini-bar, such as about consumption. This needs to be handled so that you do not appear to be accusing the guest of having stripped the mini-bar in the hope of getting away without paying for it.

If payment is by credit card the guest may have to move to the reception desk for the payment to be authorised. Alternatively, you could suggest that you attend to this while the guest finalises their packing and other matters; you should then return as soon as possible. However, be aware that most guests are very reluctant to lose sight of their credit cards and other personal belongings so close to their departure.

As guest service staff you now have an excellent opportunity to ask the guest about their stay, obtain feedback and check for guest satisfaction. If any points are raised, try to sort them out; but accept their comments graciously. If necessary, make notes and follow up. If the guest has left by the time you have done this, it may be a good idea to forward a note to their office address, apologising for any inconvenience while at the same time suggesting that you will be delighted to welcome the guest back in the not-too-distant future. On their departure, wish the guest a safe journey and thank them for coming to your establishment and staying with you. Remind them to return as soon as possible!

Late charges

Unfortunately, late charges are often the result of a breakdown in the system. Sometimes a guest will call after a stay, claiming that the 'late charges' on their account are not theirs! Provided that the hotel policy allows this, it is recommended that smaller amounts be deducted from the guest's account. Most hotels are able to 'write off' these small amounts.

However, with more substantial amounts staff should not enter into any form of debate or argument over these charges. The matter should be handled sensitively by, perhaps, saying that an investigation will be invoked and that the guest will be contacted by telephone, fax or email as soon as possible. In the meantime, an apology for the 'confusion' should be made.

Guest service staff or those checking out guests should be careful with their tone of voice and facial expression when they ask guests about items that may have been used, such as the mini-bar. It should be an inquiry, not an accusation. If there is any doubt—and you should check that the guest has time for this next step—do not ignore the situation; later antagonisms can be eliminated by making a quick call to the housekeeping department on that floor to have a quick final check done. This should only take a few minutes.

Meanwhile, the guest's possible impatience may have to be handled. Apologise for the delay and offer a small distraction such as further checking of the account or a brief, pleasant conversation. Try not to walk away from the guest; this will increase their irritation. Check again with housekeeping so that the guest is reassured that something is happening. If there is a longer delay, ask the guest if they mind a late charge being posted to their account. Most probably many guests will appreciate your concern and the fact that they are being given the choice.

Checking guest satisfaction

The person most likely to do this will be the front office cashier or the person conducting the check-out process. An inquiry about the guest's stay should be made during the check-out procedure. The question may be phrased in different ways to elicit a more detailed and honest response from the guest. Consider these variations: 'Have you enjoyed your stay with us, Mr Thomas?', 'Was everything to your satisfaction, Mr Thomas?' or 'Is there anything we could do to improve your stay next time, Mr Thomas?'

It may be too late to win a departing guest's loyalty if complaints were not made when the problems occurred. Guests should be encouraged to raise issues of concern as they arise, so as to give your operation a chance to rectify the situation. For example, a receptionist could say towards the end of the check-in procedure: 'If there is anything we can do to make your stay more comfortable, please contact me or dial Guest Services on extension 1.'

Most hotels and other operations also use guest questionnaire forms to encourage feedback from guests. The form needs to be put in a prominent place so that the guest will see it. It is worth designing a form that gives the guest an opportunity to comment on aspects of the establishment or the service that they liked, rather than just write negative criticism. A keen management team will take the time to respond quickly to guest questionnaires by acting on the feedback and by writing, or sending an email, to the guest thanking them for their input and telling them what action is being taken. It is most important to encourage all staff who come in contact with the guest to check on the state of the guest's stay. These staff should be encouraged to take action and be proactive about solving guests' problems and, indeed, passing on valuable, positive feedback about what their operation is doing well.

The subject of solving guests' problems will be tackled in greater detail in Chapter 6.

Service auditing

Achieving the highest standards of quality and service is always uppermost in a hospitality manager's mind, but perhaps the guest questionnaires and surveys are not really pin-pointing exact areas that have potential for improvement. Sometimes you need an 'outside pair of eyes' on your business—an informed person within the hospitality industry who can see things as your customer is seeing them.

Service audits represent a cost-effective means of monitoring and evaluating service. They also offer enormous benefits in terms of identifying problems early, assessing accurately your service levels and noticeably reducing the number of customer and guest complaints. Your management will spend much less time on 'fire-fighting' and 'damage control'.

Carried out very much in the background, a service audit takes one to two days, depending on the size of the establishment. It is followed up with a well-written and innovative full report with recommendations. Service audits are usually performed by people experienced at all levels including front office, guest relations, concierge, housekeeping and food and beverage service.

There are compelling reasons for service audits, not the least being the development of your service to greater efficiency. Service excellence is easily within your reach!

6
What happens if things go wrong?

Good service

In this book we have already established that creating a memorable experience for your guest—a favourable, lasting impression-requires more than simply meeting their needs and giving good service.

Customers must be made to feel welcome. They must feel that they have been taken care of, and they must feel that we want them to return. Staff and the way they present themselves, as well as their training, their ability to do the job and their interest in the customer, will have a crucial effect.

Customers and guests have a lot of expectations when they visit a hotel, bed-and-breakfast or motel. A tired business person who has been on the road all day will be looking for a friendly greeting, good service and the assurance of a comfortable night's sleep. A young couple may be looking for unobtrusive but pleasant service, a romantic setting and a sense of warmth. We can make people feel welcome by smiling, greeting them by name, and taking a moment to chat with them and put them at ease.

But what if a guest complains?

One unfortunate problem that occasionally occurs is that a guest has a complaint. Due to the familiarity guests have with the front office, they may bring their complaints, major or minor, to these staff in the hope that they may thus gain easier access to the management.

Most guests are remarkably resilient and will endure a lot before complaining, but some will flare up at the slightest provocation over a matter that may, on the surface, appear trivial. In many cases the complaining guest may have a justifiable problem that needs sorting out, but there are also 'professional' complainers, who are merely trying to obtain a free meal or a free stay. Every complaint has to be judged on its individual merits. Guests and customers don't expect you to be perfect. But they do expect you to fix things when they go wrong.

However, before we go into any detail, it should be made clear that the way in which a specific complaint may be dealt with depends heavily on the personality and experience of the staff member concerned. An inexperienced staff member who is confronted with a serious complaint can be cornered into making inappropriate decisions. In a situation like this, the junior staff member may be unable to tell if the problem refers to their area of responsibility or whether a manager should be called; if this happens, they should simply say that they are willing to listen and comprehend the extent of the problem. By doing this they can assess the situation and possible solutions. An experienced staff member with a pleasant personality—not too overpowering, but genuinely concerned—will usually find it easier to handle complaints.

Handling guests' complaints

Complaints should be accepted at face value, at least until they are proven to be unjustified. You can apologise (only once) or respond with 'Thank you for letting us know about this' or 'We appreciate your taking the time to tell us about this.' Whatever your response, keep it simple and accept that the problem is yours even if you personally may not be responsible.

In a study that was conducted by the Washington DC-based company, Technical Assistance Research Programs Inc., the following conclusions were reached:

- For every customer who bothers to complain, there are 26 others who are affected but remain silent.
- The average 'wronged' customer will tell 8-16 people. More than 10 per cent will tell more than 20 people.
- 91 per cent of unhappy customers whose problems are unresolved will never buy from you again.
- If you make an effort to remedy the customer's complaints, 82-95 per cent will stay with you.
- It costs about five times as much to attract a new customer as it costs to keep an old one.

Customers and guests who complain blame the establishment, and that is what you represent. Remember, the guest who complains is giving you a second chance: an opportunity to fix the problem.

Welcome complaints. They should be regarded as challenges worth rising to, since they teach a great deal more than is at first evident. The guest who doesn't tell you about their dissatisfaction will simply not return and you will never know why.

What happens when a guest has a dissatisfying experience? Well, research shows that people don't generally like to complain to the business that disappoints them. Three reasons most often given for not complaining include:

- 'It's not worth my time,' or 'I haven't got the time.'
- 'Complaining will not do any good because no one really cares.'
- 'I don't know how or where to complain.'

Whatever the reason, a staff member who is concerned with quality will ask what happens when a customer or guest is unhappy. If the customer or guest is upset at having to make a complaint they are often emotional, unreasonable or irate, and sometimes they may tend to exaggerate the complaint.

When you receive a complaint listen to the guest, note the details, apologise, explain the action to be taken, thank the guest for bringing the matter to your attention and do something about it as soon as possible. Sometimes the person may be so upset or emotional that they will not see reason straight away. This often happens when the complaint has been bottled up over a period of time, or when the consequences to the complainant are significant (for instance, if you failed to organise a hotel transfer and they missed their flight connection as a result).

The golden rules, therefore, are:

- Listen to the guest.
- Apologise.
- Explain the action to be taken.
- Follow up.

When you encounter an angry or irate customer, don't take it personally or become defensive. Try not to get personally involved with the angry guest. Allow them to 'blow off steam'; this will often reduce the apparent size of the problem. This is the 'cooling down' period, during which the complainant will be blind to logic or apologies. When a guest relates their story it usually sounds less important than it is. However, keep listening for any information that will help you understand the problem. Deal with the offensive situation with a positive approach. Say 'I'm so sorry you are upset. I will endeavour to do my best to sort out this situation.' Continue to listen carefully and find out the full facts. Also, if you write down the information in a notebook, the guest will feel that their complaint is being treated seriously. If the complaint has been made about a staff member, do not attempt to involve this staff member in the conversation in front of the guest. Deal with the matter privately at a later time.

In the meantime, try to follow these recommendations:
- Remain objective.
- Keep cool.
- Sympathise.
- Try to give assistance, especially if the complaint appears to be justified.
- Be tactful.
- Make an appropriate decision.
- Call in the management where necessary.

An important thing to remember when dealing with complaints is to keep a record of the solution so that, should the problem be raised again in correspondence at a later date, then a clear reminder of what actually took place will be close at hand.

If you cannot solve the problem, try diplomatically to refer the guest to a manager or other person who can. But avoid a situation where the complainant has to repeat the complaint. In handing the problem over to another person, it is up to you to pass on the relevant information, in front of the guest, with as much tact and diplomacy as possible with-out any audible tendency to put the guest down. If you have solved the problem, check with the guest if there is any further way you can be of help. At an appropriate time, later, make a follow-up call to establish that the problem is completely resolved and that the guest is now sat-isfied.

One other thing to keep in mind when you attempt to resolve a complaint is that the solution should leave the complainant satisfied. To this end, it is sometimes worth asking the complainant what they would consider to be adequate compensation. Surprisingly, this can result in an easy way out for all parties. It may be as simple as 'a com-plimentary breakfast tomorrow'.

UNIT

THHCORO1A

Training exercise: real-life situations

If you are able to work in a group, develop some 'real-life' situations and ask other mem-bers of your group to suggest how they would deal with these situations. Then take each suggested situation and in pairs develop role-plays. After each role-play, other members of the group can analyse the response and subsequent 'handling' of the guest and any improvement of techniques used can be discussed.

Written complaints

Complaints are not always delivered in person; often they can appear in writing. Usually, such letters are addressed to the managing director or general manager. The manager will either refer the letter to the head of the department concerned or deal with it personally. It is essential to reply to a letter of complaint as soon as possible. The fact that the guest has taken the time to write shows that they believe that the establishment or company is able and willing to remedy the defect that gave rise to the complaint.

An uesolved complaint can incur a real cost to your hotel or establishment in that future business could be adversely influenced by this unhappy guest.

An example from real life

[Names have been changed to protect the innocent!]

The . . . conference to be held at your hotel is a major event for us and will be attended by tax directors, international tax counsels and lawyers from around the world. It is therefore imperative that I can be confident of the level and standard of service at your hotel that has been chosen to host this conference. While I can appreciate that you have just opened and may have some teething problems, I must say the standard of service is not what one would expect from a hotel that markets itself as being a '6 star hotel'. I am therefore looking for your personal undertaking that the level and standard of service at your hotel will match your commitment to quality and service when our conference is held at your hotel in November.

. . . The first was the quality of housekeeping. In general, it was extremely difficult to contact housekeeping on the phone and requests for items, e.g. pillows, took a very long time to be delivered to the room. The service was also inconsistent—we did not get any amenities, mineral water or fresh towels on certain days and one of our pillows disappeared after 3 days.

. . . More specifically, on Friday 24 April, my husband had an encounter with a housekeeping maid who was extremely rude—when asked to return later to vacuum the room because my husband was feeding the baby and did not want her to be distracted, the maid became annoyed and raised her voice, saying 'I have other rooms to clean, you know!' She then left the room and slammed the door on the way out. The same maid had also shown her annoyance on an earlier occasion when she was asked to come back later to make up the room as the baby was asleep. Poor service can sometimes be tolerated but rude service is simply intolerable and the incident left my husband and his parents (who were in the room) extremely unhappy. My husband is a frequent traveller and cannot recall receiving such poor treatment at any other hotel that he has stayed in.

. . . The second incident involved room service. On Saturday 25 April, we ordered our breakfast from room service and waited for one hour before our breakfast was served to our room. A follow-up call about 40 minutes after the initial call was met with the response that it would be sent to our room within 5 minutes and that because of the delay, the breakfast would be complimentary. It took another 15-20 minutes for the breakfast to arrive and the bread basket had been left out. When we asked where it was, the attendant said that they were not sure what type of bread we wanted. This was either a poor excuse or room service had simply not bothered to phone and check what we wanted. It took another 10 minutes for the bread basket to be brought up. I was then asked to sign the bill for the breakfast although I indicated that we were told that it was complimentary. The attendant said that it was indeed complimentary and I had to sign to acknowledge receipt. This proved misleading, as when I checked my hotel bill carefully on the way to the airport, I discovered that I had been charged for the breakfast.

Training exercise: your course of action

This real-life situation involved many different departments and illustrates the problems that sometimes beset a new hotel. Discuss, either in a group or on paper, what your first reaction would be on receiving this letter. Then decide on your course of action, including discussion with the department heads in question and how you would approach the situation, bearing in mind the real potential cost of a complaint. Then draft a reply letter to the guest. Discuss in your group how you could avoid such an event recurring.

Summary

In summary, these points are worth considering and remembering:

- Guests' complaints should always be handled in a timely and professional manner, to ensure that the outcome is full guest satisfaction.
- Whenever possible, speak with the guest face-to-face. This is much more personal and shows genuine concern on your part. Avoid the telephone if at all possible.
- The ability to satisfy a complaint, especially one that has no real solution, often rests with the attitude of the person receiving it. Remain calm and unruffled, but be sure to show your concern.
- Never argue or interrupt. Listen attentively. Ask questions so that you get the complete picture of the situation. Get all the facts.
- Complaints should never be glossed over or taken flippantly. A simple situation can soon be magnified into a major issue without careful handling.
- Swallow that clever retort! Tact, courtesy and a quiet voice reduce the anger in the guest and open the way to a satisfactory adjustment. The louder and more abusive the guest, the softer and more conciliatory you should be.
- Give the guest plenty of time to express themselves. Sympathise with their problem. By agreeing with the guest, you are letting them see that you are trying to understand their position. You should not further aggravate the situation by taking a confrontational attitude or making the guest feel that no one is going to rectify the problem.
- Clarify the complaint and at the same time introduce something positive, such as a reassurance that you hope it will not happen again. Assure the guest that you will handle this matter personally and that you will get back to them as soon as you have a satisfactory solution.
- Always communicate with the guest and give them an update; it is vital that they be kept abreast of events. Thank the guest for bringing the problem to the operation's attention.
- Attempt to solve the problem by offering several options within your scope of authority. Never hesitate to include

management when a guest appears distraught or the problem starts to get out of hand.

- Close the situation in a sensitive, positive manner by writing a sincere note of apology. Depending on how upset the guest was, you may want to authorise some complimentary amenity to the room as well.
- Since guests usually understand that problems do occur, most are understanding. It is your responsibility to address the situation and do whatever it takes to turn the situation around. Be sure to keep a record of all complaints and the action taken in each case, and to also learn from the event for the future. Take positive steps to ensure that the problem or situation does not recur by bringing the subject up for discussion at the next meeting of the department.

Difficult situations

Occasionally you may find yourself in a situation that requires tact, quick action or initiative. The following examples are a guide to how best to conduct yourself. However, remember: if you are faced with an unusual request or situation it is best to consult with the department head or another senior member of staff before acting.

You find a stranger in a room or corridor

If you are sure the stranger is not a guest, attempt to converse with them while you take a mental note of their appearance: observe details like hair colour and eye colour as well as any unusual features. Immediately report the stranger's whereabouts and description to the duty manager, the manager (if it is a smaller establishment), another senior staff member or the switchboard operator. Security and management should come immediately to deal with the person. Do not try to escort them on your own, in case they become aggressive or violent.

A stranger asks you (or tips you!) to open a room door

Never open a room or suite door for anyone. Always ask for the person's name and explain calmly that only your supervisor is permitted to open doors to guest suites. Report the incident immediately to your duty manager, department head or another senior staff member. Record the event in your daily report.

A member of staff asks you to open a room door

No one is permitted to admit another staff member to a guest suite. Remember, those staff who are permitted access will be carrying their own set of keys. All key access to suites is recorded on the computer system and will show the time of entry and your key number, so it will be registered.

You discover a fire

If it is a small fire and can be easily extinguished without risk to yourself and guests, put it out. Follow your establishment's normal procedure in this event. If the fire presents danger to yourself and guests, go to the nearest phone and DIAL the appropriate number to speak to the operator. Clearly state your NAME, your LOCATION and the NATURE OF THE FIRE. Explain briefly whether there are flames, or smoke only. STAY CALM. Assist guests and leave by the nearest exit. The possibility of such a situation should alert you to the importance of knowing the location of fire exits.

There is a bomb threat

This sort of occurrence can happen when there are visiting heads of state or VIPs in a hotel. Should a suspicious package be discovered, or a threat made, staff must have a specific and well-rehearsed contingency plan to put into action especially if, in an extreme case, the hotel has to be evacuated. Unfortunately, hotels around the world have at times been targets for terrorist bombs, whether these have been actually placed in the hotel or sent through the post. If the threat is received by telephone or a suspicious article arrives in the mail (such as a possible letter bomb) it is often the front office staff who will be most directly involved. Virtually the same drill is used as would be initiated in the case of a fire.

If the threat is made by telephone, the telephonist or whoever is receiving the call is best advised to record the time and then allow the caller to continue their message without interruption. Exact notes should be made and any response confined to one or two words. If possible, glean as much of the following information as you can:
- the caller's sex and approximate age
- any noticeable condition affecting their speech such as drunkenness, laughter, anger or excitement
- any peculiarity such as pitch of voice, a foreign accent, mispronunciation or a speech impediment
- background noises such as traffic, music, talking or machinery.

Details like these can provide a great number of clues for the police.

They will help them gauge the strength of the threat and assess whether there is anything about the caller and the message that resembles any other such calls that have been made.

At no stage during the call give any opinions or, if you can avoid it, show any emotion in your voice. Hoax callers can waste even more of your time than they have already, simply to enjoy the effect their call is having upon you.

However, it is wise to assume that all calls of this nature need to be taken seriously. When the caller has completed the message, try to keep them talking by asking some key questions. First, ascertain exactly where the bomb is located, then ask what time it is scheduled to explode, when it was placed and the reason why it has been placed in your hotel. A member of the management team should be informed immediately, as should the police. The message should then be repeated to the police exactly as it was received.

Whether the call is a hoax or not, the police will attend and assist in the search. The police will need to be escorted by a staff member who is familiar with that area of the building and will recognise any items that may be out of place.

If a suspicious package is found, the police will hand it over to the bomb disposal squad. Under no circumstances should hotel staff try to move it or tamper with it. If a letter bomb is received, no attempt should be made to open it.

Handling guests in these situations should be done in much the same way as for fire evacuation. No staff member is expected to put themselves at unnecessary risk; however, guests will need kind and careful handling. Staff should at all times remain calm and objective about the guests' safety.

Very often on these occasions you will have to deal with complacency. Fire and car alarms are inadvertently activated so frequently that some people ignore alarms altogether. They may only believe there is an emergency if they can see the evidence for it.

Others, at the sight of danger, may scream and shout, thus causing those around them to panic. Comforting and reassuring words, spoken in a quiet manner, will have a far greater impact than loud shouts and orders that will unnecessarily cause even more alarm. It is important to keep guests up to date with some carefully filtered information. This will not only serve to calm them, but will also curb their natural curiosity, which may make them want to stay in the area of danger.

After the threat has been resolved or cleared, avoid lengthy discussions about the event in front of guests. Make sure guests are escorted safely back to their rooms and thank them for their cooperation. Check to see if there is anything more that can be done to ensure their comfort.

Guests are quarrelling or fighting

Inform the manager on duty immediately you notice an altercation between guests. Do not attempt to interfere or take part under any circumstances. Do not allow guests to involve you in their argument. Enter the incident and the time in your daily report.

There is no electrical power in a room or on a whole floor

Inform the switchboard immediately; they will get the engineering department to look into it. In a smaller establishment, an outside technician may need to be called. Stay in the area and offer assistance. As you are familiar with the layout of the building, you will be of great help to disorientated guests. Enter the incident and location in your daily report.

A guest requests a 'companion'

Explain to the guest that you are unable to assist them in this matter. Suggest that they consult the Yellow Pages or the local newspaper. Inform your department head of the request and the incident.

A guest is ill

Ask if the guest requires a doctor. If the guest is unconscious, immediately contact the switchboard. Only render first aid if you are a registered first aider. Try to be helpful and sympathetic without being intrusive. Inform your department head or the duty manager. Don't forget to ask the guest how they are feeling next time you see them! However, it may be best not to ask them this if they are in company, as the guest could have their own reasons for not wanting their friends or business associates to know they have been ill.

You think a guest may attempt suicide

If you are concerned that a guest may be considering suicide, do not interfere—this may precipitate their action. Leave the room quietly and quickly. It may be a good idea to flick the 'night latch' in order to maintain a line of contact. Alert the management immediately on the nearest phone and explain the circumstances as clearly as possible. Inform them of the room number, the condition of the guest, their whereabouts and any other relevant details. Remain outside the room until assistance arrives.

A guest offers you liquor, a cigarette or food

Refuse courteously, saying something like 'Thank you, but I am unable to accept this.' If they insist, explain politely that it is against the rules and regulations of your workplace.

A 'Do not disturb' sign is still on the door at midday

Check with housekeeping. If you have been unable to gain access to a guest room to attend to your duties, housekeeping may already have a logical explanation. If housekeeping is unaware of the situation, DO NOT enter the room but report the matter to the executive house-keeper or their assistant. If neither are available, report to the manager on duty and follow their instructions. Under no circumstances should you enter the room. Enter all details in your daily report. In a smaller establishment, notify the manager on duty.

Vermin are seen by guests

If guests notice mice, insects or other vermin, inform housekeeping and the manager on duty, who will follow up with the correct proce-dures. Reassure the guests that the situation is under control. Do not attempt to give a technical explanation. Guests tend to feel very vul-nerable and frightened of these creatures, and just need to know that they will be eliminated.

Guests make excessive noise

Report the problem to your head of department, the manager or another senior staff member. Do not interfere. Report any damage to property belonging to your establishment. Usually, if these people are treated in a quiet manner, they will respond and the situation will not escalate into a 'free-for-all'.

A guest is unruly or upset by an excess of alcohol

This situation requires the same response as that to drug use and abuse. The responsible service of alcohol rests on diplomatically stem-ming the flow of alcohol if a guest's behaviour becomes unacceptable. It is recommended that a guest in this state be separated from the 'crowd'. In this way you can gently suggest a non-alcoholic beverage such as water or lemonade. Black coffee is an alternative, but does not aid the rehydration that is needed after a high intake of alcohol.

As there is a chance that the guest may become more physically active or violent, it is important to alert a manager rather than risk danger to yourself or others by trying to deal with this situation single-handedly.

If a guest is requesting you to do something within your role or the rules of the establishment, carry it out in the normal manner. In doing so, always follow hotel policy for handling such situations.

Once an inebriated guest has been calmed, you may suggest to them that you could call a taxi-cab, if appropriate, or escort them to their room and ensure that they are safely ensconced there before wishing them good night.

A guest attempts to take property from the premises

DO NOT accept bribes to keep quiet—YOU MAY LOSE YOUR JOB! If you happen to see a guest with such property in their possession, politely and discreetly offer to put the item back in its proper place. Never make accusations. Report the incident to the duty manager or manager immediately so that the matter can be attended to BEFORE the guest checks out.

Items are missing when a guest checks out

Report the matter to front office immediately so that the guest may be billed for the missing items. Record the incident in your daily report.

Excessive amounts of money or valuables are left unattended in a room

Do not touch anything. Report immediately to your department head, duty manager or manager and follow their instructions. Security and management will handle the situation.

A guest acts suspiciously when offering a credit card

Not every guest feels confident when they present their credit card to pay their account. Sometimes a previous unsettling or embarrassing experience—perhaps one in which authorisation was not granted—can make a guest feel very nervous and appear uncomfortable in your presence. It should not be automatically assumed that this person is unlikely to be able to pay their bill. Handle the situation as normally as possible, perhaps even with more empathy.

Staff should, however, still be alert to those people who know that their card is not creditworthy. They may appear in a hurry, or anxious, and ask for certain transactions to be split or manually entered into the system. Make a point of noticing where they take their credit card from—whether straight from a pocket or directly from their wallet. When you are given the credit card, take a good look at the front and check to see if the card is damaged, whether it has a valid expiry date and if the embossing appears to have been altered.

If you get the impression that all is not quite what it seems, ask in a pleasant tone for alternative identification, such as a passport or driver's licence. Check that the details match the embossed cardholder's name. Hold onto the card while completing the transaction. When you check the signature, make sure that the card has been signed and that the signature panel has not been altered. If you are still unsure of the card's authenticity, continue to hold onto the card while you call the credit card authorisation centre; they have the facility to help you further verify the credit card's status. This call should be made away from the guest so as not to create further awkwardness. If you feel you cannot handle the situation, ask another staff member to do so. If you have to discuss matters with the guest try, if possible, to take them to a more private area.

Guests can feel quite upset if authorisation is not granted. It is important to believe guests when they say they cannot understand the situation and that to their knowledge their account is in order. It may well be that they are unaware of other authorisations that have been made against their credit card and subsequently have not been lifted. It could be that because the guests are travelling overseas, payments may not have been received by the bank or credit card company by the due date.

The most diplomatic way to handle this situation is to consider the options for the guest, and try to understand how it feels to realise that you may not be able to pay the account in the manner that you had hoped. If you can offer the local access number for the bank or financial institution, you could suggest to the guest that they call and verify the status of their account for their own peace of mind.

Mishandling a situation like this at the end of a guest's stay may well influence their choice for future reservations. In a gracious and sympathetic manner you could suggest, if necessary, that the amount be put through the system a second time in order to check that the details are correct. This will give the guest some time to compose themselves and maybe consider another method of payment. If the situation remains unresolved, it is wise to call upon the manager on duty to sort it out.

A guest behaves in a 'suggestive' manner

Leave the room as quickly and discreetly as possible. Never respond to advances. Bribes and threats are to be ignored. Generally, staff are not penalised in any way for the reported unseemly behaviour of a guest. Managements of accommodation establishments accept that this is a frequent occurrence and not the fault of the staff member, but that it can often be provoked in a guest by loneliness. Discuss the incident immediately with your department head or manager or, in their absence, another senior member of staff. Do not discuss such incidents with other members of staff.

A guest is smoking in a 'no smoking' area

If you have to inform a guest that they may not smoke in a certain area, it is probably better to take the line of suggesting an alternative area first. You could say 'Excuse me sir, but you may feel more comfortable smoking in … as this is a designated non-smoking area.' When advising the guest of a proposed move, offer to help carry any items that they may be using at the time.

You believe that a guest may be a recreational drug or substance user

This is a tricky situation, and it is becoming more commonplace. Guest service staff, or any staff members in contact with guests, must remain calm and focused. At no time should you be judgemental. However tempting this may be, it is simply not your place to do so.

To list all the symptoms and signs that may denote drug or substance use would require a whole chapter. However, there are some reasonably recognisable signs that guest service staff should be aware of.

Sometimes guests may appear preoccupied, distant or obviously distracted. Of course, this may have a number of other reasons, such as those described in the sections on body language in Chapter 4 (pages 60-63).

The use of drugs can cause symptoms such as perspiration, dilated eyes, frowning caused by a severe headache, loss of concentration or memory, loss of interest, or maybe even a little aggression. Some substances can induce an alertness that precipitates anxiety or nervousness. However, others produce a feeling of well-being, increased self-confidences and energy. It can be a very tricky area to handle.

People delivering food and beverage service, for instance, may find it difficult to gauge when guests seem to be enjoying themselves but do not want to eat. This effect can be brought about by some substances. However, be careful not to judge the situation. As said previously, there may be another explanation that has nothing to do with drugs or recreational substances.

So how do you handle these situations? The usual routine for responsible service of alcohol is a good start. If an individual's behaviour becomes unacceptable it is probably best to separate this guest from the 'crowd' and take care of their needs in a more private and sensitive manner.

It is important to alert a manager of your suspicions in these situations, rather than try to handle them single-handedly. This will reduce any danger to yourself or others.

If a guest is requesting you to do something within your role with the hotel or establishment, carry it out in the normal manner. In doing so, always follow hotel policy for handling these situations.

You believe that a colleague is using recreational drugs at work

The main consideration is not that you will be dropping your colleague into trouble but that you should be concerned for the safety of all those affected by such irresponsible actions. It is worth considering the likely outcome of not alerting management to a colleague's recreational drug use when that colleague is in charge of equipment or machinery that could cause serious injury to other staff and guests.

Although it is a difficult decision to make, it is also worth remembering that, while a hotel's policy does not usually tolerate this behaviour, you will have to live with your conscience if any serious injury or damage is caused by neglect on the part of a recreational drug user.

More information about drug-related issues can be found on the Internet or through help agencies.

Other difficult situations

Other situations that can crop up from time to time may include heart attacks, migraines, asthma attacks and other sudden illnesses. Your hotel or establishment will have a standard procedure that should be strictly adhered to.

Training exercise: What do you do if ... ?

Handling difficult and awkward situations needs some considerable thought and practice. If you are working in a group, some of the following 'What do you do if . . . ?' scenarios will offer some good examples for discussion and for formulating procedures for your establishment. Many of the situations are easily adapted for use in your own personal life.

What do you do if . . .

- you have to say 'no' to a guest without offending them?
- guests are disrupting and disturbing other guests with their noise/bad behaviour/drunkenness?
- a guest tries to date you?
- a guest refuses to show their passport/does not feel disposed to give appropriate information?
- a guest is dressed incorrectly or inappropriately?
- you cannot answer a guest's question?
- a guest has been inconvenienced and you have only just found out that they are about to leave?
- a guest makes an offensive sexual joke?
- a guest is talking to you and another staff member interrupts you?
- a guest asks you an embarrassing personal question?

'Lost and found' items

'Lost and found' items should be handled systematically to minimise guest inconvenience and to promote the professionalism of staff. Much of the time a guest is unaware that they have left any belongings behind.

It is a good idea, wherever possible, to have a quick look around a guest room as soon as the guest departs. Sometimes items can be returned before the guest has left the premises.

If a guest has checked out and there are personal articles left behind, it is necessary to verify that the guest has actually departed. Check that the items were not intended for storage, and check in the guest's history; also ask the front desk and concierge if special instructions were given.

Once you have established that the articles were left by mistake, it is imperative that they should all go down to housekeeping immediately, in case the guest calls and inquires about them. Fill out a 'Lost and Found' form and leave the items with the co-ordinator to be logged.

Also make sure that your staff do not carry 'lost and found' items around with them, and that they report them immediately.

Some articles, such as tickets for future flights, faxes and undelivered messages, should go to directly to the concierge rather than housekeeping for urgent attention. In this case the concierge should try to contact the airline with which the guest is travelling in the hope that they may be couriered to the airport before the guest leaves, or at least to acquire a forwarding address for the guest.

Day-to-day frustrations

When you deal with guests day after day, the shine can wear off! Sometimes you will feel like swapping places with the guest and being on the receiving end of all your efforts to deliver good service. This merely reinforces the point that we need to put ourselves into the guests' shoes to understand both their needs and their expectations.

Remember that the guest is paying good money for the services they expect, and it is their right to receive what they are paying for. Also try to understand that the guest may be away from home against their wishes, and they may feel strange and lost in a foreign environment.

Not all guests are holiday-makers. They may be under a lot of stress and pressure and be looking for a level of comfort and a sense of security that is beyond normal guest expectations. They may be staying at your establishment because they are visiting a seriously ill friend or relative in a nearby hospital. Sometimes you won't know the true circumstances of a guest's visit. For this reason, sensitivity and

UNIT

THHGCS03A

professionalism in your job should never be compromised. A warm welcome and acknowledgement as well as clear and polite instructions on, say, how to complete the registration card will immediately put a guest at case if it is all done in the correct manner.

If you find that you are losing your patience and your touch, take a deep breath and remind yourself that a kind, understanding, friendly approach will reap benefits for you. Guests will respond positively to your manner and you will start to enjoy your day again. The good effect will snowball.

If you find that you really are experiencing a bad day and you are having trouble turning it around, ask your supervisor if you can take a ten-minute break. Go and have a refreshing hot or cold drink and take some time to pull yourself together. This should not be necessary very often, but if you are having a really bad run it can work wonders.

If you are having one bad day after another, then it is time to take some serious action. Perhaps you need to take some annual leave—it is amazing what a difference even four days can make. You will be able to come back to work with the right attitude and suddenly you will be getting lots of positive feedback from guests and colleagues alike.

If you feel you are in a rut or an impossible situation, and you think you may have lost your hospitality edge, then there are still a few options you can consider:

- Undertake some training in another area, either within your own department or in another department of the hotel or establishment. Perhaps you need to work behind the scenes for a while in a role with less guest contact.
- Maybe you need to take action to restore a well-balanced life: work, hobbies, exercise and a good social life should all figure prominently in the big picture.
- The last resort would be a career change, but the hospitality industry offers such a diverse range of options that you may well be able to rectify the situation by taking the first suggestion listed here.

Guest service is demanding and it is not always smooth and easy going. Equipment malfunctions, unhappy guests, unexpected hiccups behind the scenes—these can all add to the demands on you in your efforts to provide outstanding guest service. Do not take the problems personally. The real satisfaction comes from providing such excellence in service that the guest does not even realise that you are dealing with all these challenges!

Now that you are armed with all the basics required for good guest service, we can move on to those chapters dedicated to creating even better, more informed and sensitive service.

7
Guest service

In this chapter you will find a lot of information that, while you may think you do not need to know it all at the same time, is the sort of information that can be stored for future reference. It is always useful to know where to find these facts quickly. For instance, knowing the different currencies could be linked to the section in Chapter 2 on geographic differences (pages 24-29). Time spent now, learning about these currencies, will save you wasting time later when a guest asks a question on this subject. Quick as a flash you will have the knowledge at your fingertips!

Familiarity with your surrounding area is crucial to the image you are presenting to the guest. Ignorance about the immediate environment of your hotel or establishment shows not only a lack of interest in your surroundings, but perhaps an unwillingness to learn vital information that would make your guest's life easier.

Foreign currency exchange

These days all hotel guests expect to be able to exchange their foreign currency at the hotel's daily exchange rate. However, they will also shop around, and some will be quite irritated by the level of exchange offered by hotels. You will need to be ready to counter some of their comments without getting into an argument.

Some form of paperwork will have to be filled out for all foreign currency. The guest may ask you to exchange travellers' cheques or cash for dollars. Reassure the guest that this can be done and endeavour to make the exchange as efficiently as possible. The exchange should be made as follows.

1 In the case of travellers' cheques, ask the guest to counter-sign the cheques in your presence and date them. Do not exchange travellers' cheques if the signatures do not match. Usually the guest's passport number is required. Refer to the hotel system for this information rather than cause further inconvenience to the guest.

2 Enter the total amount of foreign currency to be exchanged and indicate the type of currency that it is. Use the Foreign Exchange screen on the hotel system to calculate the amount to be given to the guest. Make sure you have entered details accurately so that the guest receives the correct amount and your cash float remains accurate.

3 Check the details carefully on the foreign exchange form, including the guest suite or room number, currency, exchange rate and total amount of cash given out. Ask the guest to check the details and countersign the receipt.

4 Attach the second copy of the foreign exchange receipt to the guest's foreign cash or travellers' cheques or place it in a separate envelope. Hand the top copy of the receipt to the guest with the correct currency, checking that the amount is correct. Ask the guest to check the amount so that you can be sure that they are satisfied. If possible, check the guest's details. These could show that they have only just arrived in the country and therefore may need some guidance with the currency and its denominations. It is unwise to assume that, just because some guests are frequent travellers, they are confident about a new currency.

If the guest appears to need some help, explain the currency and offer some advice about the sizes of different notes and how some traders may not accept large denominations for small payments. Offer to break these notes down into more acceptable denominations. Be sure to count out the currency slowly so that the guest can see that they are getting the same amount of cash, but in different denominations. When conversing with guests about their money, maintain a low, but still clear, volume and tone of voice. This is particularly important in busy lobbies and front desk areas, where you cannot always be sure that the 'right' people are listening in to your conversation.

The security of guests and their valuables should be of paramount importance to all staff. This level of care and understanding will be appreciated, as many guests and travellers are dubious about changing money and may be reluctant to ask questions. You may be able to gauge this from their body language and facial expression. It might be a good idea to remind the guest of the safe deposit box in their room or the establishment's secure system, so that they can see to the safety of their valuables and cash.

Training exercise: you've got the world at your feet!

This is a group exercise. Using the letters of the alphabet, choose a country whose name begins with that letter and then name that country's currency. Alternatively, have cards marked with the names of countries or national currencies. Each team should choose a card and give the appropriate answer for it. Award points accordingly to each team. This is also an ideal opportunity to display a world map and ask participants to indicate the location of each country. This will enhance the knowledge you acquired in Chapter 2.

Guest histories

Guest histories are used to maximise and ensure the guests' total satisfaction. These histories help staff when they are preparing rooms and facilities in advance of the guests' arrival. Compiling a guest history takes some skill, but it can be accomplished by simple methods. It's probably one of the more important duties you will perform, although it is unseen. It helps with future visits and enables staff to make guests feel more at home, since many of their favourite requirements are already in place and they don't have to request them.

Although almost all departments can access these histories to enter comments about guests, access to acquire information is usually only available to specific staff. It should always be remembered that this information is confidential and should be handled delicately for the sake of security.

Guests who have an extensive list of needs in their histories will often have their rooms blocked before they arrive. This means that the room is 'blocked' or occupied for several hours by guest service staff in order to place the guest's amenities and requests in place before they arrive. When showing a guest to their room, guest service staff may say something like 'I understand on your last visit we placed an extra blanket on the bed for you. We have done this, but if it is too much or there is something else you would like, please let me know or you can call extension . . .'

A guest history could include some of the following points:

- name
- nationality
- likes and dislikes
- purpose of visit
- religion
- preferred name
- preferred newspaper
- favourite fruit
- tendencies
- special requests
- activities already pursued
- room preference: non-smoking? view?
- amenity requirements
- general nature
- facilities used
- whether they use the full butler service
- previous butler
- food outlets used
- favourite restaurant
- family
- any problems encountered
- birthday
- company/purpose of visit

Training exercise: Consequences!

This fun exercise is designed to enhance your familiarity with guest history and is especially good for a group activity in communication.

Each person in the group will need an A4 sheet of paper. Leaving a space at the top, number the 'consequences', allowing a reasonable amount of space for writing each answer. The first answer is written in the second space and the top of the paper is folded over to cover the first answer; the second 'consequence' is written in the next space and folded over and so on until all the 'consequences' are finished. The object of this exercise is not to take it too seriously, since after all the papers have been handed in and collected in a box, they are then pulled out at random and read out. More often than not, imaginations have run wild and the results are hilarious. Humour is often one of the best ways to illustrate a point.

1 Name of person

2 Age of person

3 Married or single? With or without children?

4 Where do they normally live?

5 What do they do for a job?

6 What do they do in their spare time?

7 What is their favourite food?

8 What is their favourite drink?

9 Who is their favourite movie star or singer?

10 What do they dream about?

11 What do they talk about most?

12 What is their favourite movie?

13 What did they do for last Valentine's Day?

14 What is their nickname?

15 What do they like to do in... (state city or place name of choice)?

16 What is their favourite holiday destination?

17 What do they always carry with them?

18 What do they look like (colour of hair, eyes, height, shape)?

19 How do they dress? Smart, casual, rugged, rough, chic?

20 Where do you suggest they go tonight? What do you suggest they do?

1	
2	
3	
4	
5	
6	
7	
8	
9	
10	
11	
12	
13	
14	
15	
16	
17	
18	
19	
20	

'Consequences' sheet.

Airline tickets

If you are not as yet a frequent traveller, an airline ticket can be quite confusing. However, for reconfirmation purposes you will need to understand the information that a ticket carries. A list of the airline reservations and confirmations numbers is essential. There are directories and lists available that will also give abbreviations for countries and airlines. It is well worth studying an airline ticket so that you learn to recognise the following details:

- name of airline
- name of passenger
- date of travel
- flight number
- destination/outbound
- Class of travel: Y = Economy; J = Business; F/P = First class; C= Club World (British Airways only); Q = Discounted

- time of flight
- return destination/inbound
- return flight number
- return date
- ticket number.

When a guest requests that you reconfirm their forward airline reservation, all this information may not be required. However, you will need to know how to find the relevant information if you are asked. Once the reconfirmation has been made, it is wise to obtain a booking reference number and, if possible, the names of airline personnel with whom you spoke regarding the reconfirmation. This will help if there is a reason for the guest to call back to the airline office at a later stage.

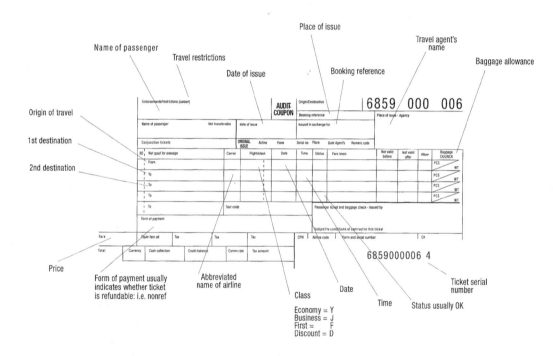

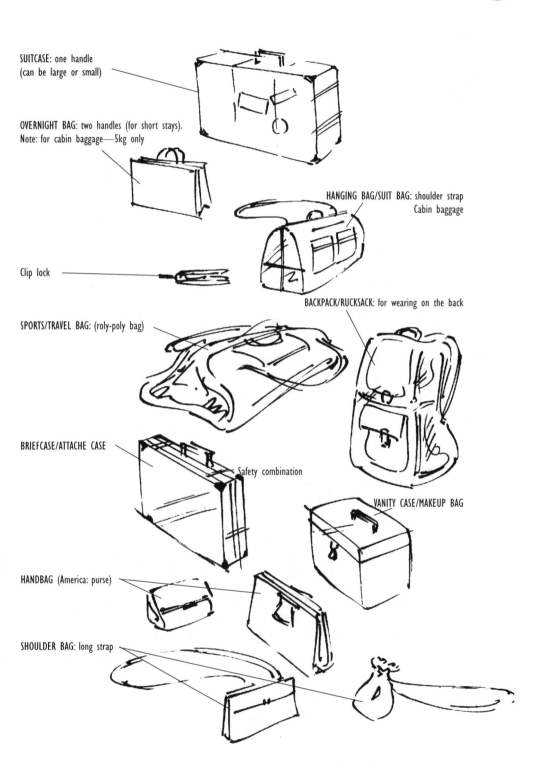

SUITCASE: one handle
(can be large or small)

OVERNIGHT BAG: two handles (for short stays).
Note: for cabin baggage—5kg only

HANGING BAG/SUIT BAG: shoulder strap
Cabin baggage

Clip lock

BACKPACK/RUCKSACK: for wearing on the back

SPORTS/TRAVEL BAG: (roly-poly bag)

BRIEFCASE/ATTACHE CASE

Safety combination

VANITY CASE/MAKEUP BAG

HANDBAG (America: purse)

SHOULDER BAG: long strap

Different types of luggage.

Training exercise: talking tickets

If possible, work with another person and develop a role-play to develop your confidence when talking with airlines and reconfirming airline reservations. If you are working in a group, each team should develop one role-play, write it out neatly and then pass it on to the next team, so that each team practises with a new role-play.

Meeting guests at the airport

Most international hotels have an airport representative who is solely responsible for meeting guests after they proceed through from immigration. This particular job calls for a great deal of understanding and sensitivity. Most guests will be tired after a long journey. (If necessary you should refresh your memory by re-reading the anecdote regarding arriving guests on page 23.) However, they will still expect a pleasant, cheery attitude without too much emphasis on personality. On their arrival most guests are aware that they will be met, so they will be on the lookout for some form of identification. After the initial recognition, the airport representative could greet the guests as follows:

- 'Welcome to ... (the paradise island/the world's most exciting city/the garden city or whatever), Mr/Mrs/Miss . . .'
- 'How was your flight from ... ?'
- 'Your hotel, the ... is about ... minutes from the airport, so if you would like to follow me we will get you and your luggage there as quickly as possible, sir.'
- 'How did you like ... (previous destination, if known)?'

At this stage check the guest's body language and expression. They may be signalling that they would like to be quiet, in which case you should take the hint and keep the chatter to a minimum. If their body language is positive, you could continue:

- 'Have you been to ... before, or is this your first time?'
- 'What sort of weather did you leave behind in your country?'

However, you may not need to ask this last question in quite this way if you followed the suggestions in Chapter 2 in relation to geographical differences (pages 24-29). Instead you may be able to say:

- 'Here in ... right now it is the high season, so you should get plenty of good weather for your stay.'

This conversation could include further information and knowledge about your surroundings to help the guest become more acquainted with the new environment. It is important that you, as the airport representative, create a good first impression of the hotel, so you could convey some basic information about the hotel and its facilities.

Local familiarisation

UNIT

THHGCS01A

All staff who have direct contact with guests should know as much as possible about the surrounding area, the city or town, points of interest and daily public events. A file should be kept available as a reference on such information as the various types of restaurants and their locations, museums, shopping, financial services, theatres, sights, available activities and industrial areas.

Never recommend just one particular shop; always give the guest a choice. This will also ensure that you aren't suspected of favouring one shop over another. Give clear and concise instructions on how to get there, giving the guest a map if appropriate. If you have the chance, contact the guest upon their return to check that all went well. Ask if they found the place, and show an interest in their outing without being too nosy or personal. Most guests will enjoy sharing their experiences, especially those who are travelling alone, and it will give you valuable feedback for future guests.

Training exercise: local familiarisation

Create your own list of questions based on the questions below:

1   The telephone numbers and addresses of:
    • the local Protocol Office
    • the local National Trust office or historical buildings
    • Parliament House.
2   Find out the opening times of . . . House.
3   Find out what shows are currently running in . . . and list three examples.
4   Which cinema is currently screening the following movies?
5   Where is the famous . . . Restaurant?
6   Suggest or seek out two good Japanese (or other style) restaurants in the city area.
7   Which store in the city would you direct someone to for the following items?
    • gourmet grocery gifts and hampers
    • locally-made gifts
    • up-market gifts
    • a good variety of top wines
    • classic clothes
8   Find out the telephone numbers and addresses of:
    • the Japanese Embassy or Consulate
    • the German Embassy or Consulate
    • the American Embassy or Consulate
9   Suggest two out-of-town tours that guests or clients might take for a day.
10 Suggest two of each of the following:
    • Australian sparkling wine
    • French champagne
    • Australian chardonnay

- Australian Beaujolais-style red wine
- Portuguese port
- Australian port
- Riesling
- French claret
- Californian wine.

11   Supply the telephone number for theatre bookings.

12   Direct an overseas guest to the tourist information office (just give the location and address).

13   Which two streets run parallel to either side of . . . Street in your city?

14   On which railway line is . . . (give two examples)?

15   What number bus or tram do you take to . . . ?

16   Which highway do you travel along to get to the airport?

17   List the forms of public transport to the airport.

18   A guest asks you to recommend a restaurant suitable for entertaining business clients in . . . Where would you suggest?

19   Suggest a couple of good late restaurants that guests might go to after the theatre.

20   Find out the opening times of . . . Market.

21   Where is the Stock Exchange in . . .?

22   Describe the . . . shopping centre to a visitor.

23   A guest would like to go to the. . . Botanical Gardens. How would they get there?

24   Where would you find . . . (place of local interest)?

Training exercise: shopping centres

'When the going gets tough our guests go shopping.' But where? And what do we know about the main shopping malls and centres in our local area?

This exercise is designed to enhance your knowledge about what is available and where you can best track it down. Every bellman, concierge, butler or service professional should be able to give this sort of advice in a commonsense fashion without assuming that the guest has a bottomless pit of cash, but on the other hand being mindful of the various labels and terminology that the guest may be familiar with and will be using.

Compile for your own reference a directory of shopping centres and malls in your local vicinity with the following information:

- name of shopping mall
- address
- style of shopping, e.g. designer shops/mainstream/food courts/restaurants/cinemas
- number of shops
- accessibility
- hours of opening.

Sometimes you may be able to contact a manager at the shopping mall and obtain a brochure.

Making theatre reservations

It is wise to do some homework in advance regarding theatre reservations and bookings. Guests will appreciate your help in finding and acquiring tickets on their behalf.

First you should become well aware of the shows that are currently running in your city. The local newspapers will have a listing of all the current shows, or the theatre will have sent out advertising handbills. Many theatres do not just make sure that hotel staff are aware of their upcoming shows; they sometimes offer them discounts and free tickets. In this way they ensure that guest service staff know what is available and how enjoyable their shows are, so that you will recommend them.

Theatre tickets should normally be booked as far in advance as possible. However, tickets can be purchased, sometimes more cheaply than usual, within a few hours of a show, as there are often late cancellations that enable the theatre to sell a seat again. Ticket agencies will take a commission from the theatre, but there are often discounts for block bookings of ten or more people.

When a guest asks for theatre reservations it is better to ask at the outset if there is an upper limit on how much they are prepared to pay for the tickets. Prices differ considerably depending on position, view and comfort. Guests will not appreciate small economies that result in uncomfortable seats. The most expensive seats tend to be in the dress circle and the front of the stalls; seats decrease in price and quality the further up and back they go. All theatres will offer a seating plan of their auditorium, which will make it considerably easier to explain to guests where they will be able to sit. Incidentally, you can also acquire seating plans for most stadiums and public entertainment areas.

When telephoning the theatre box office or agent, you should have a good idea of the requirements and how the guest intends to pay for the tickets. This will usually be by credit card. Tickets can then be picked up from the theatre in advance by the guest or at the door on arrival. The hotel can also arrange for the tickets to be picked up.

The theatre will require payment in advance on collection of the tickets. To do this, draw cash from the hotel with a requisition form. After the tickets have been paid for using a sundries voucher, fill in the appropriate details, attach the theatre receipt or docket and then request that the duty manager sign it. This in turn will be presented to the guest for payment on check-out. If the tickets are to be mailed, the box office will charge a fee for registered mail.

Most guests looking for a special night out will probably appreciate 'the works'. If this is the case, you will have the opportunity to suggest a limousine for both journeys to and from the theatre. A suggestion could be offered for a reservation for pre-theatre dinner or after-theatre supper, either in the establishment's restaurant or in an independent restaurant convenient to the theatre.

Airline and train reservations

From time to time you may be requested to make a booking for a domestic or international airline ticket or a country train or bus ticket. In most cases it is probably a good idea to use a travel agent, as this is cheaper for the guest than making direct reservations with airlines; payment also tends to be easier when reservations are made this way.

Business centre facilities and requests

For travelling business people a business centre offers welcome support with the many facilities they may need. Services that can be offered to guests include the faxing in and out of documents, Internet access, word processing, photocopying, the provision of a small meeting space, processing of incoming and outgoing mail and courier arrangements for parcels and document delivery.

The business centre staff should be familiar with the systems required to operate these services and should have a good working knowledge of where the major cities of the world are located. They should also be aware of the type of business that the guest represents—understanding the nature of the business can enhance the service they offer in the future. Other services include connecting guests for overseas conference and telephone calls, where information regarding the various country and international access codes is crucial.

Handling guests' confidential papers should be done with respect for their privacy. Guests' documents and papers should not be left in positions where other people can read them.

From time to time a business centre staff member may be requested to act as a secretary for a guest. At the outset, the guest must be informed of the costs involved. Guests are very careful about costs incurred at business centres, because these are usually quite high in comparison to office services offered elsewhere.

When handling mail on behalf of a guest, weigh items such as letters and parcels in front of the guest so that they can be sure that the correct figure is charged to their account.

When a guest requests space for a small business meeting, arrangements should be made so that the guest is shown in a professional light. Business centre staff should make sure that all facilities, such as slide projectors, function properly. Whiteboards should be clean and the provision of good whiteboard markers should be checked; the flipchart sheets should look neat and tidy; participants should be equipped with a notepad and pencil or pen each, along with jugs of fresh cold water and clean glasses. Arrangements should be made for the service of tea and coffee during the meeting, and these beverages should be served punctually at the expected time.

Business centre staff should present a good image on behalf of the hotel, since some guests will judge the running of the hotel by the professionalism of its business centre.

Requests concerning technology

Many guests will expect technological equipment that is better than, or at least as good as, they have at home. However, from time to time glitches will arise and these will need serious attention. Life can be made easier for guests if there is a member of staff who can effectively deal with more complex contingencies such as facsimile machine jams, Internet access problems and modem connections, set up laptop computers in the room or suite, and arrange the appropriate power adaptors, cables and serial ports. Some hotels are beginning to employ specially trained technology butlers, or cyber-relations staff, to manage technological problems in the recognition that some guests are technologically averse and may find themselves with a technical problem when they have checked in.

A technology butler.

Business executives, who travel with virtually their own 'offices', become very frustrated with minor technological problems if they cannot find someone who understands the local system, has a practical grasp of how various pieces of equipment work and has a good working knowledge of current and relevant software. It has become increasingly important to help guests deal with any problems that may arise with technological equipment. You can eliminate many complaints by anticipating the guests' needs in this area and asking them when they check in if they will need assistance in setting up their computers and so on.

When a guest telephones with a problem, it will usually be easier to discuss it face to face. A lack of language skills can make telephone conversations very irritating, so telephone operators and any other staff who may take calls of this kind should be ready with more detailed information.

Assure the guest that assistance is on the way. Guests usually have an understandable sense of urgency about these matters. They may even have an important deadline to reach, so they will need to know that help is coming. It is generally best not to get too technical on the telephone without actually seeing the equipment involved, since without some background knowledge it is difficult to give advice.

It is a good idea to check around for two or three reliable computer shops that you can confidently refer the guest to. The establishment should also know the 'help' numbers for local Internet providers.

If a guest complains or enquires about in-house equipment, react promptly. Take some basic notes from the guest and then go to their room to further verify the problem. But do not go to the room without some basic equipment, such as adaptors, cables and a new paper roll for the in-house fax machine. If the problem is greater than you expected, you may need to contact the hotel engineer, but you should at least be familiar with the relevant trouble-shooting techniques for any in-house equipment.

You may be asked to clarify the instructions for programming the voice mail on the telephone and producing a personal message. When dealing with guests on any such matters, be very patient and speak clearly and audibly. If necessary, suggest that they write down the brief instructions you are giving them or write them down yourself and present them to the guest.

Mobile telephones are widely used around the world on a global roaming network with the guest's home country as the base provider. Problems do occur on network selection and local access. It is a worthwhile exercise to obtain information from local telephone providers so that you can assist guests with their telephones. Battery chargers are obviously used extensively; guests may find that they have either lost or left theirs at home or at another establishment. It may be difficult to supply a temporary charger for all makes of mobile telephones, but it is possible to know of a supplier who can be contacted at any hour to courier a replacement to the guest. This can be paid for directly by the guest on their credit card.

A smooth, swift action that solves these technology-linked problems will result in a much happier guest. If you have had to hand the problem to another member of staff, be sure to follow up with the guest that everything has been sorted out and that they are now satisfied.

It is important that technologically competent staff who are called in to solve problems with computer equipment take care to erase the guest's password from their memories once the job is completed. They should also advise the guest that, for their own peace of mind, it would be a good idea to change the password.

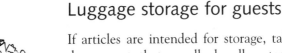

Luggage storage for guests

If articles are intended for storage, take them to the department that usually handles storage: concierge. The items will be packed in a bag or box and locked away. An itemised list should be drawn up; make sure that the entry is logged in the computer system or 'storage' book and in the guest history. A good storage record should include the precise location of the articles, for example 'shelf A2'.

Guests are not normally charged for this useful facility. It is most likely to be used if a guest is going to a hotel or resort in another part of the country. The bell desk or concierge stores the luggage or goods in a locked, secure room that can be accessed only by key card. The identity of anyone who gains entry to this room is automatically recorded. After the luggage has been entered into the system, the guest is issued with a receipt for their stored goods. A note of the guest's expected return should be made in the system. If this is done, the guest will not have to wait for the luggage to be drawn from storage; instead the luggage can be delivered to the guest's suite in advance and a follow-up call made to the guest after their arrival to check that all is in order.

Miscellaneous requests

There will of course be opportunities for you to offer suggestions to guests regarding available day trips and other outings. These may include four wheel drive charters, restaurants, yachts and charter cruises. In anticipation of such requests you should do your homework and find out the most reliable companies offering these resources.

Hot and cold towels

Hot and cold towels or flannels are sometimes offered to guests so that they can refresh themselves on arrival after a long journey or before or after a meal. The towels are well moistened, squeezed to remove excess moisture and perhaps lightly sprayed with a cologne.

Roll the towels neatly for storage prior to use. Cold towels are usually stored in a refrigerator that is specifically used for such items; hot towels can be heated in a microwave oven. They are then placed in individual plastic bags and stored in foil trays ready to supply and serve to guests.

Whether the towels are hot or cold is likely to depend on the climatic conditions. Moistened and slightly scented towels, whether they are hot or cold, will give a refreshing first impression when a guest arrives and checks in, and will provide a good start or finish to any dining experience.

The technique of serving towels

If you are offering hot or cold towels to arriving guests, first check that they are either hot or cold, and not something in between. Naturally, the number of towels you require will depend on the number of guests. The towels can be left in their plastic storage bags for the purposes of hygiene or removed with tongs and placed on a serving tray or in a basket.

Stack the rolled towels neatly on the tray or in the basket with a set of tongs or service equipment ready for service. If you are able to be creative, use a flower to decorate the tray, such as a frangipani or an orchid.

If you are offering the towels to guests in a dining situation, carry the tray on the flat of your left hand. Offer the towels from the guests' right. Please remember: you are offering the towel; do it gently and not forcefully.

Holding the tongs or service equipment in your right hand, use them to grip the edge of the towel so that, as you lift the towel, it will fall open as you offer it to the guest.

Move clockwise round the table *offering* towels to each of the guests, serving the host last. Place the serving tray on the centre of the table so that the guests can put their towels on it after use. Remove the tray with the used towels as soon as it is convenient.

The towels are usually collected and dealt with by the laundry. As little contact as possible should be made with these towels, so as to prevent the spread of bacteria and other germs.

Providing guest amenities to suites and rooms

Guest amenities are generally those items that are placed in the suite or room prior to a guest's arrival. In a way they are primarily designed to impress (or placate!) guests. However, they obviously have a practical application as well. Some considerable thought has to be given to ensure that the items will be relevant.

The main hotel system may be able to produce a guest history or profile and a list of preferences. This will give some indication of the guest's history with the hotel and will act as a guide to the guest's needs and requirements: for example, Mr Smith likes only crisp green apples or Miss Perkins prefers that no fruit at all should be put into the suite or room. Once established, this information system will direct you through a maze of indicators such as the guest's cultural background, the number of stays and room requirements such as smoking or non-smoking, extra pillows, more blankets and so on, along with a number of personal pointers like birthdays and anniversaries.

There are five main 'source' categories for guest amenities:

- food: chocolates, canapes, petits-fours, biscuits, 'special occasion' cakes and fruit
- beverages: champagnes, wines, fruit cocktails or juices, mineral water, tea or coffee
- flowers: either an arrangement or a posy, including if possible the guest's known favourite
- stationery: personalised writing paper and envelopes, postcards
- miscellaneous: gifts, perhaps from the hotel lobby shop—this might be a T-shirt, a baseball cap, golf tees, a locally-made novelty gift, or a book on the hotel, local art or the city.

Communication is vital when you are placing these amenities in a suite. It is far more impressive to have delivered these gifts, with a short note, before the guest checks in, so ensuring the correct arrival time of the guest is imperative. The amenities should be ordered well in advance. The relevant information can be logged on the whiteboard in the main housekeeping pantry, so that all staff are aware of these requirements and their pending delivery.

Creativity with these amenities is often hampered by budgetary controls. However, with the right information and a little imagination, a guest can be really impressed. For example, it is learned from the guest history that a guest arriving in two days' time has just celebrated a birthday. Would it be better to overlook this or to see it as an opportunity?

My basic philosophy, as you will no doubt have realised by now, is to turn the situation around. How would you feel? This guest may have been 'country-hopping' for several days or weeks and until now no one has recognised his or her birthday. If they walk into a suite or room to find that a subtle gift and a card have been 'delivered' they will no doubt be impressed. This simple action will be an important contribution to public relations and the guest will be bound to tell other people, both locally and at home.

Birthdays remembered!

Some years ago when I was checking into the Oriental Hotel in Bangkok, it was obviously noticed by the reception staff that my own birthday had just passed. I was subsequently offered a tour of the newly-decorated wing and a cup of coffee in the Authors' Lounge. By the time I was shown to my suite after this interesting distraction, I found an enormous arrangement of flowers that had been delivered along with a 'belated' birthday card. Was I impressed? Yes. Each year since then they have remembered my birthday with a card. Guest amenities last long after you may think they do—a valuable opportunity not to be missed.

Training exercise: special occasions

There are many occasions that can be identified and marked creatively. Drawing on the guest history and your own imagination, make a list of some of the opportunities that can be taken to create an impression with guests. Listed below are some ideas to get you going:

- birthdays
- weddings and honeymoons
- anniversaries
- national holidays of various countries such as Thanksgiving (US), Australia Day and Merdeka (Malaysia's National Day)
- religious holidays such as Easter, Christmas and other prominent days on various religious calendars
- a significant number of stays at the hotel, perhaps?

Once the occasions are established, delivering the amenities is the next important step. Obviously these amenities should be placed so that the guest sees them, but you might also keep it in mind that 'surprises' are also memorable.

Laying and lighting a fire

In some establishments a real log fire is featured in both public areas and guest rooms. Most people would agree that lighting a good fire is not the easiest task in the world. However, there are some basic tips that will help you achieve a glowing result!

First the fireplace and hearth must be clean. The ashes from the last fire should be removed. Collect together all the items you need to light the fire before you start. These will include newspapers, kindling wood, firelighters, logs, coal and matches:

- **Newspaper** Sheets can be rolled and loosely knotted (this extends the burning time).
- **Kindling wood** This consists of small bits of very dry wood that will help start the fire.
- **Firelighters** There are a few options:
  - branded: highly inflammable blocks that are useful for fast firestarting (though they unfortunately produce a slightly noxious odour)
  - natural: pine or fir cones make good natural firestarters because they contain resin and burn for a long time
  - 'recycle and re-use': candle stubs from a hotel's restaurant outlets can be used as firestarters, as they burn very well. Just place them as you would firelighters.
- **Logs** Large logs should be split lengthwise so that they can be placed safely in the fire grate. Logs should be stored in a dry storage area to ensure that they will burn readily.

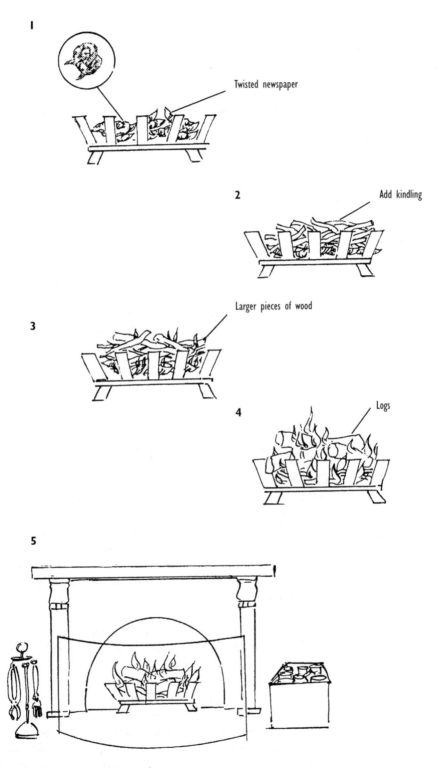

The procedure for laying and lighting a fire.

- **Hardwoods** These burn cleaner and hotter than softwoods and produce less ash.
- **Coal** Coal is a hard, black mineral. It is available in small knobs and gives a high heat when it burns. It is usually stored in a coal scuttle.
- **Matches** If possible, use long matches to avoid burning your fingers.

Lighting the fire

1 Either roll and tie the newspaper, as illustrated on page 137, or roll it into loose balls. Place the newspaper in the fire grate (the specially-shaped iron basket in the fireplace that contains the fire) and then lay kindling wood or place two or three firelighters. Strike a match and light the newspaper or the firelighters. Never wear gloves of any sort when lighting a fire, as they will cause problems if there is an accident and will exacerbate any burns.

2 When the kindling wood or the firelighters are well alight, place one or two small logs on top and allow them to settle and begin to take light. Make sure that the area under the grate is clear, as this allows plenty of air to circulate and fan the fire.

3 Once the logs have begun to burn, place another log at a different angle. Resist the temptation to pile too much fuel on top of already-lit fuel. This will have the effect of deadening the fire. As fire burns it is important to 'rake' the ash and embers under the burning logs so that air can still pass through the fire grate.

Once the fire is lit and burning well, brush the fireplace area and leave it tidy. To move any of the burning logs, use the poker as a lever. Place a fireguard around the fireplace for safety.

Do not allow the fire to burn too low, as rekindling it will be difficult and time-consuming. On the other hand, you should be aware that putting too much fuel on a fire can incur the risk of a chimney fire. Make sure there is a sufficient stock of logs beside the fireplace. It is difficult to avoid carrying in insects, ants and spiders that normally live under the bark, but if the amount of wood that is stored in the room is kept to a minimum this risk will be reduced.

Check that the fire extinguisher is either nearby or in the wood storage box.

It may be a good idea to find out tactfully if the guest knows how to keep the fire going or if they would like some assistance. Just suggest that they call you or another member of staff if they have any problems.

Finally make a quick check around the room, arrange any chairs and coffee tables so that they are positioned comfortably—but not too close—in front of the fire. Wish the guests a happy day or evening and leave quietly.

Offering beverages and food

The primary task of a good host—and everyone involved in guest service is a host—is to ensure that the guest is adequately cared for in terms of food and drink. If there is an opportunity to offer a guest a drink, don't just leave them to guess the options available: give them the choice. When the drink arrives, check that it is correct. Use this opportunity to talk about wines and beers that are currently available in the hotel. This is an ideal opportunity to ask the guest their preferences; this is valuable feedback. Also offer the different options available in the hotel restaurants and bars for such drinks.

With food, take the time to guide the guest to the buffet. Do your homework. Check which kitchen supplied the food for the occasion, and then explain relevant items to the guest if this is appropriate. This is another valuable opportunity to list the hotel's restaurants and to let the guest know that all the menus are available for perusal in the club or private lounge or at the reception desk of the hotel.

Tray set-up for a wake-up beverage.

Serving a wake-up beverage

The wake-up beverage is the first issue of the day that the guest has to contend with, so it should always be served professionally, discreetly, punctually and exactly to the guest's requirements.

Poor service at this stage of the day may well affect the guest's entire day, and therefore may affect their encounters with other staff members as well. When a guest requests a wake-up call with the operator or the butler, they could be offered coffee or tea with the wake-up call (see Chapter 8, pages 160-1 and 165-6 for ways to make that perfect cup). This will be served by the butler or room service assistant at the wake-up time specified on the order form completed by the operator.

When there are extra requests, such as for orange juice, croissants or muffins, a copy of the order form should be passed to the room service department unless the guest specifies a preference for the butler's coffee or tea service. Don't forget that some guests may even like a glass of champagne—they may have something to celebrate.

Prepare the wake-up beverage tray, remembering that the items should be placed for the guest's ease, not necessarily yours. If it is appropriate to do so, serve sweet biscuits. If you notice that the guest frequently leaves these, offer an alternative or simply serve just the beverage alone.

Bear in mind that the tray may have to be carried some distance, so it should be well balanced, as well as neatly presented. Make sure all the handles of cups, pots and jugs are pointing the same way; this is not only easier for the guest but also makes the tray look neater. Always make the hot beverage at the last minute and place it on the tray accordingly; this ensures that it will arrive piping hot for the guest. Make sure you arrive at the suite or room a few minutes ahead of the requested wake-up time. This will have allowed for any lift or elevator delays and ensures punctuality.

Pick up the newspapers in front of the door and fold them for more comfortable delivery. Ring the guest's doorbell or knock. Wait at least 30 seconds before repeating. Listen carefully for any movement within the room. If there is no response from the guest, remember that they may be in the bathroom and may not be able to hear you. In this case, return to the pantry, telephone the guest and gently inquire when they would like the beverage to be served.

When you enter the guest room, say 'Good morning, Mr/Mrs ...', using the guest's name. Be as brief and subdued as possible; it is best not to start a conversation unless the guest makes the first comment.

Walk discreetly into the guest room and place the newspaper on the table or the bed, depending on where the guest decides to sit. Remember that your body language will be clearly on view, particularly if the guest has returned to bed.

Place the tray (or unload the tray) on the main table or, if appropriate, the bedside table. Offer to pour the beverage for the guest. Never place food and beverage items on the desk if there is quite obviously some business activity there. Once this is done, move on. Don't linger, or guests will feel awkward.

At this stage you could offer to open the drapes. If possible, do this in a very gentle manner and resist the urge to open them more than necessary or comment on the weather unless you are already in conversation with the guest.

Be alert, but in a discreet way, looking for laundry that has been placed in a laundry bag ready for removal. If this is the case, offer to take it to be laundered. Perhaps shoes have been placed in the shoe basket waiting for polishing; take these at the same time.

Make a point of asking if there is anything else that you can do. After checking with the guest for other possible requirements, wish them a pleasant day and leave the room discreetly. Close the door as quietly as possible behind you.

Fixing a hangover

It is important to rehydrate the body after an excess of alcohol, so offer the guest plenty of pure cold water. They should take at least two glasses of water before retiring to bed and again when they wake in the morning.

Some recommended remedies include Berocca or a patent brand of salts in soda water and blended carrot and tomato juice. For a headache offer honey, either in hot water or on its own.

Avoid offering coffee, as caffeine will dehydrate. Instead, offer easy-to-digest foods such as cereal and milk and toast spread with butter.

Gently suggest fresh air and a good brisk walk around the block, or a light swim.

Training exercise: setting the stage

If you are to become adept at this task, role-playing during training is essential. Go through the whole process as accurately as possible. If you act out the entire scene, including being in the bathroom with the shower running, or being in the room with the television blaring, or actually lying in bed, you will see just how good the service looks and feels. In fact, in your own individual situation, you may find that your management of both the service delivery and the 'vocal and body' script may need a few slight changes to make it both more practicable and acceptable to the guest.

Setting up and delivering in-room dining

In-room dining in many hotels is not always treated with the importance it deserves. For a guest it provides an opportunity for privacy and the continuation of business and work. Many guests do not like to eat alone in a restaurant. If this is kept in mind, it offers a challenge to promote the service as something rather special. Nor should a call for 'in-room dining' or 'room service' be viewed as laziness on the part of the guest; often it is quite the reverse.

When guests order room service, they are usually trying to re-create some of their home comforts. If the opportunity to set the table in advance is there, take it. If, however, it is a straight request for 'in-room dining', consider how it must feel for the guest when you enter the suite or room with the room service trolley. Rather than just asking the guest 'Where would you like the trolley?' when you come in, do some

UNIT

THHBFB08A

homework beforehand, check out the suites and rooms and make a note of the configuration. This will enable you to offer guests some suggestions.

Maybe the guest is working at the desk and does not want to be interrupted by stacks of questions. However, a logical suggestion could be made to help them enjoy their meal. Perhaps they would like the coffee table set for their meal or the table taken out to the balcony? All this can be done with style. It also makes the job far more enjoyable if you can offer these options. Other guests may prefer to sit up in bed, in which case positioning the room service trolley for their ease and comfort could be tricky.

With some homework—even role-play—you can easily achieve an imaginative and practical style of in-room dining service that should give the guest an experience they would like to repeat.

Group discussion: imaginative room service

In a group—either large or small—discuss the different ways in which food and beverages may be served, imaginatively and with creative flair, in the room or suite. List these ideas and develop role-play situations. After these role-plays have been viewed, allow other participants to analyse these suggestions from a practical and economical point of view.

Room service quality check

As far as possible the same staff member or butler should provide all services to the same floor, including delivery of breakfast and other meals, mini-bar service, guest requests and services, but this is not always possible. However, checking that the following details are in order will make the task easier.

Trays and trolleys

Make sure that trays and trolleys are spotlessly clean before setting them. Trays should be clean and dry on both the top and the bottom. As guests will be left with this piece of equipment, it is important to remember that they will have more time to notice things. Trolley surfaces, flaps, legs and wheels should be clean and dry. A tray is often used for service of one cover. A trolley will be used for service of one, two or more covers.

Linen trays are covered with a clean, laundered and ironed tray cloth with one clean napkin neatly folded. The trolley should also be covered by an appropriate cloth, laundered and ironed. There should be one clean napkin per cover neatly folded. Always check linen for stains, holes, bleach marks and so on and replace it if necessary. Never use items that are not in a pristine condition.

ELF'S SHOE

Fold napkin in half, and half again lengthwise.

From top centre fold both sides down diagonally. Fold into centre again, diagonally. Fold in half with smooth edge on top. You will find two 'wings'.

Twist one 'wing' up and into the centre and bring other 'wing' around the back and tuck into the side pocket. Sit on place setting.

The top may be turned down like a cuff.

FLEUR DE LYS

Fold napkin diagonally,
Take outer points down to bottom centre.
Fold lower points in half to meet at top.
Take remaining bottom point in half to meet line and then fold in half again.
Take another fold, this time over base of flaps.
Fold the top points down diagonally and tuck into collar.

Holding base firmly, fold back to form a circle and tuck one point into other side.

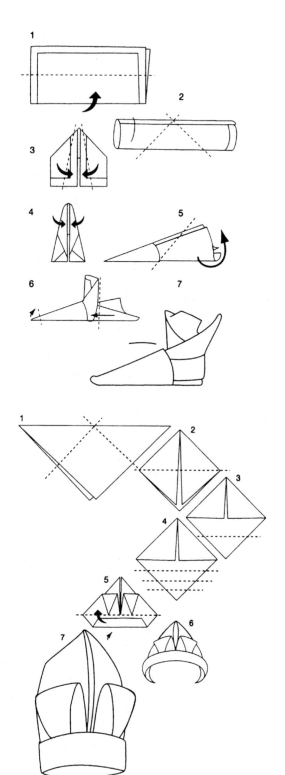

Four popular napkin styles. On this page, the Elf's Shoe and the Fleur de Lys. To increase your repertoire, refer to the author's *Table Napkin Folding: An Elegant Art* . . . (see bibliography).

continued

VICTORIA

Fold in half and then again lengthwise.

With dotted lines in mind, fold down top corners diagonally to form cones.

Turn over and fold cones in to centre to meet.

Place on plate or setting.

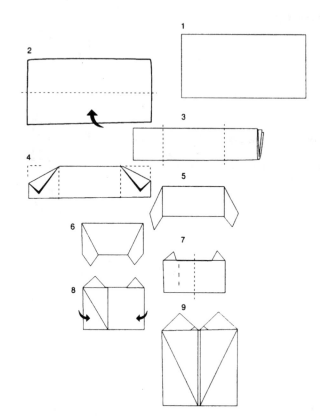

DOUBLE SWAN

With napkin folded into four, take one corner back diagonally and concertina pleat as in (2).

Repeat with second layer.

Pick up napkin and fold in half with pleats on outside.
Fold back to form circle and tuck one point into other.

Napkin styles (continued): the Victoria and the Double Swan.

Sample checklist
A breakfast tray or trolley will require:

- bud vase with flower (no water)
- salt and pepper (checking that they are full)
- sugar bowl with sugar and spoon
- milk jug
- plate for preserves
- butter plate and knife
- teapot/coffee pot/hot water pot
- container for bakery items
- juice glass
- side plate and knife
- cup, saucer and spoon
- cereal bowl and spoon (for cereal, fruit or yoghurt)
- card indicating instructions for clearing of tray or trolley
- all relevant cutlery
- toothpicks.

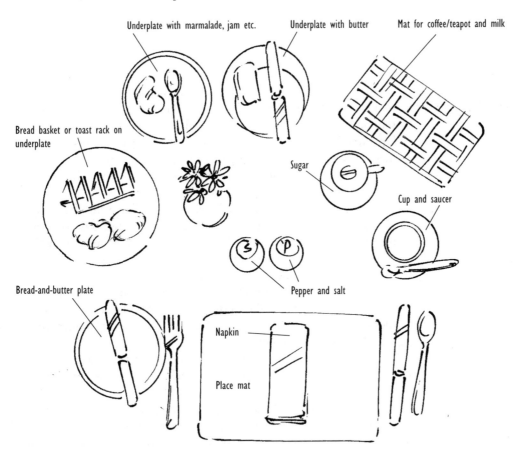

An in-room breakfast service tray setting.

A cooked breakfast will require these additional items:
- main course knife and fork
- main course plate, heated
- silver cloche (plate cover), clean and polished.

'Hot box' room service

'Hot box' is the term given to the heated box unit that fits under the table of a room service trolley. Hot boxes are kept heated to a regulated temperature in the room service kitchen department, ready for food to be placed in them prior to delivery to the guest.

When delivering room service orders to a guest it is important, after positioning the room service trolley, to offer assistance to the guest regarding the hot box. When you lift the tablecloth and indicate the hot box you can also offer the guest advice about opening it. It is probably a good idea to open the door and show the guest the various dishes as a way of checking that the order is correct. Be sure to remind the guest that items stored in the hot box will require care when they are removed; perhaps they will need to use a napkin to hold the hot plates.

Delivery to guest suites

The success of in-room dining relies on the final check to make sure that all necessary cutlery, crockery, condiments and food items are present and properly arranged. Guests will find it particularly irritating to have to call the room service department to request a missing item or make a complaint about any part of this service, especially since they will be well aware that their food is getting cold while they wait for replacement items to be delivered.

Many in-room dining preparation areas will have the space to display photographs or diagrams of correctly presented trays or trolleys ready for delivery. The tray or trolley should be prepared well in advance, so that it can be delivered as close as possible to the time requested by the guest.

On arrival at the door of the room or suite, ring the doorbell and announce your name and purpose, for example: 'John, your butler (or room service) here, Mr Brown. I have your breakfast/ dinner/ drink.' Wait for the guest to reply.

If there is no reply, ring or knock again and announce yourself. NEVER enter a room or suite unannounced and without first ringing the bell.

If a 'Do not disturb' light or sign is showing, go to the nearest floor, telephone the guest and alert them to your arrival.

On being invited in, enter the suite and address the guest by name: 'Good morning/afternoon/evening, Mr Brown, your breakfast/

lunch/dinner.' Once you are in the suite, ask the guest where they would like to have their meal or offer them an option based on your background awareness of the possibilities.

Training exercise: your average hotel room plan

Draw a diagram of an average hotel room with all the usual prerequisites of furniture, fittings, bathroom and balcony. Then consider the options available to the guests as to where they can eat their meal or have their drink. It is important to remember the practicalities of your suggestions. Creativity at this stage will impress the guest, particularly if you can create a calm, relaxed atmosphere. This is all very much part of making the guest feel at home.

Position the trolley carefully. If it is appropriate to do so, set up room service trolley flaps and rearrange the items on the table. Avoid making too much noise and try not to be too chatty. Observe the guest's body language; it may be conveying their impatience for you to leave the trolley and run, or they may be absorbed in the television or their work and will be reluctant to allow anyone to interrupt their train of thought. Be sensitive to these observations. Once the meal is set up to the guest's satisfaction, check with them whether there is anything else you can do. Leave the suite or room quietly.

Upselling

If you are serious about giving good service, you may find other opportunities to exercise a professional approach, apart from delivering the trolley. You may recognise a good opportunity to 'upsell'. You will need to know and be able to recommend some extra dishes or daily specials. Cleverly constructed questions will give you an idea of what the guest is in the mood to eat or drink.

In order to do this you will need to have a good working knowledge of the ingredients, preparation procedures and price of every item on the room service menu. Study the room service menus and ask questions. The Food and Beverage Manager or the Chef will be able to answer these questions and will appreciate the value in your being able to communicate this information to the guests. Menus should not always be relied upon to convey the exact meaning from the kitchen. However, there are words that you can use when describing certain dishes that will help the guest make their choice: words such as 'delicious', 'fresh', 'home-made', 'healthy' and 'crunchy'.

Training exercise: scripted sentences

Using menu suggestions and ideas from your own research, devise some scripted sentences that use more interesting words to describe certain dishes. Be careful not to go overboard with these descriptions, or guests will either lose interest or be suspicious about your motives.

When you deliver a room service and only a main course has been ordered, it may be worth suggesting a dessert to follow. Here some persuasive selling may be involved, but it is a good opportunity to use the previous training exercise. At the same time offer to take the order, so as to save the guest calling through to the room service department. Leaving them to do this alone might mean that the 'sale' could be lost through some distraction such as a telephone call or an interesting program on the television.

You could also say, 'We have a great selection of wines by the glass or bottle on the list. I'd be happy to help with any questions you may have.' Again you will have to be able to back up your offer with good product knowledge. Alternatively, you could use some suggestive selling by saying, 'Would you like me to bring you a pot of fresh coffee in about thirty minutes, sir?'

If a guest requests an item that is no longer available, simply reply 'Sorry, sir, we were unable to offer …. but perhaps we can tempt you with something just as good/delicious such as. . .' Be mindful of the fact that the guest may not always know or understand everything on the menu, so you can suggest items or 'side orders' that may make the meal even more enjoyable. Always take time with guests to ensure that they are happy with their choices; you may even try to make suggestions before the guest has to ask.

Time spent on role-playing exercises in room service delivery will be worthwhile. The result will be service that is more confident and, hopefully, more profitable.

Removing room service tables

Room service tables should be removed in a discreet and timely manner with the minimum of fuss and disturbance to the guest. Generally room service staff will remove tables, but if requested, the butler will remove them.

First of all, do not knock, enter or ring if a 'Do not disturb' sign is displayed. Many guests prefer to relax after having a meal; others will simply put the tray or trolley out in the corridor hoping that someone will remove it. However, if a request has been made to clear the trolley, ring the doorbell and wait. Allow time for guests to collect themselves and open the door. Again, remember to consider what you may be interrupting. Resist the urge to be impatient and allow at least thirty to forty seconds before ringing or knocking again.

When the guest opens the door, introduce yourself and ask them if it is convenient to remove the room service table. Inquire, sincerely, if the meal was enjoyable and to the guest's satisfaction. Make a mental note of their comments, if appropriate, to relay back to the kitchen. If a guest has not been satisfied, obviously action towards resolving their complaints should be taken immediately.

Arrange all the dishes in an orderly and neat fashion, being careful not to make too much noise. Avoid accidents, fold the table down carefully if this is appropriate, take the tablecloth over the dishes as a cover and move the guest's chair back to its original position.

While preparing the table to be removed, you could offer to take an order from the guest for some tea or coffee. Also, take the opportunity to ask the guest if they would like their room to be serviced.

If possible, avoid showing your back to the guest. If the guest waits at the door when you are closing up the table, inform them that it will take a few moments and make sure that you thank them.

Again, ask the guest if there is anything else you can do. While pushing the table out of the room, wish the guest a pleasant day or evening and remind them to call on you if you can be of any further assistance.

When you return to the kitchen or room service pantry, if there are comments to be made about a particular room service order pass them on to the relevant department before they are forgotten. Remember that all colleagues and staff are our 'internal customers' and have feelings just as guests do.

So be careful how you deliver these comments. Consider how you would like to be informed yourself and act accordingly. A sharp '2016 said the veggies weren't cooked!' sounds harsh but if you said, for instance, 'Chef, the guests in 2016 loved the chicken in garlic and herb sauce and the potatoes but thought the vegetables were a bit under-cooked for their liking' you will find that the response is quite different.

Serving 'alcoholic drinks

Sometimes a guest prefers to have someone serve their visitors drinks or cocktails in their suite or room. Often these drinks can be prepared in the room (see next chapter, pages 167-175), but it may be simpler to arrange for the room service department to prepare larger orders. Before embarking on taking down the guests' preferences for drinks, check with the host how many rounds of drinks they would like offered, or whether they would prefer only certain drinks to be available. It is far less embarrassing to know all this in advance than to have to apologise to the guest for the unavailability of such drinks. When taking the orders use a system that will allow you to be organised and appear even more professional. Take the orders down on a notepad, if necessary, in the clockwise order in which guests are seated or standing. If you take the order in this way you can then arrange the drinks on the tray in the same order to make delivering them easier.

Walking with confidence is not always easy when you have a tray laden with twenty or thirty glasses of liquid. However, with practice confidence will come easily. Carry the drinks on the correct drinks tray to the guests or the table and do not carry more than you can comfortably cope with. Hold the tray on your left hand (or on the right hand if you are left-handed) with the flat of the palm under the centre of the tray. Trays should be carried on one arm only with the other hand to offer some support, should this be necessary. Serve the drinks in sequence: clockwise or anti-clockwise, serving the host last as a matter of correct etiquette—unless of course it is a king or queen, in which case they are served first.

When offering the drink or cocktail to the guest, be aware of their current physical position and make it as easy as possible for them to take the drink. Hold the tray at a comfortable level for them and indicate their drink, or hand them the drink carefully. Sometimes it is necessary to place a drinks coaster or mat on the table before you serve or place the drink. This can be an awkward movement and it may be better to put coasters or mats on the tables first to cope with any spillage of drinks from your tray.

Once the guests are comfortably settled with their drinks, allow them to enjoy them without further interruption until you see that they require more attention. People relax when they have drinks and interruptions can be irritating. By all means check that ashtrays are emptied and any drink snacks are topped up, but resist the temptation to keep returning to the table or people will think you are deliberately trying to distract them.

When it is appropriate offer more drinks, bearing in mind the host's requirements as far as availability is concerned. Take only the number of replenishments of guests' drinks that you can remember at a time. When taking a glass from a guest or a table avoid holding the glass by the rim, and wherever possible replenish and serve all drinks in fresh glasses.

If you only take a few glasses for replenishment at a time, you should be able to ensure that each guest is served with the correct drink without having to ask them which is theirs.

Serving spirits

When offering spirits to guests who may eventually be paying for their own drinks, it is a good idea to tactfully offer some guidance on how much some of the more specialised spirits will cost. The wise thing to do is to produce a wine and spirit list for the guest to consider. This gives them the chance to absorb the prices and the different qualities available; it often influences their choice and sometimes encourages them to spend more money. The next chapter (pages 167-8) will deal with spirits in more detail.

Buffet layout.

Buffet service

In buffet service, like smorgasbord service, guests select what they want from a presentation of food items, hot or cold. The difference is that buffet service staff serve the guests with the food that they have selected, whereas in smorgasbord service the guests help themselves.

Butlers or service staff are positioned behind the buffet to assist the guests by plating their food for them as they select it. Butlers or service staff can use silver service technique to plate the guests' food.

Hold the guest's clean plate in your left hand and, using a serving spoon and fork with your right hand, transfer the food items selected from the service plates to the guest's plate. As with silver service at table, you must carefully place the selected items on the plate so that it is visually well balanced and convenient for the guest.

Packing a picnic hamper

Guests who are on holiday or have a few days' break between business commitments sometimes like to have a meal packed to travel with them. This may be a day trip, a day at the races, a simple lunch in the park or a more romantic dinner or supper by the beach. The contents of a picnic hamper can be very simple or quite luxurious, depending on the guest's needs and budget.

First determine the occasion, the time of day for the meal and the time that the hamper will be required to go. A picnic hamper should

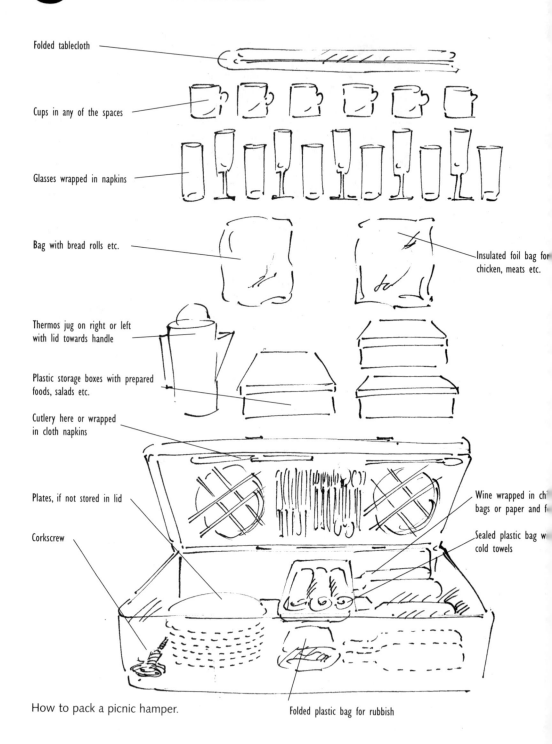

Folded tablecloth

Cups in any of the spaces

Glasses wrapped in napkins

Bag with bread rolls etc.

Insulated foil bag for chicken, meats etc.

Thermos jug on right or left with lid towards handle

Plastic storage boxes with prepared foods, salads etc.

Cutlery here or wrapped in cloth napkins

Plates, if not stored in lid

Wine wrapped in ch bags or paper and f

Corkscrew

Sealed plastic bag w cold towels

How to pack a picnic hamper.

Folded plastic bag for rubbish

be a properly constructed container made either from basketwork or lightweight wood; however, for the sake of convenience many establishments use a waxed cardboard variety that is disposable. A basket-style hamper usually has compartments for the cutlery and various other requirements such as plates and cups.

A well-packed picnic hamper should represent both the practical and the whimsical. It should arouse a pleasant feeling of expectancy in the guest. The menu can comprise the guest's favourite dishes, be ordered from the room service menu or be chosen from a list prepared by the establishment's chef. Once the menu has been agreed upon, the food should be ordered from the kitchen with definite instructions for its packing and the time it is required. It is important that delivery of picnic hampers is punctual, since many guests will have a car or transport waiting for them and will not want to be delayed.

Foods that are to be eaten cold should be packed into suitable containers such as plastic boxes or polystyrene foam insulated containers. A 'chill bag' that fits into the hamper will be useful for the storage of foods that need to be kept chilled. This is particularly important if the picnic is to be eaten in a hot climate. Food is far less palatable when it is not kept at the right temperature and has begun to deteriorate.

Conversely, foods such as soup or hot dishes will need to be packed into insulated flasks with good, secure screwtop lids. Any food that is likely to spill in transit should be reconsidered and an alternative, more suitable item chosen in its place.

Since picnics are regarded as special occasions, popular choices for picnic fare can include smoked salmon, caviare, paté, a meat or fish terrine and sliced meats with appropriate accompaniments of chutneys, mayonnaise and some style of dressing or sauce packed separately (unless a chicken, meat or fish dish is already prepared with its own sauce). These items should be packed into appropriate containers and stored in the chill bag.

Salad items are best kept separate, either in sealable bags or small plastic containers, so that the salad ingredients remain crisp and appetising. Fresh bread rolls should be wrapped in a fresh clean napkin and butter wrapped and kept in the chill bag.

Desserts usually consist of fresh fruit, a pastry pie or small cakes that are convenient to eat. If cream is to be included this should be well chilled. Unless you are very confident of the chilling or freezing capabilities of the freezer bag, do not attempt to pack any frozen item such as ice cream unless your establishment and the picnic location are at the North or South Pole!

Beverages can range from the most expensive champagne to a good wine or well-chilled beer. Bottles of non-alcoholic beverages such as soft drinks and mineral water should be included, particularly in hot climates and if any children are going to attend the picnic.

Once the food has been arranged and collected from the kitchen and before you pack the hamper, a tablecloth and napkins should be provided. (Always supply plenty of napkins—picnics have a habit of needing more of these than normal meals!) Appropriate cutlery should include a spare set in case one piece is dropped or lost. Other necessities include a corkscrew and bottle opener and sufficient plates. China is better, but paper will be lighter to carry. For glasses, again glass is better but the plastic variety is usually safer. Pack a couple of extra glasses; sometimes guests team up with other people and would love to be able to offer them a drink, but cannot because they don't have enough drinking glasses.

Condiments such as pepper and salt are essential; without these a picnic can be ruined for some people. A large plastic bag for storing the soiled plates and so on will make your job easier when you have to unpack the hamper. For the guests pack some refresher towels, and allow at least two per person. Preferably these should be of the cloth variety, stored in resealable bags and placed in the chill bag.

Bottles of champagne, wine and beer should be pre-chilled. To keep them chilled, either use a chilled sleeve wrapper or several layers of paper or newspaper and maybe a clean napkin. Alternatively, if the guest has the space (and energy!) they may appreciate the loan of an insulated wine carrier. Unfortunately, the practicalities of this loan usually involve charging the guest a deposit against its safe return and this can be a disincentive.

Packing a picnic hamper sensibly means packing it in reverse order so that all the right items are to hand when they are needed. Of course, as with packing a suitcase (see pages 204-5), the heavier items are best packed on the bottom to create a better-balanced hamper for carrying and unpacking. For instance, the tablecloth should be laid on the top of the hamper so that this can be spread out at the picnic site first.

Making the occasion even more special for guests could mean including a candle that will fend off the mosquitoes on a dinner picnic (don't forget the matches!), mosquito-repellent spray, suntan and sunblock lotion, a blanket and cushions (these will probably be very useful to those guests with their own transport). You could include a platter of pre-dinner crackers and appetisers, chilled chocolates and sweets, a well-constructed cheese platter, or strawberries dipped in chocolate. If you have enough time and you know that the picnic is a special occasion, you could include a greeting card. The list is limited only by your imagination, and guests will have a wonderful and memorable experience as a result of your careful planning and thoughtfulness.

What do you do when a guest asks you to take photos?

Although this may be an innocent request, the situation should be handled professionally and with care and consideration for other guests. When a large group require a photo, it can disrupt the entire area if you are not careful. Ask the group to form themselves into the pose before you stand waiting with the camera.

Once the 'subjects' are ready, do a quick check on the peripheral surroundings to ensure that the hotel or establishment is being portrayed correctly. If there are other guests straying into the frame, ask them if they mind. A simple question like this will give these guests an opportunity to decide whether they need to be recorded on someone else's film. For both security and private reasons a lot of people do not wish to be photographed; their need for privacy should be respected.

If a guest requests that you be included in the photograph, be flattered. Check the impression you are giving, particularly with regard to your facial expression and body language, and be utterly professional.

Gift wrapping

A professionally wrapped gift always impresses. If a guest requests wrapping paper, take the opportunity to offer this service if you can make the time to do so.

- When collecting the guest's gift, inquire as to the time the guest wants it returned.
- Always handle the gift with care and reverence.
- Wrap the gift neatly, using paper of a sufficient size only. Take the ends into the parcel as neatly as possible. Roll the sticky tape to produce a double-sided roll that will be hidden from sight.
- As much as possible, ensure that the ribbon and paper are matching.
- Return the gift to the guest as soon as the task is completed. Ask the guest if they require a greeting card. If they do, suggest the hotel lobby shop, adding the opening and closing times of the shop for their information.

With practice this becomes a very useful skill, especially if you have to provide a gift or amenity to overcome an awkward guest situation or if you are providing a gift for a birthday or anniversary. Everyone, especially guests, loves to receive a thoughtfully-packaged gift.

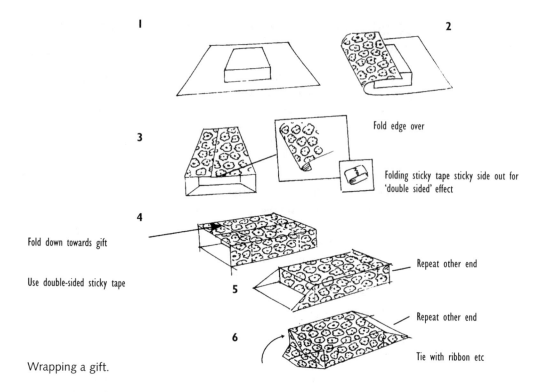

Fold edge over

Folding sticky tape sticky side out for 'double sided' effect

Fold down towards gift

Use double-sided sticky tape

Repeat other end

Repeat other end

Tie with ribbon etc

Wrapping a gift.

Flower arranging

When a guest has cut flowers, a bouquet or a posy delivered, it is essential that the butler, or a member of housekeeping staff, offers to arrange and present these flowers professionally.

Take the flowers to a pantry or other suitably convenient place, having ascertained from the guest any preferences for the style of arrangement. If the flowers are meant to be a surprise, though, make sure that they will be.

- Select a vase or container, ensuring that it is scrupulously clean and appropriate for the flowers in question.
- Fill it to two-thirds with fresh cold water. Please note that if boxed or posy flowers include 'cut flower food', you should use it. Check the instructions and use it accordingly.
- Unpack the flowers carefully, removing all string and bands. For single cut roses, stems should be squashed lightly to prolong their life.
- Take the foliage and 'bulkier effect' flowers, such as gypsophila, first. Place one piece in the vase and assess the correct length for flowers and foliage.
- Cut the foliage accordingly and place it in the vase, arranging it so that the stemmed flowers will sit well amongst the foliage.
- Using trimmed stemmed flower blooms, arrange them evenly

according to colour and texture. The effect should be balanced and pleasing to the eye.

- Continue arranging the flowers, avoiding over-filling the vase or container. Assess the overall look of the finished arrangement. Check that the base of the vase is dry.
- Spray the arrangement with plain chilled water. If this is suitable, tie the ribbon with the gift card around the vase, always ensuring that the gift card is returned with the flowers to the guest.
- Place the flowers in the suite or room in an appropriate position for the guest's enjoyment, while avoiding the possibility of the flowers being in the way or knocked over. Resist the urge to wait for the guest to compliment you on your flower arranging skills!

Anniversary gifts

If you are required to choose an anniversary gift on behalf of a guest, the table below will be of use.

Year	Traditional	Modern
1	Paper	Clocks
2	Cotton	China
3	Leather	Crystal, glass
4	Fruit, flowers	Appliances
5	Wood	Silverware
6	Sweets, iron	Wood
7	Wool, copper	Desk sets
8	Bronze, pottery	Linens, laces
9	Pottery, willow	Leather
10	Tin, aluminium	Diamond jewellery
11	Steel	Fashion jewellery
12	Silk, linen	Pearls
13	Lace	Textiles, furs
14	Ivory	Gold jewellery
15	Crystal	Watches
20	China	Platinum
25	Silver	Silver
30	Pearl	Diamond
35	Coral	Jade
40	Ruby	Ruby
50	Gold	Gold
55	Emerald	Emerald
60	Diamond	Diamond
75	Diamond	Diamond

8
Beverages

The well-handled delivery of guest services is crucial to the success of all establishments, regardless of the level in the marketplace. This chapter deals with some of the basics involved in the successful preparation of food and beverages. Although you may already be aware of many of these, some of the points raised and suggestions for improving service techniques are very worthwhile. For instance, you may believe that you do not need to know how to serve cocktails, but at least, just as the last chapter prepared you for any eventuality, you will now know just where to go for reference.

Hot beverages

The following pages will help you master the art of preparing the various kinds of coffees, teas and other hot drinks that are normally served to guests.

Coffee

Coffee is produced from the beans of the coffee tree, and is grown and exported by fourteen countries including Brazil, Colombia, Kenya, Indonesia, Papua New Guinea and the Ivory Coast. The varieties of coffee are named after the areas where they are grown, for example Mysore, Kenya, Brazil, Mocha and Java.

Coffee can be brewed to suit individual tastes. The great variety of pure blended and instant or soluble coffees, which can be brewed in different types of coffee makers and in various special ways, makes it possible to provide brews that suit everyone. However, regardless of the type of coffee used, the length of time the beans were roasted, the fineness of the grind or the brewing method chosen, there are some basic rules you will need to follow if you are to make a good cup.

Different styles of coffee

Different styles of coffee that are commonly served are as follows:

- **Long black** Freshly percolated coffee served without milk or cream in a large cup.
- **Short black** Usually an espresso served in a small coffee cup or demi-tasse.
- **Café au lait** Coffee served with milk; also known as white coffee. Cafe au lait is usually made with hot milk (au lait is French for 'with milk'), whereas ordinary white coffee has cold milk added. Sometimes cream is used instead of milk.
- **Espresso coffee** Coffee made in a machine that uses steam pressure (literally 'pressed out' coffee). An espresso (without qualification) usually means a 'short black' made using an espresso machine. Espresso coffee should have a creamy golden froth. This is a mark of a well-maintained machine and freshly ground coffee used in the right quantity.
- **Cappuccino coffee** Coffee that is made using an espresso machine with frothed milk added. It should be strong and milky with a creamy, frothy crest. It is usually garnished with a sprinkling of chocolate or cocoa. Cappuccino coffee is so named because its appearance is reminiscent of the white-on-brown cappuccio or cowl worn by Capuchin friars.
- **Caffe latte, or flat white coffee** This is also made with an espresso machine, but with a higher proportion of milk than a cappuccino. (Latte is Italian for 'milk'.) The milk is not frothed. Caffe latte is the Italian version of the French café au lait. A popular breakfast coffee, caffe latte is frequently served in a glass rather than a cup.
- **Macchiato** An extra strong espresso served long or short in a glass with a dash of cold milk. Macchiare means 'to stain' in Italian. A macchiato is a very strong coffee just 'stained' with a little milk—barely enough to change its colour.
- **Vienna coffee** Coffee topped with thickened cream; it is very rich.

Coffee being dried
on drying mats,
Papua New Guinea

How to make good coffee

Your ability to make a good cup of coffee is crucial to the guest's
enjoyment of it. These are the basic rules for making good coffee:
- Use freshly-roasted ground coffee.
- Always use freshly-drawn, cold water. Remove it from the heat
  immediately it has boiled.
- Measure the coffee carefully.
- Remember to strain or filter the coffee within 30 minutes, or it
  will taste brewed or stewed.
- Water that has been artificially softened should not be used to
  make either coffee or tea, since this will affect the final
  taste.

Plunger method

The most popular way to make coffee these days is with a plunger. The
plunger pot is designed to stop the coffee grounds from pouring into
the cup. The method is very simple:
1. Warm the plunger pot before adding a measured amount of fine-
   to medium-ground coffee—usually four heaped tablespoons per
   half litre of water.
2. Once the water has boiled, wait ten seconds before pouring it
   over the coffee. This prevents the coffee from being 'burned',
   which causes a bitter taste.
3. Fill the pot with water, lifting the plunger.
4. Leave the coffee to brew for about 4-6 minutes.
5. Push the plunger down carefully and firmly before pouring the
   coffee into the cups. The plunger will hold the grounds at the
   bottom of the pot.

'Jug' method

To make coffee by the ordinary 'jug' method, use a china, earthen
ware or enamel jug.

1   Before making the coffee, scald the pot with boiling water and dry it. This heats the pot.
2   Add medium-ground coffee, using the same measurements as for the plunger method above, with just enough freshly boiled water (remember to allow ten seconds for water to go off the boil) to make the grounds wet.
3   After about a minute, add the remaining water and stir the mixture.
4   Keeping the jug warm, let it stand for about 10 minutes before pouring the coffee. Usually the grounds will sink to the bottom of the jug, but a strainer can be used if desired.

Espresso method
Another way to make coffee is with an espresso pot. This is a pot that forces steam and water under pressure through the coffee grounds. This produces a similar brew to that made with a commercial coffee machine. Fine-ground dark roasted coffee is preferable. The result has a characteristic, slightly bitter taste with a strong 'espresso' flavour.

Milk, cream and sugar

If you serve milk with coffee, it can be hot but should not be boiled. Serve it separately in a jug. Cream is served chilled in a jug. Sugar is a matter of taste and personal preference. Demerara or coffee sugar has a flavour of its own and fine white sugar or lump sugar is acceptable, but unrefined brown sugar is probably the most popular choice.

Serving

When serving coffee, you will need the following equipment:
•   tray or salver
•   tray cloth or paper mat
•   cups and saucers
•   teaspoons
•   sugar basin and tongs or teaspoon, according to choice of sugar
•   coffee pot
•   jug for warmed milk or chilled cream
•   stands or mats for coffee pot and milk jug.
When setting the tray, position the items for the ease of the drinker. Bear in mind, however, that the tray may have to be carried some distance, so it should be well balanced. Make sure all the handles of cups, pots and jugs are pointing the same way; this is not only easier for the guests but also makes the tray look neater. Always make the hot beverage at the last minute and place it on the tray accordingly—this ensures that it will arrive piping hot for the guest.

Tea

Styles of teas from China and India

These are as follows:

- **Lapsang Souchong** This is a large-leaf China tea from the province of Fujian with a highly individual smoky aroma. This unusual flavour is obtained after normal processing by smoking the tea in large baskets over oak chips.
- **Jasmine** The classic tea of Chinese cuisine, this is traditionally served with dim sum dishes. It is an exotic green tea from the province of Fujian, scented by the addition of real jasmine flowers. As with other teas, you need to experiment with different quantities to find the strength preferred.
- **China Oolong** This well-known green tea, also from Fujian, is a semi-fermented, large-leaf tea with a lower caffeine content than black tea. Delicate, like most China teas, its flavour can be likened to that of peaches.
- **Keemun** or **China Black** From the province of Anhui, this is a traditional black tea from Imperial China and is an ideal accompaniment for Chinese food.
- **Traditional Gunpowder green tea** This tea from the eastern province of Zhejiang produces a delicate straw-coloured liquor and has the lowest caffeine content of all teas. It is only available as loose tea because its large leaves make it impossible to place in teabags. Be prepared to experiment with quantities to find the strength preferred. As a guide, you will find you need less tea than normal.
- **Chunmee** This is a superb green tea from Zhejiang. It is widely consumed in China every day. This delicate tea is ideal after a Chinese meal.
- **Yunnan** Yunnan comes from China's remote south-western province of the same name, known as 'the Kingdom of Tea'. It is distinguished by its great wealth of long, golden, finely twisted tips and clear, bright liquor. Twinings has a 'China' teabag, which contains Yunnan tea.
- **Lychee** From the Guandong province of southern China, lychee is a fragrant black tea scented with the oriental lychee fruit. The aroma and flavour of the fruit are allowed to infuse into the tea and then the fruit are removed.
- **Rose** or **Rose Pouchong** This comes from Guangdong. It is made by interspersing flower petals with the leaves. The subtle rose perfume blends with the large, delicate leaves to form classic China tea.
- **Sichuan** This is a fragrant black tea from Sichuan province. It produces a golden liquor.

Blends of China tea

There are various blends of China tea:

- **Russian Caravan** This tea was cherished by the old Russian aristocracy, and was traditionally brought across Asia to Russia by camel caravan, which is how it got its name. It contains a fine blend of China teas.
- **Earl Grey** A world-wide favourite blend produced by Twinings. Legend has it that the second Earl Grey (former Prime Minister of England) was presented with the recipe by an envoy on his return from China. This fine blend of China teas flavoured with bergamot can be enjoyed at any time of the day.
- **Prince of Wales** This contains a bright, leafy tea from the Anhui province of China. It was originally blended in 1921 exclusively for the former Prince of Wales, who later became King Edward the Eighth and then Duke of Windsor. Today, because of its royal connection and the strict rules regarding the royal warrant, this tea can only be bought outside the UK.
- **Lemon** Another classic flavoured tea, this combines a blend of fine oriental teas with natural lemon flavouring, giving a bright golden liquor of medium strength.

Blends of Indian and Ceylon teas

From India and Ceylon come the following blends:

- **Darjeeling** Grown on the foothills of the Himalayas, this fine, pure tea has a well-rounded, mellow flavour and can be enjoyed at any time of the day.
- **Vintage Darjeeling** This tea for connoisseurs, considered by some to be the champagne of teas, is an exclusive blend of pure Darjeeling flowery orange pekoe teas. Picked during the first and second flush, it has a delicate muscatel flavour.
- **Queen Mary** This is a special blend of fine orange pekoe pure Darjeeling teas, which Twinings supplied to the late Queen Mary of England in 1916.
- **English Breakfast** This blend of small-sized Ceylon and Indian teas results in a full-bodied liquor. Its brisk flavour makes it an ideal tea for any time of the day, but particularly the morning.
- **Irish Breakfast** A rich, strong tea from the Assam region of India. Perfect on a cold, wet day or taken in the morning with a hearty breakfast.
- **Assam** Also from Assam, as its name indicates, this tea gives a bright-coloured liquor with a distinct malty character. It is enjoyed by lovers of strong tea world-wide.

Tea country,
Sri Lanka.

- **Ceylon Breakfast** A tea from the high regions of Sri Lanka
  (formerly Ceylon). A delicate broken orange pekoe tea with a
  golden liquor and delicious bouquet. This is a particularly good
  tea iced, as it does not 'cloud' when cold.
- **Ceylon Orange Pekoe** A medium-sized leaf tea with a
  smooth flavour, from the high area of Sri Lanka.

Other teas

- **Lemon-scented** Lemon-scented tea has a high-grown,
  medium-sized leaf specially selected for its lemon scent. It is
  perfect as a refreshing tea for hot weather, served hot or iced.
- **Blackcurrant** This is a selected blend of China and Darjeeling
  teas that are further blended with the flavour of blackcurrant.
  It can be served with or without milk, hot or iced.

Herbal teas

Herbal teas are also called herbal infusions or, in the French terminology, tisanes. Herbal infusions have been popular in Europe for many
years and have for a long time been served alongside the more conventional teas and coffees. Herbal infusions contain no tea
whatsoever! They are totally natural beverages based on traditional
recipes. They usually contain no preservatives or artificial colourings
and are caffeine-free. This is probably why so many health-conscious
people prefer them to conventional teas.

Although they are not strictly teas, they are brewed in the same way.
Use fresh boiling water and let the bag steep or infuse for 3-5 minutes
according to taste. Herbal infusions can be sweetened in the usual way
or with honey. Herbal teas and infusions should be stored in airtight
containers as they tend to pick up other flavours and aromas from the
kitchen or surroundings. Most herbal infusions are taken without milk,

although there are some exceptions and, of course, personal preferences. Some people prefer the bag to remain in the cup while they drink the infusion, to add further strength.

- **Camomile or chamomile** This is one of the oldest herbs and is known to have been used by the Romans in Europe over 2000 years ago. It is a low plant that has daisy-like flowers and will grow virtually anywhere. Camomile is also used in cosmetics, soaps and shampoos. However, many people who enjoy camomile tea do so because it has excellent soothing qualities for migraine and other headaches. It is claimed to lower nervous excitability and in some cases helps to lower blood pressure.
- **Peppermint** Peppermint was cultivated as a herb by the Ancient Egyptians. The plant has broad leaves and spiky flowers. Peppermint oil contains menthol, which some people find excellent for clearing head colds. Other people use it as an anti-spasmodic to help ease stomach pains and aid digestion. It can be sweetened with honey or flavoured with a slice of lemon.
- **Rose hip** Rose hip tea comes from the dog rose, whose flowers are white or pale pink. Rose hips, particularly in Europe, are well-known for their value in cooling fevers and easing coughs. For that reason they are good infusions for people with respiratory problems. It is a very popular herbal infusion and nowadays it contains the more exotic hibiscus as well, which gives it a bright red colour when served.
- **Mixed fruit** This is a blend of herbs and fruits such as apple, orange peel, peppermint and rose hips.

How to brew the perfect cup of tea

Here are the golden rules for making perfect tea. Follow them and you will never go wrong.

- Always use freshly-drawn, cold water.
- Never use a teapot made of aluminium or chipped enamel as this will affect the taste of the tea. The best teapots to use are either plain glazed earthenware or porcelain.
- Use a clean teapot. Ignore the old tradition that teapots should never be cleaned. However, never use washing-up liquid, as this sours the pot. Clean it with two dessertspoonfuls of bicarbonate of soda, fill it with hot water and leave it for three hours before rinsing thoroughly unless, of course, it is requested by the guest.
- Pour a little hot water into the pot to warm it and then pour it out.
- Use one teaspoon of tea (or one teabag) per person and one for the pot as a guide.
- Always take the pot to the kettle and pour the water onto

the tea as soon as it boils. Don't allow the water to overboil, as this will remove the oxygen in the water and the tea will taste flat and dull.

- Allow the tea to stand and brew, stir it once and serve. As a rule, small-leaf teas need about three minutes to brew; larger-leaf teas need from five to seven minutes. If the strength is not to your liking adjust the amount of tea, not the brewing time.
- Always use the best quality tea and never use a tea cosy, as this causes the tea to 'stew' unless you have decanted it into a warmed pot and removed the teabags or the infuser (teabag) after the brewing time. The tea can also be decanted through a strainer. Green tea, however, can be allowed to stand without straining, as it does not become bitter.
- Don't be afraid to create your own blend by using loose tea or even teabags. For example, two teaspoons of English Breakfast and one teaspoon of Earl Grey (or two teabags of English Breakfast and one of Earl Grey) make a very pleasant brew. There are endless permutations!
- Finally: it is not necessary to even use a teapot to make perfect tea! Just follow the above rules, whether you use a cup, mug, jug or even a clean coffee pot.

'Milk and sugar, ma'am?'

The addition of milk and sugar to tea is purely a matter of personal taste. Strictly speaking, sugar should not be used as it numbs the taste buds and therefore affects the flavour of the tea. However, there are some teas that benefit from the addition of milk, while others are better appreciated without milk or with a slice of lemon. Cream should never be used in tea.

When milk is used it should always be added first. Years ago, when chinaware first came into use, people were so afraid of shattering the delicate tea bowls that they put the milk in before the scalding tea to prevent the bowls breaking. As it happens, adding the milk after the tea has been poured can result in greasy globules floating on the surface if the milk is not perfectly fresh. Here is a rough guide:

- teas best served with milk: English Breakfast, Irish Breakfast, Assam
- teas best served without milk: Lapsang Souchong, Rose Pouchong, Jasmine, Traditional Gunpowder, Chunmee, Lychee, Sichuan, Vintage Darjeeling, the herbal infusions and fruit-flavoured teas.

Other hot beverages

These include hot chocolate and malted milk drinks. Hot chocolate is almost always made from pre-prepared instant powder. The chocolate powder is mixed with hot—but not boiled—milk, usually in the cups in which the hot chocolate will be served or prepared in a service jug. Other malted milk drinks are made in a similar way, but check the instructions on the packet before you make the drink. The Europeans favour strong hot chocolate made with very high quality cocoa powder; this can be mixed with a little cold milk prior to adding the hot milk. Pure luxury! This cocoa powder, though, has to be of a very high quality. The ultimate hot chocolate includes marshmallows and cognac and is dusted with more of the pure cocoa powder.

Alcoholic drinks

You have already studied the in-room service of alcoholic beverages on pages 149-150 in the previous chapter. Now is the chance to refine your skills even further!

Aperitifs

An aperitif is a pre-dinner drink taken to whet the appetite. Most aperitifs are dry in style because dry beverages stimulate the appetite, while sweet drinks tend to dull it. In spite of this, some guests may prefer to have a sweet drink as an aperitif.

A good butler or host will never make guests feel uncomfortable because of the drinks they have chosen, no matter how inappropriate they may seem. Popular aperitifs include:

- dry champagne served in a tulip champagne glass
- a pre-dinner cocktail (acidic or dry rather than creamy) served in the appropriate shaped glass
- dry sherry served in a sherry glass
- dry (French) vermouth served in a highball or stemmed glass
- a proprietary aperitif (for example Campari, Fernet Branca, Dubonnet or Rosso Antico) served in a tumbler, highball or stemmed glass.

Serving spirits

The following information is just a brief guide to the 'accepted' ways of serving spirits. Of course there are many other spirits and drinks; you should be able to find out more about these from a specialised book on bar service.

Whisky

Scotch whisky is usually served in a tumbler or an 'old-fashioned' glass. Since most whisky drinkers have decided preferences of their own, care should be taken to serve it so that it is just right for the drinker. It is a good system to serve the measure of whisky first (the standard measure is 30 millilitres) and then offer the other options, such as ice in a bucket or dish, soda water in a syphon or bottle, and water in a jug, separately. All other mixers can be served from the bottle. If the request is for whisky 'on the rocks', place a generous amount of ice in the glass and then pour the whisky over it to chill it thoroughly. Usually guests requesting 'a whisky' will expect a blended Scotch whisky. Malt whiskies are usually served neat and often in short-stemmed, plump glasses.

Gin

Gin is a distilled grain spirit that has been redistilled with various herbs and fruits, particularly juniper berries. The word 'gin' is a corruption of the French word *genievre*, which means 'juniper'. Gin is usually served in a tumbler (but can be served in a stemmed glass) with ice, lemon and tonic water, although some people prefer to have bitter lemon or some other fizzy beverage added, such as tonic water.

Rum

Like gin, rum is distilled—but from diluted sugar molasses—and is made wherever sugar cane is a major crop. White rum is matured for one year only and gold rum for three years. Brown rum is richer because of its even longer maturation and added molasses caramel.
Rum is seldom taken neat. It is usually diluted and mixed with other drinks such as Coca-Cola. It is often used as the base for punches and cocktails. Serve it in a tumbler or highball glass with ice and a slice of lemon.

Vodka

Vodka is a popular spirit in Eastern Europe. It is distilled from mashed grain. The best vodkas are charcoal filtered, which ensures the purest spirit. Known for its odourless, tasteless, colourless, smooth qualities, vodka is very popular in mixed drinks. It adds strength but not flavour, which can be a disadvantage to the inexperienced drinker.
   It is often served with orange juice for younger drinkers.

Cocktails

Although cocktails, and the making and mixing of them, appears to be a very specialised area, you may find this section useful. A cocktail is a short, mixed drink of about 75 to 100 millilitres, usually served in the early evening prior to dinner. It can be alcoholic or non-alcoholic; in the latter case it is often referred to as a mocktail. Most cocktail bartenders are flamboyant and enjoy the glamour of their job. It does require a certain flair as well as excellent skills in customer relations. Being able to gauge the guests' needs and inspire them to choose a cocktail instead of their usual beverage is essential. Even if you are working in another department, you can still inspire guests with your knowledgeable suggestions.

A lot of ingredients and equipment are necessary for successful cocktail mixing and serving:

- standard shaker
- Boston shaker
- strainer
- mixing glass
- bar blender
- bar mixer
- barspoon
- glasses in a variety of shapes and sizes
- clean, clear ice
- muddlers (stirrers)
- decorations and garnishes.

The basic rule is that the appearance of a cocktail should be pleasing. There is a saying: 'When you please the eye, you please the palate.' The cocktail should be a carefully-balanced combination of ingredients, not just a randomly-selected group of liquids. Always make sure that the glasses and all the other equipment are kept clean and polished. Some ingredients that should always be to hand include:

- olives
- silverskin onions
- maraschino cherries
- Worcestershire sauce
- tabasco sauce
- salt and pepper
- nutmeg
- angostura bitters
- cube sugar
- cream
- fruit
- mint
- sugar syrup.

Fans of James Bond will remember that he always insisted that his dry martini be stirred, not shaken. However, since most cocktails are shaken, the shaker is the most basic piece of cocktail-making equipment. It can be of any size, shape or material, but for convenience it should have a built-in strainer. This prevents the ice, whose only purpose is to chill the cocktail, from falling into the glass with the drink. Always shake the shaker vigorously with both hands; this is how you bring the cocktail to life. Fresh ice should be used for each mixing.

Always use large ice cubes for shaking or for serving drinks. Never use small cubes, as these will dilute the drink too much. Make sure that the cocktail mixing area is laid out properly before you begin to mix cocktails. An important point to remember is that the least expensive ingredients are placed in the container first; this eliminates any unnecessary wastage if you make a mistake. Finally, never fill the glass

to brimming point. Space needs to be allowed for the garnish, and also it is more difficult to drink if the glass is too full. Most cocktails are served with a garnish; this should be appropriate to the contents of the cocktail.

Useful cocktail terms

Blend Put all ingredients in the container and blend to the required consistency. Pour unstrained.

Build Pour ingredients direct into the serving glass. Add ice and a muddler.

Frosting The glass rim is moistened with lemon juice and rimmed with salt or sugar.

Mix Put all ingredients into the bar mixer container. Mix to the required consistency and pour strained or unstrained.

Shake Put ice in the shaker, add ingredients, give a short, sharp shake and strain the drink into a glass.

Spiral A complete peel of a fruit cut in a spiral.

Stir Put the ice into the mixing glass and add the ingredients. Stir until cold and strain.

Stir in Use the bar spoon to stir in a final ingredient.

Twist A long piece of zest, twisted in the centre and added to the drink.

Zest A small, thin piece of citrus peel (no pith), which is squeezed over the top of the completed drink to extract its oils.

Cocktail recipes

There are many cocktail recipes, but the following represent the most popular ones. I suggest you check out the recipes for your own use; an appropriate book is suggested in the bibliography (page 259).

Between the Sheets	Kir
Black Russian	Kir Royale
Bloody Mary	Mai Tai
Brandy Alexander	Manhattan
Buck's Fizz	Margarita
Champagne Cocktail	Pina Colada
Daiquiri, Frozen	Rusty Nail
Daiquiri, Frozen Fruit	Screwdriver
Dry Martini	Singapore Sling
Golden Dream	Tequila Sunrise

Harlequin   Tom Collins/John Collins
Harvey Wallbanger   Whisky Sour

Opening a bottle of champagne

Treat every bottle as if it is worth $10 000.
It is the respect champagne deserves!

Always point the bottle away from your body, and never point it at anyone else. Unwrap the top of the foil and remove the wire muzzle
carefully, keeping your hand over the cork at all times.

Put one hand over the cork and grip it firmly and tightly. Hold the
bottle near its base with the other hand and gently turn the bottle, not
the cork. Keep the bottle at an angle of 45 degrees. The turning
motion will free the cork, which you can now slowly ease out. Keep
holding the cork while you do this and keep the bottle at an angle.

Pour a little champagne into each glass carefully, as the foam will be

1
Use a clean glass (glass is sometimes chilled)

2
Hold bottle above glass

3
Pour a little champagne into each glass, carefully allowing foam to subside

4
Top up to just over halfway and serve immediately

Pouring champagne.

very frothy. Let the foam die down and then top up to the half-way
mark.

Sometimes you will come across a difficult cork; this is often the
result of incorrect or poor storage. When this occurs, try using a service cloth over the cork to gain a better grip and follow the above
procedure.

Decanting red wine

Certain wines, particularly aged and distinguished reds, develop sediment. This sediment is made up of tartrates that crystallise into a layer
of what looks like silt or dust in the bottle. According to one wine

expert, sediment is an excess that the wine itself gets rid of naturally. Modern processes are used in wine-making to remove the unwanted sediment from white wine before it is sold. However, because red wine is more 'precarious' in the making, the sediment is left alone.

If you do not remove sediment from red wine by decanting it, there will be a difference in taste and texture between the first and the last glasses. The nearer the sediment is to the bottom of the bottle, the coarser and more gravelly the taste and the cloudier the appearance. Decanting wine should ensure a brilliant clarity in the glass.

While the main purpose of decanting the wine is to clear the sediment, there are other reasons too. The traditional custom, particularly in England, of buying claret by the gross and laying it down in the cellar meant that over a period of time bottles became encrusted with grime. Wine was decanted into crystal for presentation purposes.

Young wine is decanted to get air into it—to 'kick it into life'. It should be poured into the decanter in a thin stream so that as much of it as possible makes contact with the air. This will help it breathe and improve its flavour. There is no set time when a wine may be considered old. This depends on the style of wine and its potential to improve with age.

To decant wine successfully, first know where the sediment is. If the bottle has been kept in one position, say with its label facing upwards, you will know that the sediment will cling to the side of the bottle opposite the label.

If you know in advance when the wine is going to be drunk, bring it to the dining-room a couple of days ahead and stand it upright on the sideboard to allow the sediment to settle to the bottom of the bottle. This will make it easier for you to remove the cork than if you try to do so when the bottle is placed horizontally in a basket or cradle.

Draw the cork as gently as possible half an hour before you plan to decant the wine, because your movements are likely to shift the sediment. Decant in the following way:

- About an hour before you plan to the serve the red wine, hold the wine bottle in front of a candle so that you can watch the sediment as you pour. Keep the bottle as steady as you can. Do not allow any sediment to spill into the decanter; this means that a little wine should be left in the bottle.
- Alternatively, you can pour the wine very gently through a strainer into a round glass decanter. (Square decanters are for spirits only, by the way.) You can, if you choose, rinse the bottle with pure water and pour the decanted wine back into its original bottle.

The older the wine the less time it requires to breathe before opening. Some very good red wines of age may only require 3-5 minutes, while their younger counterparts may need up to an hour to 'come to life'.

Wine coolers and ice buckets

Ice buckets are used to keep white and sparkling wines cool in the more formal and usually more expensive restaurants, while simple insulated wine coolers, sometimes placed on the table, are used in less formal establishments.

Ice buckets, when required for use, should be half-filled with a mixture of crushed ice (two thirds) and cold water (one third). The water allows the bottle to sink into the ice instead of balancing on top of it. The bucket may be placed in a tripod stand.

A quick tip for chilling champagne and white wine

Sometimes the particular champagne or white wine that is required is not sufficiently chilled. While an ice bucket and chilled water will do the trick, it is not always quite quick or effective enough. Take a clean tea towel, thoroughly dampen the cloth and wring it out well. Wrap the wet tea towel around the bottle and place the bottle in the freezer compartment of the refrigerator. After ten to fifteen minutes in a good freezer the tea towel will begin to freeze, thus chilling the bottle and its contents.

Serving port and liqueurs

Port and liqueurs are generally served at the end of a meal with coffee. Port takes its name from Oporto, the town at the mouth of the river Duoro in northern Portugal. Port is nearly always a sweet red wine fortified with brandy. Often an establishment will offer more than one brand of port. The styles of port generally available include:

- **Ruby** A basic young blended port that has been matured for only a short period of time, and usually aged for 3 to 5 years. It has a bright ruby colour, a fruity bouquet and a sweeter taste.
- **Tawny** Another blended port which is well matured in the wood. This produces a change from ruby to tawny. The bouquet and flavour reflect the oak ageing, so the resulting palate is sweet but the port has a nutty, dry finish.
- **White port** Only a very small percentage of all port is white. A dry, fortified wine, it is made from white grapes and is usually served as an aperitif in a similar way to sherry.
- **Vintage port** Vintage port is taken from the oak casks before all the impurities have had time to settle. It is then matured in the bottle. A hard sediment forms a 'crust' in the bottle, which means that almost all vintage port should be decanted before being served. Although it is blended, 80 per cent of the blend must be from wines of only one good year.

As a result of its limited maturation before bottling, vintage port retains its rich red colour. Vintage ports should be stored on their side and, as with all red wines, drunk soon after opening.

Serving port

Port is served at room temperature. Traditionally port was served at large formal functions in a clockwise direction—in other words it was always passed to the left. It was considered bad manners to stop the progress of the bottle of port and even more so to pass it in the wrong direction. However, in a less formal environment port is served by the glass, the normal measure being 60 millilitres, taken around the table on a tray and served to each guest. The same style of glass is usually used for both sherry and port.

Serving liqueurs

Originally better known for their medicinal properties because many of them were developed from herbs, liqueurs are served at the end of a meal as a digestif. They are designed to be lingered over, particularly since some of them have a very high alcohol content.

Liqueurs can be served neat in a small liqueur glass, topped with cream, added to coffee or layered. Layering is done by carefully pouring different liqueurs into a very tall, narrow glass to create coloured layers (usually five, but always an odd number). They can be layered in this way because of the differing densities of the liqueurs. Another way to serve liqueurs is frappe. Here the liqueur is poured over crushed ice in a wide-bottomed glass, such as a brandy balloon or a champagne saucer, and served with a straw.

Serving cognac and armagnac

Cognac is one of the most famous brandies. Brandies are blended and matured by cognac houses. The traditional markings on the bottles of cognac are:

- *—one star
- **—two star
- ***—three star
- VO—very old
- VOP—very old pale
- VSP—very superior pale
- VSOP—very superior old pale
- XO—extra old.

'Fine champagne' cognacs are blended only from brandies produced in the Grande and Petite Champagne regions of France. Armagnac is another type of French brandy. It comes from the Armagnac region in southern France, near the mountainous border with Spain. The production of armagnac is much like that of cognac, but it is fuller-bodied and much drier than its counterpart. Good armagnac has a firm, nutty, fruity taste because it is matured in dark-wooded Monlezun oak, which is grown locally in the Armagnac region. Most armagnacs are sold in a very distinctive-looking flat-faced bottle called a 'basquaise'.

The normal measure for cognac and armagnac is 30 millilitres. Fine brandies are served in wide-bottomed brandy glasses or balloons. Sometimes the brandy glass is warmed gently over a special warming lamp before the brandy is poured, or guests rest the brandy balloon in their palms to warm the brandy.

Glasses

The question as to which glass should be used for which beverage can be a vexed one. Rules are not necessarily hard-and-fast; a champagne glass, for instance, can have one of several shapes. The diagram below will help you if you are in any doubt about choosing the right sized glass.

| Liqueur | Port | Sherry | White wine | Red wine |

| Goblet | Champagne: 'Marie Antoinette' | Champagne flute | Tall hock |

| Brandy balloon | Tumbler (9 oz) | Hi-ball (12 oz) |

A range of commonly-used glasses. Frequently one glass size is used for both port and sherry, and one size for both white and red wines.

Cleaning and polishing glasses

Although glasses are hygienically washed and sterilised by the high temperatures of the washing cycle in a dishwasher, it is still necessary to wash and polish all glassware by hand before it is placed on the table or used to serve drinks.

- A lint-free tea towel or polishing cloth should be used to polish glasses and to make sure they are spotlessly clean.
- Hold the glass over boiling water so that steam fills the bowl of the glass. To polish well, hold the bowl of the glass in the palm of your hand, with the stem between your thumb and forefinger. Carefully push the corner of the tea towel into the bowl of the glass and move it around the bowl in a circular motion.
- Polish the base of the glass last and place the glass down, holding it by the stem.

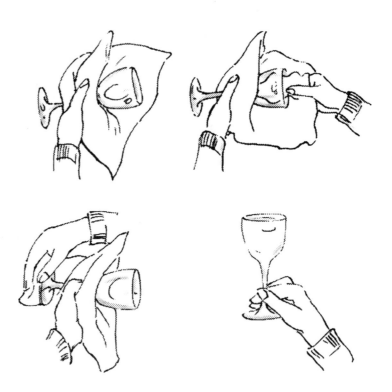

Polishing a glass

9
Giving that extra special service

Butler or valet service

UNIT

THHBH06A

Recognising that a hotel guest may require several different levels of service, many international five-star hotels offer butler service. The butler can be regarded as a key element in delivering a level of personalised service that exceeds the expectations of the guests and gives the hotel that edge of difference. A butler can be either male or female.

Butlers are almost always attached to the housekeeping department—although there are areas of crossover into the food and beverage department—and often act as 'mini-managers', developing other staff members and offering a style of service that is quietly confident in its delivery. The main role of a butler is that of a personal assistant who can anticipate the guest's needs without waiting to be asked. In addition to housekeeping and food and beverage service, a butler needs to be well versed in personal care and valeting.

The criteria for such a position are high. A butler needs to be prompt, courteous, organised, well-groomed, honest, trusting and trustworthy, friendly but not familiar, reliable and low-key in demeanour. A butler is an unobtrusive hotel professional committed to the highest standards of service. He or she is very often the first and last point of contact for the guest and represents the best the hotel can offer—an ambassador! An attention to detail and the ability to anticipate the needs of the guest, coupled with an appreciation of the finer things in life, make the butler a consummate hotel professional with impeccable standards.

Integrating butler service into an existing hotel style requires putting a considerable amount of time and thought into just how much butlers should offer in terms of service. Each butler will play a critical role in developing and maintaining a total quality focus within the department and the entire hotel. Since much of the role of butlers depends on attention to detail and using their own personalities to create a standard, it is difficult to chart all the tasks that they may be requested to do.

Most butler and valet services operate on a central call system that alerts the butler, by pager or with word text, to call the main switchboard or housekeeping department if there is a request. On receiving the request, the butler is expected to make every effort to expedite the task as soon as possible.

Quality awareness

Every establishment strives to set and maintain standards to the best of their ability. Success, however, usually comes from aspiring to one notch beyond excellence.

It is usually the responsibility of the housekeeping supervisor or butler to check a room or suite for quality finish in preparation for the guest. Spot checks should also be carried out by management, and it is sometimes beneficial to ask a member of another department to do one of these spot checks.

UNIT
THHBH01A

Whoever is doing the inspection should use a checklist to ensure high quality and a satisfactory finish. The primary thought should be: 'Would I be happy checking into this room?' Check as many details as possible, and settle for nothing less than the highest standard. It is quite enlightening to find just how much you can notice if you look at the room or suite from a guest's point of view. To carry out a more thorough room inspection, see what you can see by lying on the bed, sitting on the lidded lavatory or standing with your back to the window looking into the room. Sit in the armchair or on the sofa—not just for a minute but for five minutes; guests will be glad that you did!

To maintain a consistently high standard, you require a checklist. Each room or suite will have a different configuration, but a checklist that follows the room or suite around in a clockwise direction makes sense. When a room or suite has been designated 'OK', it should be ready to 'sell'.

In each guest room or suite check the following.

Bathroom
- Check the front, sides, back and drain of the bathtub.
- Check the shower head, nozzle and drain.

- Check the shower curtain and the area around the base of the shower.
- Check towels and appropriate linen for numbers and correct presentation.
- Check that the vanity unit, shelves and mirror are clean and smear-free.
- Look underneath the bathroom vanity unit.
- Check the washbasin, drain and soapdish.
- Check that chrome fittings are clean and polished.
- Check glasses.
- See that amenities are completely replenished.
- Check the tissue box and toilet paper—VIP fold at the end of the toilet paper roll.
- Check that the toilet bowl, seat and lid are clean and disinfected.
- Check that light switches, wall fittings, walls, floors and so on are cleaned.
- Check behind the bathroom door and the back of the door; see that they are clean and free of hairs and dust.

Bedroom

- Check the bed by lifting the bedspread and blankets to ensure that it has been made properly. Look under the bed in case items have been left or lost.
- Lamps: these should be in working order and dusted.
- Check walls, ceiling and carpet for marks.
- Wardrobe or closet: no baggage marks on walls; shelf and floor clean; clothes rail dusted; correct number of hangers; spare pillow and blankets. As the safe is usually located in the wardrobe, check that the safe door is open and the safe is empty.
- Valet area: laundry processing; bag and appropriate forms replenished; shoe cleaning mitt and basket for shoe collection; clothes brush or lint remover pads; slippers and dressing gown or bathrobe.
- Bedside tables: clean and dust-free; memo pad and pen; breakfast reminder card; telephone clean and in working order, including mouthpiece. Check radio is working. Switch off alarm if it is set.
- Sofa table or writing desk: table lamp clean and in working order; telephone books present and properly placed; stationery wallet replenished; ashtray polished.
- Check waste baskets.
- All chairs, baggage racks and standard lamp should be clean and dust-free.
- Doorknobs and handles should be polished.

The Royal Suite,
Hotel Windsor,
Melbourne.

- Curtains and drapes should be checked by opening and closing.
- Check television cabinet and screen; CD player; remote controls; refrigerator; mini-bar; tea and coffee making equipment: all dusted and in working order.
- Fire and safety card; 'Do not disturb' sign on knob on inside of door; eye viewer glass in door; entrance light; general condition of front door.

Parlour

In the parlour check all the same items that you would in the bedroom excluding the bed and wardrobe, of course.

Finally

Check flowers and fruit amenities; current magazines should be neat and not dog-eared from use or from the effects of air-conditioning.

The following extract is taken from a delightful book written by Jeffrey Robinson and titled *The Hotel*.

Now he [the Duty Manager] went through what he hoped would be his final chore of the evening—'snagging' [checking systematically] the room.

He inspected it for dust behind the mirrors and opened the magazines on the end table to see that no kids had drawn black teeth or spectacles on the pictures. One of the pre-set stations on the radio needed tuning—he retuned it—but the pre-set stations on the television remote were okay. He found an ink mark inside a lampshade, looked at the stock of stationery and counted the postcards. One window seemed stuck, so he gave it a tug and unstuck it. He then opened the mini bar to see that no seals were broken on the spirits. It seems some people drink the vodka, then refill the bottle with water or drink the Scotch and refill the bottle with tea. He also checked the sell-by on the jar of mixed nuts and, sure enough, it had passed.

Because a hotel room didn't always 'work', it was necessary for someone who knew how it was supposed to be to sleep in the bed, to take a shower in the bathroom, to push the floor waiter button, to look for draughts, to check if any furniture needed to be repaired. By design, the Duty Manager slept in a different room each night. It meant that, over the course of six or seven months, someone from the senior staff snagged every room of the Hotel. Any redecorated room was snagged within a week of the work being finished. The more exigent the Duty Managers were, the sooner the faults showed up. And as long as it was the staff who found those faults—before a paying guest did— Touzin [the General Manager] believed the room would always be up to standard.

Having found those things, Pierron [the Duty Manager] honed in on the rest of the room. The paint work below the wardrobe door was chipped. Paint was flaking high up on one wall in the bathroom. There was no on-off knob for the towel rail.

Everything was recorded in his log for Touzin's attention. Minor faults would find their way into a memo from the General Manager to the Chief Engineer or the Executive Housekeeper. Major flaws would be discussed at the morning meeting. And nothing ever seemed to fall by the wayside. Touzin followed up on everything.

If a guest discovered that the radiator wasn't turned on, or the air conditioning didn't work, or the shower curtain didn't keep the water off the floor, or the lights above the mirror were not bright enough, or the phone was too far from the desk to reach, or there wasn't a waste paper basket under the dressing table or there weren't any notepads next to the phone—Touzin figured it was directly down to Housekeeping not doing their job or Engineering not doing theirs or the Duty Manager not doing his.

When guests were paying for a room, Touzin insisted, guests had a right to find it in perfect condition and the Hotel had an obligation to make certain they did.

This extract illustrates more than adequately the need for attention to detail by all staff. It is much easier to handle guests' queries if the room and suite inspections and checks are consistent. Each staff member should have a thorough understanding of the required standard of the establishment. The main philosophy of quality awareness embraces total guest satisfaction.

Making a comfortable guest bed

An essential part of a guest's enjoyment is a comfortable bed that has been well made. It is better to have two people make a bed. If only one person is assigned the task, do one side at a time to eliminate walking back and forth around the bed; this saves time and energy.

Having stripped the bed of linen, check under the bed and the mattress for items left behind by previous guests. Turn the mattress if appropriate, observing safety instructions to avoid back strain. Mattresses should be turned on a rotating basis, side-to-side or top-to-bottom—or this can be done in a clockwise routine.

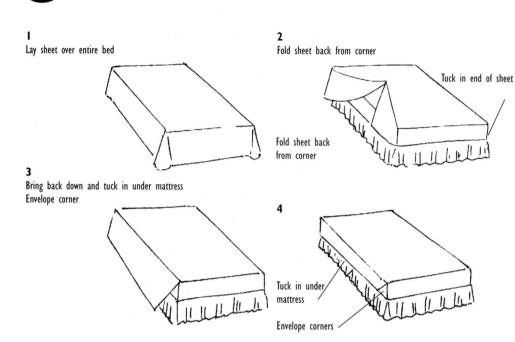

I
Lay sheet over entire bed

2
Fold sheet back from corner

Tuck in end of sheet

Fold sheet back
from corner

3
Bring back down and tuck in under mattress
Envelope corner

4

Tuck in under
mattress

Envelope corners

A bottom sheet
with envelope
corners

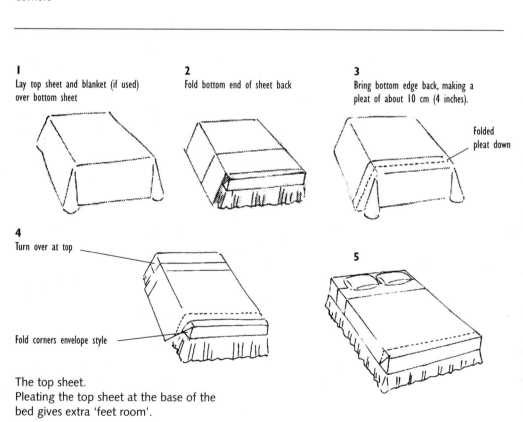

I
Lay top sheet and blanket (if used)
over bottom sheet

2
Fold bottom end of sheet back

3
Bring bottom edge back, making a
pleat of about 10 cm (4 inches).

Folded
pleat down

4
Turn over at top

5

Fold corners envelope style

The top sheet.
Pleating the top sheet at the base of the
bed gives extra 'feet room'.

A mattress protector or undersheet will help keep the mattress in better order. The bottom sheet is then placed over the bed and smoothed. Tuck the top of the bed first and form envelope or mitre ends neatly.

Tuck in the bottom of the sheet, repeat the envelope or mitre ends and lightly tuck in the sides. Place the top sheet over the base sheet and smooth it all over. Standing at the base of the bed, pleat the sheet neatly towards you by about 10-15 centimetres to allow extra room for the feet of tall guests.

Tuck in the bottom of the sheet, making envelope ends. Place the blanket or next layer—the duvet or doona—on the bed over the top sheet, tuck in the bottom and make envelope ends.

Fold down the top end of the top sheet and blanket neatly and evenly. Tuck in the sides of all layers. Place the pillows. Complete the bedmaking with a counterpane or bedspread, ensuring that this layer is folded under the pillows and brought over the top of them. Smooth the bedspread neatly.

When repositioning the bed, take care not to disturb any electrical wiring or telephone connections. Make a final check around the bed for any untidy finishing to the bedmaking—this is often one point that is easily noticed by guests.

Evening turndown service

The evening turndown service is another opportunity for an accommodation establishment to convey a sense of comfort to its guests. It should not be forgotten that the primary commodity that the operation really sells is sleep. If a guest gets a good, uninterrupted, comfortable night's sleep, they will be much happier in the morning and often a lot easier to handle. Don't you feel the same?

A good turndown is a practical way to create a calm environment that will enable the guest to relax without too much difficulty. In other words, the guest's suite or room should be 'good to come home to'! The 'goodnight' amenity is very often chocolate, some sort of sweet or biscuit or a flower. Another creative idea could be a small, locally-made souvenir. Placing different amenities over a number of nights adds interest to this guest service; providing the same item every night can get very boring for a long-stay guest.

The turndown service should also be used as an opportunity to make a final check on the suite or room before the guest retires for the night. If the guest is in the suite or room, ask them if they would like the bed turned down. If they would, carefully remove any items the guest has placed on the bed and put these to one side. Treat this time in the guest's suite with respect for their space and privacy; it is not necessarily an appropriate time for cheery conversation and gossip.

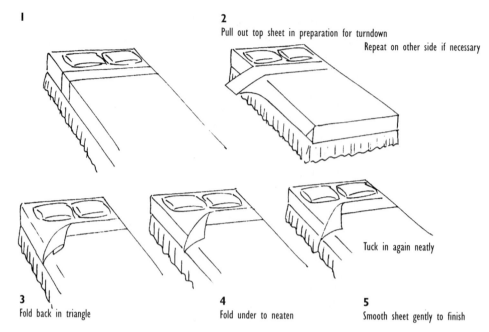

1

2
Pull out top sheet in preparation for turndown
Repeat on other side if necessary

3
Fold back in triangle

4
Fold under to neaten

Tuck in again neatly

5
Smooth sheet gently to finish

Ask the guest if they would prefer the bedspread on or off the bed. If they prefer it off, pull back the bedspread or counterpane to reveal the pillows. Fold the bedspread in a three-way fold—top towards bottom and bottom over to the top fold—and then fold it in three the other way for neat storage. Store it for the night in an appropriate place.

Turn back the sheets, blankets and duvet or doona to give the bed a neat, inviting look. Plump up the pillows and arrange them either flat or propped against the headboard. Check with the guest to see if they require any more pillows or extra blankets.

Place the 'goodnight' gift or amenity in an appropriate place: either on a bedside table or on the pillow along with the breakfast menu and a pen.

Any items that are left around the room should not be touched unless the guest requests some assistance with them.

Check that any flowers in the suite are still fresh. Some guests may prefer to have flowers taken from the suite or room overnight. Flowers, lovely as they are, take oxygen from the air and reduce the levels often needed to induce a good night's sleep.

Quietly empty rubbish containers, remove any dirty or used china and glasses and replenish them accordingly. Straighten and plump cushions in armchairs and settees. Ask guests if they would like the curtains or drapes to be drawn. Some guests actually prefer to look at the view, and feel shut in by closed drapes.

Switch bedside lights to the 'on' position and dim other lights if appropriate. Check the bathroom; replenish towels, toilet paper and any other bathroom amenities.

Make a final check around the suite before asking the guest if there is anything else you can do. Leave the suite quietly.

Group discussion: the 'inspired' turndown service

Discuss the different options for developing a 'superior turndown service' and suggest some ideas for improving on the guest's amenities, such as the item placed on the pillow.

Running a bath

The emphasis on running a bath is a discreet but sincere aspect of service that makes the guest feel special, comfortable and relaxed. It usually falls to the butler's responsibilities and should be carried out in a very natural way, without making the guest feel any intrusion on their privacy.

ACTUALLY I THINK HUMANS LIKE THEIR BATH WARM

First ensure that the bath is clean and free from chemical detergents. Place the plug or stopper firmly. Run the cold water up to 5 centimetres. This method works on the principle that, since running a hot bath often involves having to cool it down after filling it, it is actually simpler to warm up a bath of water rather than go through the lengthy process of cooling it down.

Ask the guest for their temperature preference. They may prefer their bathwater to be very hot, hot, warm or lukewarm, depending on their needs and the climate. Also ask whether they would like any particular product added from the establishment's range of amenities.

Continue filling the bath with hot water blended with some cold water. Bath water should be just above blood heat, but this really depends on the guest's preference. At this stage bath salts or bath foam should be poured into the stream of hot water so that it dissolves.

Check the temperature of the water in the bath again. Adjust the taps accordingly. Fill to at least 20 centimetres from the top of the bath. Bear in mind the size of the guest who will be taking the bath and allow for overflow levels! Check the temperature again.

Place the bathmat in front of the bath. This should always be done after you have run the bath so that you do not stand on it in your working shoes. If appropriate, float rose petals or frangipani flowers on the top of the water.

Check that there are enough bathrobes and fresh towels. Tactfully ask the guest if anything else is required—for example you could suggest that a bottle of champagne or relaxing drink be delivered to the suite. Withdraw discreetly from the guest's suite.

Unpacking suitcases

UNIT

THHBH06A

As a service to a busy traveller, this is invaluable. The unpacking of a guest's luggage should be handled as efficiently and professionally as possible to ensure guest satisfaction, giving consideration to the guest's personal space.

As a butler offering the unpacking service, you have to do this sensitively. A standard, subtle suggestion could go like this: 'If you would like, sir/ma'am, I can unpack your suitcase, and on departure I can repack it for you. There is no extra charge.'

If the guest agrees, assess how many bags or pieces of luggage are to be unpacked and calculate the time that will be required. If many items need refolding or hanging, allow extra time. If necessary arrange for extra hangers in the wardrobes. Move the luggage rack close to the bed for easier working. Never open a suitcase while it is on the floor. Apart from the inconvenience and hard work that this method creates, it looks very unprofessional.

If the guest is present, ask them: 'Is there any special way you would like your clothes unpacked and stored, sir/ma'am?' If the guest is not available at the time, continue to unpack the suitcases methodically, using the diagram below as a guide to where the items should be stored.

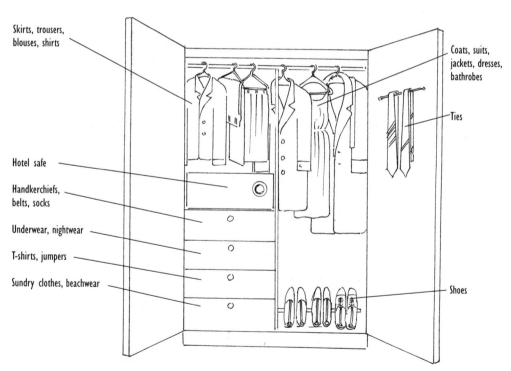

Skirts, trousers, blouses, shirts

Coats, suits, jackets, dresses, bathrobes

Ties

Hotel safe

Handkerchiefs, belts, socks

Underwear, nightwear

T-shirts, jumpers

Sundry clothes, beachwear

Shoes

Hanging clothes in a wardrobe.

Well-travelled guests nearly always have laundry requirements, so offer the guest the laundry and pressing service: 'May I press (or arrange the pressing of) a garment for you to wear this evening, or perhaps for a business appointment tomorrow, sir/ma'am?'

Unpack the clothes carefully and individually, placing each item on a hanger or in a drawer. Do not unpack everything onto the bed all at once—be methodical. Do not unpack personal items such as toiletries bags.

Ensure that clothes and garments are hung correctly in the wardrobe; they should all face in the same direction and hanger hooks should all match. If possible, keep ladies' and gentlemen's clothes separate. It is essential to hang clothes properly, otherwise unwanted creases will form and the garments will sag. Hang trousers on the appropriate hangers with the jackets and coats over them. The flat part of the trousers should hang against the back of the jacket—not just for neatness, but so that when they are in the wardrobe bulky areas with buttons, pockets and zips are not pressed against the smooth areas of other garments. Do not hang trousers at the knee; rather, hang them about 15 centimetres above the knee.

When placing garments with sleeves in the wardrobe, gently hold the sleeves together in front of the garment while you hang the hanger on the rail and then allow the sleeves to fall naturally into place. This ensures that the sleeves will not be caught up with other garments.

Hang trousers approximately 15 centimetres above the knee.

Hanging a garment with sleeves. Make sure the crook of the hanger is central.

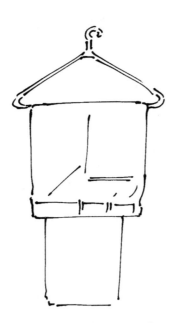

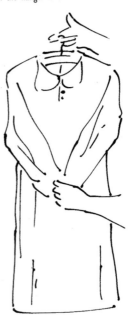

Hanging clothes.

If gentlemen's ties are already knotted, leave them that way and place them neatly on a hook or separate coathanger. Place any books or magazines on bedside tables. If there are any items you are unsure about, these should be placed on the table or desk for the guest to arrange.

Shoes should be placed in the wardrobe or near it. An offer can be made at this stage to polish shoes, or to arrange repair of any damaged items.

Do not feel shy about conversing with the guest—it will help to relax them—but keep the conversation general. Don't be too personal or ask too many questions.

Training exercise: unpacking—a script

Start with a packed suitcase. Unpack the suitcase, but develop a 'script' for conversation that is general and interesting without being personal. Consider how you would feel at this stage—having just checked into the hotel and perhaps feeling a bit tired. Refer back to the anecdote in Chapter 2 about the guests who had had a long journey (page 23). If you had packed your own suitcase, would you feel nervous about another person unpacking it and perhaps making a judgement?

Fold up the guest's luggage bags or close the suitcase. If necessary, place smaller ones inside larger ones for easier storage. If there are quite a few bags, offer to store the luggage for the guest, especially if they are staying for a long time.

Work neatly at all times. Whether the guest is in the room or not, make no judgements about the content or quality of the suitcases. Treat every item with care and reverence.

Where do you put everything as you unpack?

Towels/swimwear/beachwear	Bottom drawer
Evening dress	Wardrobe
Toiletries bag/hair drier	Bathroom
Shaver	Bathroom
Heated rollers	Dressing table
Lightweight dresses/blouses/ties	Wardrobe
Underwear/bras/stockings	Top drawer
Dressing-gown	Wardrobe
Belts	Top drawer
T-shirts/shirts/pyjamas/singlets	Top drawer
Trousers/skirts	Wardrobe
Socks/handkerchiefs	Top drawer
Sweaters/cardigans	Bottom drawer
Shorts	Top drawer
Jackets/coats	Wardrobe
Shoes	Shoe rack/bottom of wardrobe
Suits/dresses	Wardrobe
Ties	Tie rack/hanger/rolled neatly in drawer
Items for laundry	Laundry/dry cleaning bag

Brushing and pressing clothes

Once the clothes and other items are carefully hung in the wardrobe or stored in drawers other services can be offered, in particular pressing or brushing clothes.

Brushing

Brushing clothes is actually the first step to good clothing care. With respect to your own clothes, you can save a lot of dry cleaning bills if you brush them regularly. All clothes will look better for brushing; it seems to restore them and freshens them at the same time. Brushing primarily removes dust and grit that attaches itself to the fibres of the clothes. Dust and grit can be damaging to the surface of fabrics, acting as an abrasive element that will wear out the clothes quite quickly.

UNIT

THHBH06A

Brush in long, sweeping strokes, brushing in the same direction throughout. To brush inside leg of trousers, fold the other leg back as shown. With the jacket, fold the sleeves out of the way in a similar fashion. Also fold pockets out of the way as much as possible.

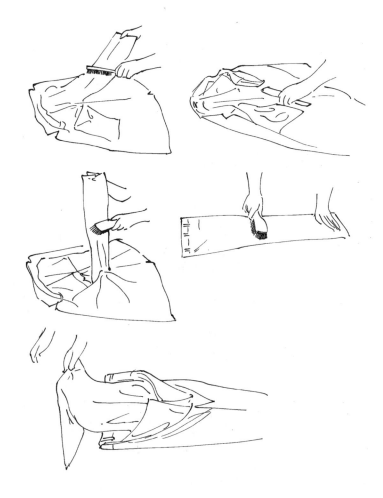

Natural bristle brushes are the best, but many people prefer to use the synthetic variety. One of the most useful brushes is the one designed to be used in one direction only. This type is particularly good at removing fluff, hair and clinging particles, although some of these particles are often better removed with sticky tape. Wind the sticky tape around your fingers with the sticky side on the outside and carefully dab at the fabric. Lint removers are worth having, especially to remove the little bobbles that appear on woollen clothes.

It is the correct use of the brush that really removes the dust. The ideal place to brush clothes is on a large table; but if that is not possible use a bed, although beds are very often too low and cause backache.

Brushing requires long, sweeping strokes rather than a scrubbing or circular motion. Take all brushing strokes in the same direction, otherwise your newly-brushed garment will look like a newly-mown lawn! First, brush up the nap (this is the surface given to the cloth by raising and then cutting and smoothing the short fibres—it is sometimes known as the pile).

If clothes are suitable for this treatment and need freshening, take a slightly damp clothes brush, simply dip the bristles lightly in cold water and shake the brush well so that it is only slightly damp. Once the nap has been raised, you can either brush it back down or press in that direction to bring the fabric back to its normal state.

Knitted woollen garments should be brushed lightly with a soft brush or shaken well. Extra care should be taken with mohair and particularly fluffy or fine woollens.

Light pressing

Pressing one or two garments on the guest's arrival is very often the normal procedure and is offered in most cases as a complimentary service. The items requiring pressing should be collected from the guest's suite or room as soon as they are identified or pressing is requested.

When collecting items for pressing from the guest, ask if there are special instructions for any of the garments. Be as well-organised as possible—you should be able to press these garments immediately. If there is to be a time delay, make sure the guest knows. If the guest asks for clothes to be returned by a certain time, only agree to do it in the time required if you know that you can do so. Otherwise you will later have to handle a difficult situation if the guest is upset by the delay. Take the garments to the ironing room or butler's pantry, if appropriate, and label them with the guest's suite or room number.

Check the label for any special instructions; make sure that the iron is not too hot for the fabric in question. Remove any hairs and fluff with a clothes brush or sticky tape.

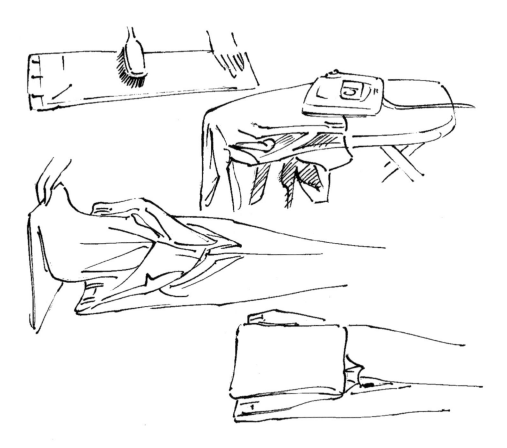

Light pressing.

For a really professional effect, always use an ironing cloth. This cloth is about 60 centimetres square and can be either a piece of cotton fabric or part of a former sheet. It is mainly used to protect garments from high temperatures, but it also produces better results because a higher iron temperature can be used without leaving a tell-tale shine on the garment.

Spray the ironing cloth lightly with plain cold water if necessary, or immerse it completely in warm or cool water and wring it well. When the damp cloth is used over garments, this will aid the removal of more stubborn creases.

Follow the guidelines of the garments: line up the creases in pants, skirts, jackets and the like. Carefully press, using firm pressing movements, to avoid any extra creasing. Avoid making a circular motion with the iron—smooth, straight strokes are best.

When you have finished, check that you have ironed all areas of the garment; it can be very frustrating for a guest to find that there are still creases or folds present. Also, it not only wastes their time but yours as well.

Place the pressed clothing on the appropriate clothes hangers: clip hangers for skirts and trousers; satin hangers for the more delicate garments (silk blouses and so on) and shaped plastic or wooden hangers for suits and jackets.

Return the garments to the guest's room and hang them in the wardrobe so that they are in easy view of the guest when they open the wardrobe. Human nature seems to dictate that when guests are expecting laundry or pressing to be returned they straightaway check the wardrobe when they return to their room. If you wish to bring the guest's attention to anything about a garment, leave a polite note (for example: 'The left pocket in the trousers has a hole in it; when it is convenient I could fix it for you.')

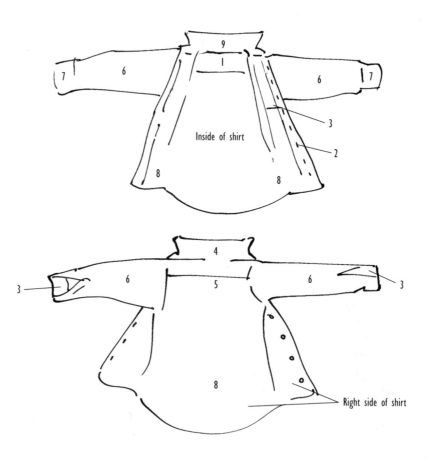

Pressing shirts and blouses.

Suggested ironing temperatures for different fabrics

Silk/chiffon (material can be slightly damp)	Low/cool/no steam (unless very creased)
Satin	Low/cool
Nylon	Low/cool
Polyester	Medium/steam
Crêpe, wool/polyester	Medium/high with cloth/steam
Cotton	High/steam
Linen	Press on inside if necessary; high/steam/cloth
Denim	Damp cloth; high/steam/cloth
Microfibre	Low/medium/without cloth; hot/damp cloth
Fine lawn/muslin/cotton gauze	Medium
Wool (flannel, wool blend)	Damp cloth/hot/steam
Mohair	Inside out; warm
Lace: cotton/nylon/polyester	Damp or dry cloth/medium or cool
Trims: leather/suede	Do not press
Linings: acetate/nylon taffeta	Cool/medium
Applique	Iron on inside; damp cloth/hot

As with all pressing and ironing jobs, you should check the manufacturer's instructions before putting the iron on to any fabric. Don't forget to check the base of the iron to make sure it is clean and also the temperature before you begin ironing.

Gentlemen's ties

Tying a bow tie

From time to time guests may request some assistance with tying a bow tie. Although the clip-on or ready-made bow tie is convenient and saves time, the old-fashioned bow tie that is tied each time it is worn is really much more attractive and stylish.

1   Place the tie around the outside of the raised collar. The tie should be flat against the collar and one end should be about 200 millimetres longer that the other end. Cross the longer end over the shorter end.

2   Form a knot by threading the longer end behind the shorter end. With the longer end hanging over the shorter end, fold the shorter end at the point where it flares to its bow tie width. Position the folded shorter end in the centre.

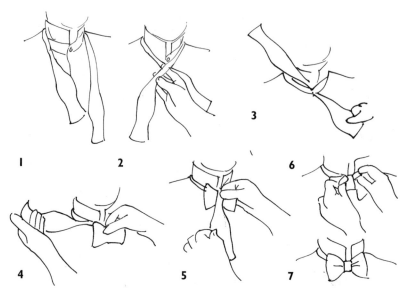

Tying a bow tie.

3 Bring the longer end down over the shorter end. Fold the longer end and thread the shorter folded end to form a bow. Pull through the longer end and, holding both sides of the bow, pull firmly to tighten the bow.

4 If necessary, pull the ends slightly to loosen the bow and retighten the tie so that the centre of the knot is tight enough to make a good-looking bow.

Tying a Windsor knot or a four-in-hand knot

To tie a Windsor or four-in-hand knot, follow the diagrams below and opposite. As you can see, the Windsor knot is a much fuller knot. It is purely a matter of choice which one is preferable; whatever style feels most comfortable or suits the individual's taste is best.

Tying a four-in-hand knot.

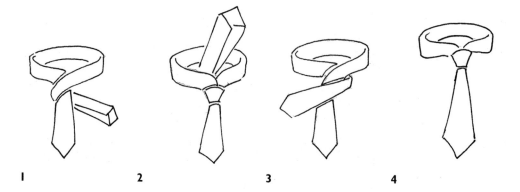

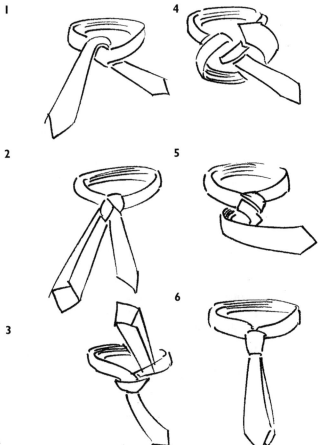

Tying a Windsor knot.

Cleaning and polishing shoes

Polishing guests' shoes should be done professionally and speedily to ensure the guest's satisfaction. Check your own shoes first. A guest may notice them. While you may be prepared to polish their shoes and offer this special service, they may be judging the quality of your shoe-cleaning by the state of the ones you are wearing!

In many international five-star hotels, guests are encouraged to place their shoes in the appropriate basket to be polished overnight. This is then done by the appropriate department staff member, who is either the overnight bellman or the floor butler. A guest may also request to have their shoes polished during the day. The butler or housekeeping staff on duty will usually be responsible for this task.

UNIT

THHBH06A

The basic steps

It should take only about four or five minutes to polish shoes properly—once you learn the true basics, that is. You will need two to three brushes or a double brush, a duster, a chamois leather and maybe a soft rag. Polish can be wax or cream. Shoe cream preserves the leather and keeps it supple, whereas wax polish creates a protective film and is water-resistant, so you should use cream and wax alternately.

First inspect the undersides of the shoes to ensure that they are clean. Remove any mud or soiling. Check the inside of each shoe for fluff or residue and remove it.

Remove any marks caused by accumulated polish with a transparent wax. Rub this wax into the spot with the corner of a duster. If the colour appears lighter, rub in a little of the self colour and shine accordingly. You can apply polish with a small circular brush, a second polishing-style brush or a soft rag.

Always polish shoes on a table, with shoe trees in them to hold them steady if you prefer.

Always remove the shoelaces, but make sure you remember which way the shoelaces were threaded; some people are very particular about how their shoelaces are re-threaded. By removing the laces you are protecting them from being covered in shoe polish, which would cause them to dry out and become brittle. If the laces are worn, you may wish to offer replacements or leave a note with the polished shoes to that effect.

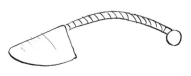

If there are shoe trees, use these to support the insides of the shoes; otherwise, put your hand inside each shoe to hold it in position. Remove all dirt and dust from the shoes before you begin rubbing gently with a cloth or brush.

A shoe tree

Select the appropriate colour cream or wax for the guest's shoes. Apply cream polish with a shoe cloth or rag; otherwise it will fall between the bristles on the brushes and be useless. For a wax polish use a bristle brush and be careful not to put too much polish on the shoes, or you will spend hours trying to 'polish' it off again. Drag the polish brush across the polish in the tin, scraping off on the edge of the tin any lumps that may have accumulated on the bristles.

Take the brush round and cover the leather upper of the shoe with polish, using a circular motion. This ensures that you work the polish into the surface of the leather. Allow it to dry briefly while you put polish on the second shoe. Hint: with gentlemen's shoes an old toothbrush is handy for getting into the welts and stitching areas.

Using a second, large shoe brush, brush the shoes with light skimming strokes until you have achieved a sheen or polish. With practice this will become an easy task, but never underestimate the importance of brushing off as much polish as possible. Guests will not be impressed with polish marks on their trouser cuffs or inside ankles. To test, run a soft, clean cloth over the surface of the leather. There should be very little residue on the cloth if the shoes have been polished well. Give the shoes a final polish with a soft, clean duster.

If shoes are suede, use only suede spray; never apply any cream or wax. Brush with a special suede brush, then spray and brush again. Patent leather shoes are cleaned with a cream polish or Vaseline. Refer to the chart below for more detailed information about cleaning various types of shoes.

When you have finished, lightly deodorise the shoes with a shoe freshener or a damp cloth slightly impregnated with disinfectant, taking care not to mark the shoes in any way. Insert shoe trees, if appropriate. Place the shoes in the wardrobe of the guest's suite or room, or in a suitable place where they will be visible to the guest.

Type of shoe	Preparation	Cleaning	Finish
Leather shoes or boots	Prepare shoes by removing dust with soft cloth or brush. Remove shoe laces.	Using a good brand of wax polish, polish the leather. Allow a few minutes to dry before polishing with a second brush.	Polish well with clean, soft duster. Return shoelaces in same fashion as previously threaded. Place shoe trees in shoes if appropriate. Place in basket, box or bag for return to guest.
Leather shoes or boots: high shine	As above.	As above, then rub in a little lemon juice and buff.	As above.
Suede shoes	Remove dust with a roll of pantyhose or similar fabric or with the dust attachment of a small vacuum cleaner.	Hold suede over steaming (boiling) water to raise the nap; brush lightly.	Allow to dry. Place shoe trees as above and then in basket, box or bag for guest.
Buckskin shoes	Brush lightly to remove dust.	Use fine sandpaper over surfaces of shoes.	Place shoe trees in shoes and then place shoes in basket, box or bag for guest.
Sneakers, fabric tops and rubber soles	Remove surface dirt.	Place each shoe in pillowcase or laundry bag and place in washing machine. Set machine for gentle wash with half cup of detergent per load.	Stuff sneakers with newspaper and allow to dry for 24 hours. Place in basket, box or bag for guest.
Tennis shoes	As above.	As above or try gently brushing, using a nail brush with soap under a running tap. Steel wool with soap will take off the more stubborn stains.	As above
Man-made fibre shoes	Dust with soft cloth to remove dirt and dust.	Use good quality spray polish and buff well.	Place shoe trees and place shoes in basket, box or bag for guest.

Type of shoe	Preparation	Cleaning	Finish
Black patent shoes or evening shoes	Dust gently with soft cloth.	A branded preparation, a spray polish or a light film of Vaseline will clean and protect patent leather.	Place shoe trees and place in basket, box or bag for guest.
Smelly shoes	Use a good quality antiseptic disinfectant such as Dettol; dilute and gently wipe inside of shoe. Test interior of shoe first in case the lining will stain, in which case the next suggestion may prove more useful.	Alternatively, put a layer of bicarbonate of soda in the shoe and leave for a few hours (the longer the better).	Shake out and air. Place shoe trees and place shoes in basket, box or bag for guest.
Badly scuffed leather shoes	Use a raw potato and rub all over shoe; this will eliminate many of the scuffs.	Proceed as for leather shoes.	Proceed as for leather shoes.
Grease-stained shoes	For white shoes rub very gently with nail polish remover; try a patch that is out of sight to check first. For other colours rub on cleaning fluid with a soft cloth.	Polish as appropriate.	Place shoe trees and place shoes in basket, box or bag for guest.

Extra valet services

Hand sewing and emergency repairs

Small sewing tasks are very often offered as a 'no charge' service. However, it should be remembered that some tasks may take considerably longer than they seemed to at first glance. When a guest requests this service, it is advisable to assess the task before saying that you can fulfil it. Zip replacement or a 'tear' style mending task needs professional attention and most definitely will be a chargeable service, whereas a simple hem mend or button replacement is a lot easier to do.

Mending a hem

Check with the guest if there is a time when the garment is required to be returned after collection. Write down the guest's name, room number, the time the garment was received, the time it should be returned, the type of garment, the colour of the garment and the repair required. With the correct coloured thread, use fine stitches so that the resulting repair will not be visible.

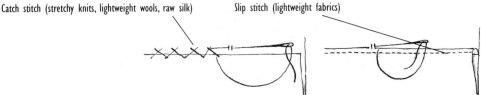

Catch stitch (stretchy knits, lightweight wools, raw silk)　　Slip stitch (lightweight fabrics)

Stitching a hem.

With the threaded needle, take up about two strands of thread from the main fabric and then two strands from the hem of the garment. Repeat until the repair is complete.

With hem repairs, always check the outside for visible stitching. When you are satisfied with the result, press lightly on the inside of the garment with an iron and return it to the guest. Record the time the garment was returned to the guest in your report book.

Button repairs

When replacing buttons, make sure that you have the correct type and size of button. It is worth checking the garment for spare buttons, which may be located in another part of the garment—usually the inside of a seam or hem. For button repairs, the thread is doubled and the ends knotted together well.

Take the thread through the fabric of the shirt or blouse in the exact position of the previous button. Push the needle through the holes of the button and then through the fabric again. Do not pull the thread too tightly—some allowance should be made for the thickness of the fabric once the button is fastened.

Sewing on a button　　Repeat this step several times to ensure that the button is securely fastened, then take the thread through the button and bring it between the fabric and the button. Wind the thread around the 'stalk' (the name given to the sewing threads between the button and the fabric) several times; this strengthens the stitching. Take the threaded needle through the stalk two to three times and cut the thread. Check that the finished sewn button will fit the buttonhole and lie flat against the closed fabric. Close all buttons and buttonholes and press lightly if necessary; sometimes clothes become creased as you work on them. Return the finished garment on a hanger to the guest. If you were not able to match a missing button, leave the guest a small note of apology.

Processing a guest's laundry

Guests always hope to experience an efficient dry cleaning, pressing and laundry service that returns all their garments cleaned and on time. The hotel's laundry service is very important to the comfort of the guest—housekeeping and laundry are definitely two of the most important departments. Many guests, particularly long-staying guests, need reassurance that their clothes will be well cared for while they are away at the laundry.

Using the appropriate form, usually in triplicate, fill in the guest's name, suite or room number and the date and tick any of the boxes for options. Write clearly and, if appropriate, put your name on top for guest referral.

If no specific time is requested by the guest, state 'regular service', 'overnight service' or 'same day service'. Do not commit the laundry to an impossible turnaround time. Enter each number in the guest count column and, if possible, check the list through with the guest.

To avoid confusion, it is advisable to add the colour of the garments. If there are marks or stains ask the guest, politely, if they know what the stain is and mark the laundry form accordingly.

If, on checking the garments, it appears that a repair of some nature is necessary, it is worth offering the guest the service of button or hem stitching as described on pages 198-9.

Some items to be dry cleaned or laundered are often referred to by different names, as shown in the following list.

tuxedo suit	formal suit, dinner suit
safari suit	two-piece gentleman's suit with both pieces in the same colour
sweater	jumper
slacks	trousers, pants
nightgown	nightdress, nightie
underpants	pants, shorts, jocks
singlet	vest, undershirt
waistcoat	vest
pyjamas	two-piece nightwear
swimming trunks	swimsuit, costume, togs, bathers
long or knee-length pants	bermuda shorts, dress shorts
panties	pants, knickers
stockings	stockings, pantyhose, tights

95 Normal	95 Delicate	60 Normal	60 Delicate	40 Normal	40 Delicate	30 Delicate	Hand wash only	Do not wash

Symbol (°C)	Laundering	Symbol (°C)	Laundering
95	Normal mechanical action Rinse at normal temp. Normal spin-dry	40	Normal mechanical action Rinse at normal temp. Normal spin-dry
95	Reduced mechanical action Rinse at decreased temp. Moderate spin-dry	40	Reduced mechanical action Rinse at decreased temp. Moderate spin-dry
60	Normal mechanical action Rinse at normal temp.	30	Extreme reduced mechanical action Rinse at normal temp. Moderate spin-dry
60	Reduced mechanical action Rinse at decreased temp.	(hand)	Hand wash only Careful and gentle treatment

Different 'care labels' and their meanings.

If a guest requests different times for different garments, it is better to split the order. For example, if a guest has one laundry bag full of clothes and requests that one of the suits be returned earlier, place that suit in a separate bag with separate paperwork.

Remember to remove the suit from the original paperwork to reduce any confusion that may arise when the butler or valet on the next shift is looking for a suit that has already been delivered. The third copy of the laundry slip should be assigned to the notice board in the butler's pantry ready for cross-reference at a later time.

Folding clothes and packing suitcases

More guests are appreciating the opportunity to have their suitcase packed; it is a prominent role of the butler or valet and a task that should be practised as frequently as possible. Otherwise, a guest may ask you 'out of the blue' to pack for them, and you may not have time to run for the book to brush up your skills!

UNIT

THHBH06A

As is often the case, there is always a right way and a wrong way of doing a job. On the following pages there are instructions and illustrations for folding clothes, whether for storing or for packing when travelling.

Results are greatly improved if the hotel can supply tissue paper or 'bubble pack'. However, being able to fold clothes properly will help

TROUSERS

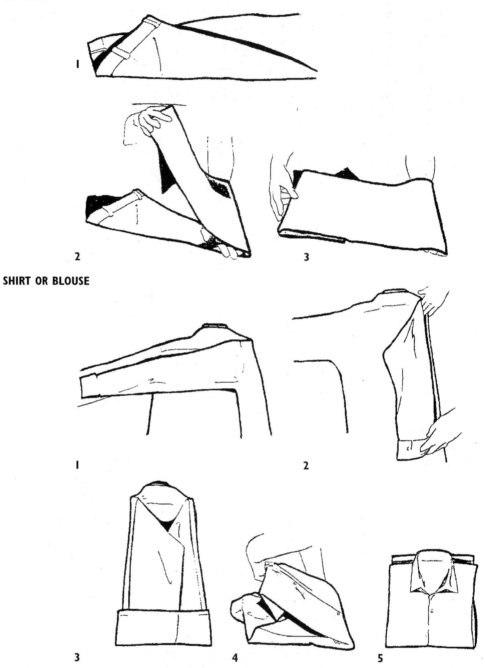

SHIRT OR BLOUSE

Folding trousers, blouses and shirts. Dresses and blouses can be folded along similar lines to shirts.

prevent many of the folds and creases often found in packed clothes, with or without tissue paper. Tissue paper is preferred over bubble pack because it takes up less space.

JACKET

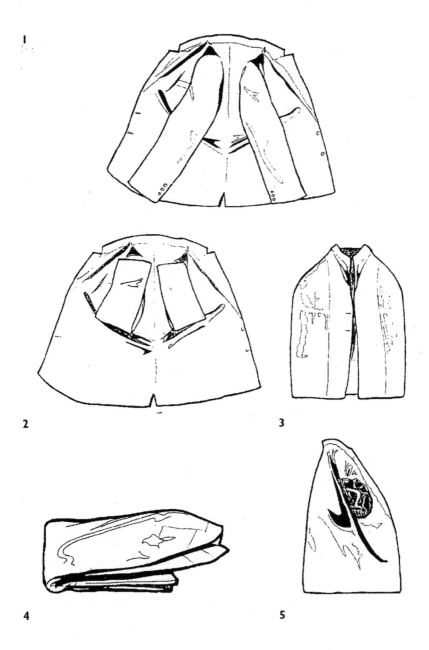

1

2

3

4

5

Folding a jacket. For tips on folding other types of garments, refer to the author's *By Jeeves!* (see bibliography).

There are two types of tissue paper: acid and non-acid. Acid tissue paper is ordinary tissue paper, which is often used to wrap foods such as bread. It is fairly soft and tears easily, making it unsuitable for packing. The other type, non-acid, is tougher and thicker. It is better to use white non-acid tissue paper rather than coloured, in case of moisture or condensation, which may cause discolouration or running of colours into clothes. The object of using non-acid tissue paper is to create space and eliminate any harsh creasing. In effect, folds are thus rounded rather than flat. Tissue paper should be placed wherever you feel that a fold needs support and space created around it.

Bubble packing is a very useful medium, particularly if clothes are to be folded for long periods of time, but it can be over-bulky.

Packing a suitcase

The object of packing a suitcase, apart from the obvious, as you can imagine, is for clothes to arrive in as crease-free a state as possible. The following points will assist you in reaching that objective.

- Collect all the items to be packed. At this stage the suitcase is not relevant to the packing process. Fold all the clothes first according to the diagrams on pages 202 and 203. Lay them on a bed or table for easier folding.
- Protect clothes from shoes by placing the shoes in shoe bags or plastic bags. Shoes travel better if they have shoe trees in them, incidentally. Whatever the style of luggage to be packed, the basics are the same: heavier items on the bottom; lighter, delicate items towards the top.

With all the items ready and folded, packing is simple. Start loading the suitcase with heavy, flat items such as trousers, skirts and jackets. Make sure, where possible, that the fronts of garments such as trousers and jackets are placed facing the handle side of the suitcase.

Shoes are placed in the suitcase with the flat surface or sole to the outside of the suitcase (see diagram). Then follow through with toiletries bags, sweaters and T-shirts, filling in the spaces with belts, hair driers, underwear and socks.

When loading shirts it is easier to lay one shirt flat with the collar upwards and then turn the next shirt over, allowing the collars to create a space while balancing the height. Continue loading with the more delicate items, followed by ties and silk scarves and finishing with a towel or sarong to neaten the packing before connecting the elastic straps across the top of the packed suitcase.

When the suitcase is packed, ask the guest if they would like to check the suitcase. At the airport they may be asked whether they packed their own suitcase and they will need to be able to see that you packed it responsibly. Just before closing the case, you may wish to leave a small, personal handwritten note thanking the guest for staying at the hotel, saying it has been a pleasure to assist them and that you look forward to seeing them on their return to the hotel. Whether the note is discovered before or after departure, it will be a pleasant surprise.

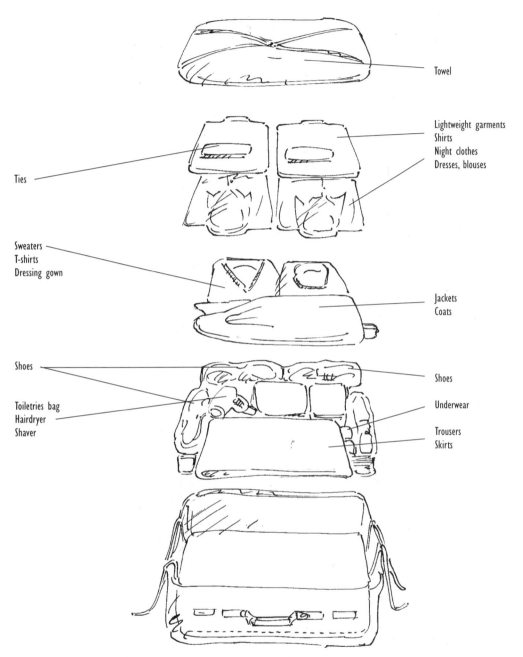

Towel

Lightweight garments
Shirts
Night clothes
Dresses, blouses

Ties

Sweaters
T-shirts
Dressing gown

Jackets
Coats

Shoes

Shoes

Toiletries bag
Hairdryer
Shaver

Underwear

Trousers
Skirts

The order of packing for a suitcase.

Training exercise: pack your bags

Practise packing as many different styles of luggage as possible and then, using the packed bags, reverse the practice session to incorporate unpacking procedures.

A butler's pantry emergency kit

In order to be prepared for almost any eventuality, the butler's pantry or office should be equipped with not just the routine 'hardware', but should also have in stock various items that guests may require in an emergency. The following list offers some idea of the sorts of items that have been requested:

hair spray	wrapping paper
toothpaste	stockings
tissue paper	toothbrush
clear nail varnish	razors
hairbrush/comb	deodorant
shaving gel/cream	tweezers
tampons	scissors
eye mask	sanitary pads
hair gel/mousse	Vaseline
shoelaces	disposable nappies
batteries	condoms
dummies	safety pins
string	baby feeding bottles
plastic gloves	hair elastics
baby powder	heavy-duty sticky tape
selection of buttons	baby lotion
earplugs	black/brown belt
baby wipes	fly spray
icepack	children's amusements
disposable lighters	tie/bow tie
socks	magnifying glass
water filter	cufflinks—plastic
breath freshener	hot rollers
baby bouncer	nail clippers
white shirts:	shoulder pads
2 x 38	curling wands
2 x 40	clothes pegs
2 x 42	black stockings
2 x XL	washing detergent
pantyhose	hot water bottles
inner soles for shoes	cotton handkerchiefs
sticky tape	

This store of items need not be prepared all at once; very often they are acquired over a long period of time, thereby offsetting the enormous expense involved. All these items should be carefully recorded so that any one of them can be, if appropriate, charged to the guest's account. Alternatively, some of these items could be offered on a loan system only. However, retrieving borrowed items may require a lot of extra tact and diplomacy, and discretion on the part of the butler will be very important.

10

'Top flight' luxury

Introduction to 'top drawer' shopping

Recognising luxury and high-quality products is an essential part of understanding more about guests who stay in five-star accommodation. It helps us give them top-quality service. Chapter 2 has provided some insights into where some of our guests come from. This chapter will build on that knowledge, and the many other aspects of service that we are now familiar with, by dealing with those items that are part of the everyday lives of so many of our guests.

In normal conversation it is easy to be overawed by the sense of luxury that is conveyed by these goods and the way guests use them. However, after a time these luxury goods fall into perspective, particularly since many of them had quite humble beginnings.

Subtlety always seems to be the key to overcoming any nervousness we may feel when a guest arrives bearing every imaginable label of luxury. Their first impression of service care can be a 'make-or-break' situation for the hotel. These guests will quite naturally want some recognition of their position in society, and many think highly of the impact that their goods and chattels have on other people. It's human nature. There is one way to deal with this situation successfully: arm yourself with some background knowledge of these products and you will feel more confident about handling them.

Your first reaction needs to be a subtle blend of confidence and acceptance, rather than awe. You should not give the impression that you handle this level of quality so often that you are bored by it; you do need to show respect for the guest's wealth and how they use it. It is true that accepting other people's wealth can sometimes be difficult, but it is an important step towards giving the ultimate service. In the service industry there is very little room for jealousy or envy. If you can't afford to own so much luxury, the next best thing is to work with it—besides, it is much less of a headache. Most moneyed people will readily admit that being rich can be the basis of many of their headaches!

Creating the right impression when approaching guests pays huge dividends. Take your time, make eye contact, smile and talk to the guest, not at them. Learn to generate excitement in your voice without any hint of envy. Incidentally, this can only happen if you feel it genuinely. Although this profession is very often about acting, real insincerity can be detected quite quickly. Acknowledge to yourself in a quiet, confident manner that these guests are looking for the same 'human' element as everyone else, even if they are much richer. One good way to overcome any nervousness about dealing with such guests is to be able to distract yourself from the trappings of their wealth. Chapter 2 can help you here. Refer back to it if necessary and use your knowledge of current affairs and your ability to converse with guests at their level.

Gaining more information about luxury items can be an interesting exercise in customer relations. Apart from what you learn in this book, you will be able to find out a lot by visiting some of the shops personally and asking questions, looking around and becoming more aware not only of what is available, but also of current trends among the rich and famous.

Product knowledge is a key element of better service and increased sales. Good product knowledge does not just mean knowing the basics; it also means having some hands-on experience. Visiting fashion shows, targeting the perfume counters, checking out the top-quality china and glass companies and browsing though antique shops can give you an amazing amount of conversational knowledge.

This chapter is not about becoming a know-all or an expert, necessarily—it is designed to whet your appetite to know the guest even better and find out what makes them tick. It should also enable you to offer imaginative and well-informed suggestions that can only come with experience. Indeed, you may find the subject so absorbing that you will forget your own financial limitations and see the whole thing differently.

The true art of being gracious about wealth often consists in admiring something not just for its monetary value or the wealth of the owner, but for the fact that an artisan crafted a piece so beautiful that its worth is irrelevant to its value. It becomes an opportunity to praise the artist and admire their faith in themselves for persevering with something they clearly enjoy and love creating.

Luxury and quality

Luxury can be described as enjoying surroundings, food and dress that are both choice and costly, but not necessarily essential; *quality* can be described as a characteristic that expresses a level of excellence. An appreciation of both can be developed by knowing how some of the originators of luxury products succeeded in producing these items, so that their names are now household words. This very fact illustrates their acknowledged success and popularity. It would be impossible to list all the famous products, but the following represent just a few names that are frequently seen.

Perfume, clothes and accessories

Louis Vuitton

Louis Vuitton is a name synonymous with luxury. The finest luggage, handbags and small leather goods are the basis for the fame of this company, which was founded in Paris in 1854. It is interesting to note that the original founder, Louis Vuitton, was not only a luggage-maker; he was also a clothes-packer whose reputation was such that the Empress Eugénie employed him as her personal packer. In those days, clothes were kept laid flat in presses ready for either the next wearing or the next trip. The heirs of Louis Vuitton have maintained their ancestor's standards by striving for the best design while never sacrificing quality.

Over the years Louis Vuitton has become active as a supporter of artistic endeavours (the Louis Vuitton Foundation for Opera and Music) and to major sporting events (the Louis Vuitton Cup and Challengers Races for the Americas). In 1987 the company broadened its scope by acquiring Veuve Clicquot champagne and Givenchy perfumes, adding in 1989 Hubert de Givenchy's 'Maison de Couture'. Louis Vuitton Moët Hennessy, otherwise known as LVMH, is a major force in the world of luxury in the fields of luggage, champagne, cognac, perfumes and fashion.

Limoges

Limoges is the largest producer of porcelain dinnerware in France. It has been in operation for over two hundred years and has been run by the family of Bernardaud at Limoges since 1883. Limoges is a town about 200 miles south of Paris. Its name has been synonymous with the finest quality in porcelain since 1768 when large deposits of kaolin, a fine white clay essential for producing lightweight translucent porcelain, were discovered in the local soil.

Harrods,
Knightsbridge
store.

One of the unique features of Limoges is, on top of its capacity to customise a dinnerware service to the individual's needs, the fact that each pattern (there are over 200) has 61 pieces available to accessorise any table setting, whether it is formal or informal.

Harrods

The famous Harrods green-and-gold emblem is well known and often copied, but there is, thankfully, only one real Harrods in the world—in Knightsbridge, London—although branches have been opened in duty-free areas at airports and in certain stores around the world. From the Harrods personal taxis through their umbrellas to their gold roped caviare bags, the name is a recognised benchmark of quality. Harrods sells pretty much everything. There is a dress code for entry to their Knightsbridge store. Some people feel this is unfair, but understandably the Harrods management in their own wisdom prefer to see well-dressed shoppers around the store.

The food hall is not just a sight for sore eyes—it offers the greatest temptations in the modern world; the fashion floors offer the best of British and overseas design; if you cannot find the perfume you want at Harrods it has probably not been created.

Christofle

Christofle is another name synonymous with luxury. The presence of Christofle silverware on the tables of the Elysée Palace in Paris and other elegant dining rooms around the world attests to its international reputation. The company was formed in 1830 when Joseph-Albert Bouilhet, a Parisian jeweller, teamed up with his brother-in-law, Charles Christofle, originally to make jewellery. Their work attracted the patronage of King Louis Philippe. Taking advantage of their resulting increase in prosperity, they began to develop silver and gold tableware.

The business continued to flourish under the new Emperor, Napoleon III, who commissioned the company to gold-plate the statues for the new Paris Opera House. The factory at St Denis, just outside Paris, remains their main headquarters. In 1986 the company returned to jewellery-making, producing collections that blend sterling silver and 18-carat gold. Incidentally, the company motto is 'Only one quality: the best.' Not a bad motto—one that could easily be borrowed by the hospitality industry!

Chanel

Making the famous 'little black dress' the basis of every woman's wardrobe was the brainchild of none other than Miss Coco Chanel. Her tweed suit trimmed with braid and gold buttons has gone beyond fashion and become a lifestyle. Founded in the 1920s, the Chanel company has always been a leader in trends. The famous Chanel No 5 fragrance caused quite a stir in the twenties and is still one of the most popular perfumes. Today there are many other products in the range, plus a collection of timepieces and watches. In the 1980s Karl Lagerfeld joined and continued to keep the company at the top with the classic Chanel style.

Christian Dior

Christian Dior is often regarded as the ambassador of French luxury and elegance. The four letters of his name remain synonymous, even for the least fashion-conscious, with the magic of Paris fashion. The success of Dior owes nothing to chance. Back in 1947 the Dior company launched their 'new look', just at a time when women were gaining a political voice and a right to their own professional lives. The company quickly spotted a niche market in licensing, notably in the US. Now there are more than 200 licence agreements that link the House of Dior with the world's leading manufacturers. The creations of the House of Dior comprise not only ready-to-wear clothes and *haute couture* (high fashion) but also a large range of perfumes and cosmetics including Miss Dior, Diorissimo and, of course, Dune.

Jean Patou

Not many people realise that the owner of this celebrated name, Jean Patou, invented sportswear and swimming costumes in the 1920s and later created Chaldée, the first suntan oil. In 1930 he launched Joy, at that time the costliest perfume in the world. The House of Jean Patou remains an independent family-run business.

Waterford
Wedgwood's
'California' range.

Over the last few years Jean Patou has relaunched the most prestigious fragrances created between 1925 and 1964 one of which, Normandie, was offered to each passenger in 1935 during the maiden transatlantic voyage of the famous ocean liner of the same name.

Hermès

The Hermès family has successfully guided the company from its simple beginnings as a small exclusive harness-maker for horses to its current status as a symbol of elegance. They have diversified from the original harness to the hand-rolled silk scarf, introduced in 1937; the range now includes jewellery, watches, fragrances and ready-to-wear fashions and accessories. The company's rise to fame was greatly helped by the design and production of the famous Kelly and Birkin bags. It is one of the few companies of its kind to boast a museum at its address at Rue du Faubourg St Honoré, in Paris, which features one of Napoleon's original overnight cases.

Calvin Klein

Calvin Klein is New York's version of the casual chic look, famous for silk print dresses, soft tailored suits and good-quality casual clothes such as T-shirts, which are frequently copied. The accent, and probably the reason for the high cost, of these clothes is summed up in their comfortable, understated wearability. Like most fashion houses Calvin Klein has now expanded into fragrances for both men and women.

Waterford Wedgwood,

Wedgwood and its founder, Josiah Wedgwood, commenced trading in 1759. The words on Josiah's memorial tablet near his grave in Stoke-on-Trent, in England, perhaps best summarise his life's achievements. They state that he '. . . converted a rude and inconsiderable manufactory into an elegant art; an important part of national commerce.'

Perhaps he is best known for his Jasperware, the traditional blue-and-white ceramic style commonly recognised as 'Wedgwood'. Today the company is better known for its vast selection of stunning designs in tableware. Since its merger in 1986 with Waterford Crystal, it now offers magnificent pieces of crystal stemware and a superb range of tabletop and giftware. Westminster Abbey, in London, celebrated its 900th anniversary with the hanging of sixteen Waterford chandeliers.

Training exercise: the Best Hotels Guide

Before reading the next section on champagnes and wines, do some research on your own or in a group and discuss hotels such as the Oriental in Bangkok, the Raffles in Singapore, the Peninsula in Hong Kong, or the Ritz or Savoy in London, which have become famous names. Compile a directory of perhaps twenty top hotels that come to mind. Then in a group discussion analyse what has made these hotels so great.

Wines, champagnes and cognacs
Laurent-Perrier

The House of Laurent-Perrier was founded in 1812 in Tours-sur-Marne at the heart of the three renowned French vineyard regions of Champagne: the Montagne de Reims (pronounced 'ronce'), the Côte des Blancs and the Vallée de la Mame. The House benefits from a very privileged location at harvest time—it is able to select its supplies from the best vineyards. Only the product of first pressings of Pinot Noir and Chardonnay from the best classified vineyards is used to make up the thirty or so wines that comprise each blend.

These wines have allowed Laurent-Perrier to gain a long-standing world-wide reputation for consistently top-quality champagne. Over 175 years after it was founded, Laurent-Perrier is today the largest family-structured champagne house, in spite of a rather unsettled market situation. Fiercely attached to this region and its traditionalism and deeply rooted in the history of the vineyard, Bernard de Nonancourt remains one of the most illustrious figures in Champagne. His drive to perpetuate the House doubtless serves as a token of genuine guarantee for the products distributed by Laurent-Perrier throughout the world. Laurent-Perrier is an ultra-brut, 'bone-dry' style of champagne.

Roederer

This champagne house is not like the others—but just what is it that distinguishes it from its competitors? First, the company's 450 acres of vineyards are an exceptional mosaic of the finest growth areas of France, with an average rating of 98 per cent on the official classification scale.

This alone is a rarity. Added to the fact that these 450 acres, plus another 100 acres that rate 100 per cent, meet approximately 75 per cent of Louis Roederer's needs, it becomes an exception in Champagne, where only 12 per cent of the vineyards belong to the great champagne houses.

This house, founded in 1776, is no newcomer to the international marketplace. As early as 1876, Louis Roederer was a purveyor to the Russian Tsars, who were connoisseurs of the precious cuvées. Indeed Cristal, the first prestige cuvée, was created at the request of Tsar Alexander II.

Remy Martin

A family-owned business in France for more than 260 years, the House of Remy Martin is the world's most prominent producer of fine champagne cognac. The artistry of Remy Martin lies in the intricate process of turning wine into cognac.

The result of the House's strict adherence to its centuries-old production standards, from grape to bottle, is a family of the finest cognacs in the world. First in line is VSOP (Very Superior Old Pale), the standard by which all VSOP cognacs are measured and the largest selling VSOP in the world. Next is Napoléon, aged longer and possessing a finer flavour than VSOP. Aged longer still is Remy Martin XO, a perfect balance between oak and grape and considered by many to be the richest and most complex cognac in the world. The crown jewel in the Remy Martin line is Louis XIII (100 per cent Grande Champagne), with its incomparable mellowness and bouquet.

Château d'Yquem

Back in the sixteenth century, the world's most famous sweet wine was the property of the Bazas family. Yquem was brought into the Lur Saluces family by marriage in 1785. It is still their property. Today Count Alexandre de Lur Saluces is head of the domain. He represents the sixth generation of his family to assume the destiny of the 250-acre Domain d'Yquem, which nature ordained great, and which the family has continued to render in an exemplary style.

It is this constant attention to detail, and all the care taken to ensure the quality of the wine, that allowed Yquem to be classified in 1855 as 'first of the first', since it was the only one to be classified 'Premier Cru Supérieur'. Today it is still considered to be the first of the great wines of Sauternes, the premier white wines of the world.

On average, the yield from Yquem is one glass of very strong, intense, luscious wine per vine per year, or an annual average of only 500 bottles per acre. It is kept in the barrel for four years and most vintages improve for fifteen years. In some years, the property selects a very small quantity of dry white wine containing 50 per cent Sauvignon and 50 per cent Semillon; this is named the 'Y' which, by its bouquet, is a drier version of their beloved Château d'Yquem.

Courvoisier

Courvoisier was born among the splendours of the French Imperial Court and appreciated by the Emperor Napoleon and his field marshals. Courvoisier has displayed from its very beginning the attributes of success, good taste and personal accomplishment.

The story of Courvoisier dates back to the early nineteenth century when the enterprising Emmanuel Courvoisier became a supplier to the Emperor Napoleon I. By 1811, when Napoleon visited Courvoisier's warehouses in Bercy, Paris, the association was proving a commercial success.

Soon after this, Napoleon tried to escape to America in a ship stocked with his favourite cognac, Courvoisier. However, he had to abandon his plans and surrender to the British. While the ship was being unloaded, British naval officers sampled the haul of cognac and were so impressed that they referred to it as 'Emperor's Cognac' or 'le Cognac de Napoléon'.

By 1869 the greatly-expanded business was proclaimed, by special appointment, purveyor to the court of another emperor and Courvoisier aficionado, Napoleon III. From this evolved the famous Courvoisier trademark—the silhouette of Napoleon—and the slogan 'le Cognac de Napoléon'. To complement the cognac, Courvoisier created the distinctive 'Josephine' bottle. Today the bust of Napoleon appears on the bottles of all the styles of Courvoisier cognac.

Bollinger

Since its founding in 1829 by Jacques Bollinger, four successive generations have run the company. In order to guarantee the quality of their production and the consistency of their style, the Bollingers have patiently tended their own vineyards in France, which are now over

140 hectares (346 acres) in area. It is rare for champagne houses to grow as much as two-thirds of their grape requirement, and even rarer for them to rate an average of 98 per cent on the legal classification scale; Bollinger can boast both of these achievements.

Much of this is due to Madame Bollinger, who was a familiar figure in and around Ay, where Bollinger is based in the Champagne region. She took over the company after the death of her husband Jacques Bollinger in 1941. Her perfectionism was legendary; her only weakness was fierce brown cigarettes, rolled by her head vineyard worker. She rode every day to the company's vineyards on her bicycle and is fondly remembered and often quoted as saying 'I drink [champagne] when I am happy and when I am sad. Sometimes I drink it when I'm alone. When I have company I consider it obligatory. I trifle with it if I am not hungry and drink it when I am. Otherwise I never touch it—unless I am thirsty.' Nowadays Bollinger is affectionately referred to as 'Bolly' and is best described as a dry, very full-flavoured style of champagne.

Rothschild (Château Lafite)

It is the land at Lafite, in the Bordeaux region of France, that makes the property unique. Nature performed a miracle when it created the perfect combination of soil, subsoil and exposure, plus that certain *je ne sais quoi* that makes the wines of Lafite so admired.

Already recognised as outstanding in the London markets of the sixteenth century, Lafite received recognition at the court of Louis XV when Alexandre de Ségur, well known as the 'Prince des Vignes' and also the owner of Latour, Calon and Phelan, introduced the wines to the King and to his favourite, the Marquise de Pompadour.

Three classical grapes of the Médoc—Cabernet Sauvignon (70 per cent), Cabernet Franc (10 per cent) and Merlot (20 per cent) are cultivated by traditional methods and harvesting is done by hand. It is still the Maître de Chais who is in charge and it is his palate that determines the length of fermentation. The wines are bottled at the château after 18 to 25 months in the barrels.

Ruinart

At the beginning of the eighteenth century, at the abbey of Hautvillers in the Champagne region of France, the Benedictine monk Dom Thierry, friend and confidant of Dom Pérignon, became acquainted with the precious secret of the elaboration of 'the wine that sparkles'. He passed this secret to his nephew Nicholas Ruinart, who founded the first House of Champagne in 1729.

The directors of the House of Ruinart blended political life with the commerce of Champagne. In this way Claude Ruinart, son of the founder, became counsellor to King Louis XVI. Some years later, he not only received Napoleon I at his château Grand Sillery, but also Charles X, the last King of France to be crowned at Reims Cathedral.

Ruinart is a very noble champagne, which is presented in an elegant, long-necked bottle characteristic of the style of the eighteenth century. Incidentally, Dom Ruinart blanc de blancs, or rosé, is made only in excellent years; therefore it is always a vintage and is notably a fine crisp wine.

Veuve Clicquot

Champagne Veuve Clicquot, today enjoyed in more than 135 countries, has maintained an international reputation for excellence since 1722 when the House of Veuve Clicquot was founded at Reims, in France. Owner of paralleled vineyards, the House produces champagnes noted for their classic style: dry and full flavoured, with elegance, crispness and a lingering aftertaste.

Bottles of this famous wine patiently reach their peak in Veuve Clicquot's Gallo-Roman chalk cellars. Long ageing gives the champagne its well-known finesse and its guarantee of quality. The Veuve Clicquot champagnes owe much of their long-standing and far-reaching renown to Madame Clicquot who, when widowed at 27, took over the business and confidently guided it to a position of world-wide importance. While her agents succeeded in spreading throughout Europe her champagne's popularity, Madame Clicquot personally supervised the cellars and ultimately invented the 'fiddling' process essential for removing cloudy deposits from champagne.

This remarkable woman, known as the Grande Dame of Champagne, dedicated her life to 'One quality—the finest': the motto that guides Veuve Clicquot to this day. Veuve Clicquot is well-known as a full-bodied, almost rich, champagne.

Krug

Since 1843, Krug (pronounced Kroog) has been the one house producing solely prestige champagnes. Here dedication to quality takes precedence over quantity. Using traditional methods, the Krugs combine three grape varieties that contribute to the enormous complexity of the champagnes: Pinot Noir for fullness and ability to age beautifully, Pinot Meunier for fruitiness and bouquet and Chardonnay for finesse and elegance.

Krug is the only firm still fermenting all its champagne in the age old way—in small oak casks—which is necessary for developing Krug's intense bouquet and complex flavour. Since there is no precise formula for Krug champagne, the memory of the original Krug taste has been passed through generations of Krugs who personally supervise every phase of the production, tasting and blending.

The Krug Clos de Mesnil vineyard. This vineyard is exceptional in the Champagne region in that it belongs entirely to the House of Krug and is situated in the very head of the village of Mesnil-sur-Oger.

Four out of every five bottles of Krug are Grande Cuvée, a non-vintage champagne. A Krug vintage is produced which is similar to the Grande Cuvée, but less uniform in style. However, the world's most expensive champagne is Clos de Mesnil. This is a blanc de blancs produced uniquely from a small walled vineyard inside the village of Le Mesnil-sur-Oger; the first wine from this vineyard was the vintage of 1979. Those who have tasted it speak lovingly of its delicate scent and rich, honeyed flavour—yet at around the same price as a London-to-New York air ticket it seems to offer its value for money only to the very rich. The end product is a dense, full-bodied, very dry champagne best suited to those really special occasions.

Standing outside the entrance to the famous Krug cellars you would never believe that beyond those gates lies the birthplace of Krug champagne. Its understated cellars have none of the grandeur usually expected from such a fine product, but Krug champagnes not only look, but are, the grandest that money can buy.

Pol Roger

Champagne was the favourite drink of Winston Churchill, the famous English wartime politician, and Pol Roger was his favourite champagne; which explains why there is a Sir Winston Churchill label on the list of Pol Roger champagnes. The Épernay-based house has been family-owned since its foundation in 1849 by Paul Roger ('Pol' is the local dialect for 'Paul'). There are five champagnes in the Pol Roger range, each distinguished by its neck foil.

White foil-brut non-vintage is a plummy wine with a crisp finish. Bronze foil indicates the vintage Pol Roger, a slightly drier wine. Lilac foil signifies the rosé, and gold foil the blanc de blancs; both are vintage dated. The black foil signals the Cuvée Sir Winston Churchill, a complex but earthy wine often described as graceful.

Pommery

In 1858 the House of Pommery suffered in the same way as Clicquot had. Louis Pommery died, leaving his wife to continue running the business. Madame Pommery had watched with keen interest Veuve (widow) Clicquot, knowing that she could achieve the same. When she died thirty-two years later her company was just as important as that of Clicquot.

The Pommery style of champagne is lively and elegant. Brut Royal, light, fresh and palest yellow-gold in colour, is the biggest-selling of Pommery non-vintages. Vintage Brut has a fuller, firmer flavour. A speciality of Pommery is its use of larger bottles, particularly those up to salmanzar sizes. Incidentally, Pommery Brut Rosé, because of its blending, is ideal as an accompaniment to food.

Mumm

Many people may be startled at the number of Germans who founded some of the French champagne houses. Geographically the Champagne region was closer to Cologne in Germany than it was to Marseilles. Thus it attracted many workers and investors alike. Peter Mumm began trading as a wine merchant in Cologne in 1761. The city's position was ideal for supplying drinkers of the north. Later, his sons decided to open an office in Reims in the heart of the Champagne region.

As soon as they had established themselves, most of the Germans in Champagne became French citizens. Not so the Mumms, who were proud of their German origins. The rest is history, as they say, and the consequences tragic: family control was severed by the two World Wars.

Mumm's biggest-selling champagne, notable for the distinctive red diagonal band on its label denoting the Légion d'Honneur, had the same problems that so often affect its main rival, Moët et Chandon's Brut Royal: inconsistency. When it is good, Cordon Rouge is a lively, well-rounded champagne. Mumm's style is that of light, crisp and biscuity wines, reminiscent of its German origins.

Moët et Chandon

Moët et Chandon is the one name that would most likely come up if you mentioned 'champagne' in a word association game. The pronunciation causes much confusion, but if the name is shortened to Moët, the t is silent; if the full name is used, the t immediately before 'et' (French for 'and') is said very quickly.

Claude Moët was born in 1683 and inherited the vineyards at Hautvillers in the French Champagne region. Moët et Chandon is now the biggest champagne grower and merchant with the largest cellars in Épernay in the Champagne region. It was Claude Moët's grandson who achieved an international reputation for the company. His very good friend was Napoleon Bonaparte. In spite of this close connection he managed to entertain, and sell to, the Emperor's enemies as well, including Tsar Alexander I and those nations whose soldiers were dying at the hands of the French. Even after Napoleon's fall, war for Moët was definitely good for business—Queen Victoria became a customer.

Moët et Chandon is now one of the crown jewels of the giant LVMH (Louis Vuitton Moët Hennessy) group, with no fewer than seven great champagne houses under its umbrella. Moët et Chandon dominates the French export market; one out of every four bottles leaves France for consumption abroad. Moët et Chandon at its best is easy and straightforward as a champagne, with sweet vanilla scents and well-balanced flavours. Its most celebrated vintage is the Dom Pérignon, named after the famous cellarer, who claimed he was drinking stars when he tasted the very first 'champagne'. Dom Pérignon is consistently good, with its flowery apple-blossom aroma and vital fruit flavour.

Training exercise: checking out the top brands

Most wine merchants, given the time, are only too happy to share their knowledge. If you source the best wine merchants in your area, you will not only be able to recommend these wine shops to guests, but you should also be able to check the labels, obtain a reasonable amount of information and also find out the recommended and discounted prices for most of the champagnes described in the previous section. Construct a checklist of the various champagnes and their availability, both within your hotel or restaurant and at the local wine merchant's.

How to enjoy champagne

The valuable background information about champagne that you gained in the previous section should help you feel more confident about discussing some of these top names and should also help you understand why they are so revered. Good champagne tastes wonderful. As Napoleon once said: 'In victory you deserve champagne; in defeat you need it!'

There always seems to be something faintly absurd about telling anyone how to enjoy champagne. It's a bit like telling people how to laugh, or how to have fun on a luxury holiday. Whatever the occasion when you find yourself serving champagne, it will always be an occasion, regardless of the initial intention! It seems to encourage relaxation and celebration.

Pouring champagne

The enjoyment of champagne should be effortless. However, if it is not served properly, the occasion will be marred. Since champagne is one of the world's most expensive wines, it is wise to know how to prevent this happening. If it is served properly you will be remembered for having helped create the right atmosphere for the celebration.

Champagne at its best will taste clean, fresh, foamy, scented, incisive, rousing and inspiring—altogether more than the sum of all its parts. Since champagne is both sensitive and fragile, shocks of transport and storage will inevitably affect it when it is served. Store it properly in a dark, peaceful spot without any large temperature variations and make sure it is lying flat.

There are often arguments about what glasses to use. These days the most common style is the flute. The bottom of the bowl ends in a point. The top of the bowl should be narrower than the middle, so that the weaving ribbons of fine-beaded bubbles can wend their way to the champagne's foamy surface. With a clear glass of this shape the drinker can fully appreciate the intensity and delicious impact of the champagne.

Champagne must be thoroughly chilled, since the bottles are twice the thickness of conventional wine bottles. The indentation in the base—called the 'punt'—is essential to the bottle fermentation of champagne, and it should be well noted that the pressure in the bottle is four times that of a truck tyre (just a bit of trivia for you!), so it is not hard to understand why the champagne cork needs the extra protection of the *museler* or wire muzzle under its final wrapping of foil.

The chilling of champagne has two purposes. First, champagne tastes much better at 8 degrees Celsius than it does at 18 degrees. The second purpose of chilling is to subdue the sparkle: it is easier to open the bottle in a controlled, safe manner when the pressure has been reduced by chilling. Instructions for opening a bottle of champagne can be found in Chapter 8 (page 171).

The language of champagne

The word itself comes from the name of the Champagne region in France. Many of the terms are, needless to say, in French. In the glossary at the end of this book you will find a section of these terms, including the names and descriptions of the various bottle sizes used for champagne: balthazar, jeroboam, magnum, methusalem, nebuchadnezzar, rehoboam and salmanazar.

Caviare: those tiny 'black pearls' of luxury

Caviare is one of those wonderfully unusual foods that a lot of people absolutely adore; the rest dislike it and cannot understand why anyone would eat it. It's also one of those foods that has not been mentioned much in literature. However, Shakespeare referred to it in *Hamlet*: 'The play, I remember, pleas'd not the million; 'twas caviare to the general' ('general' in this case meaning the general population).

Served properly this expensive commodity is delicious. Caviare consists of the eggs of fish, salted or pickled to preserve and flavour them. It is most commonly made with the roe, or eggs, of the sturgeon. Sturgeon is native to the Northern Hemisphere, though in principle caviare can be produced wherever there are appropriate species.

Until recently, caviare production was an Iranian and Russian monopoly based around the Caspian Sea and its river systems. However, a promising start has now been made in caviare production in the American north-west and in China. Making caviare is a slow process, since a female sturgeon must be 15 to 20 years old before her roe can be converted into caviare. Furthermore, there is a wide variation in roe quality from fish to fish and from species to species.

Caviare usually carries the description *malossol*, which is simply Russian for 'lightly salted', along with an indication of the type of sturgeon from which it comes. The largest eggs, grey in colour, come from the beluga. Darker and smaller, but of fine flavour, are those of the sevruga sturgeon, the most common caviare type. While both Russian and Iranian sturgeon are caught in the same sea, there are differences in the processing of the roe. Russian caviare tends to have more salt added than Iranian and the Russians add a little borax to the salt which enhances the flavour, preserves the caviare longer and sweetens the eggs a little. This also makes the eggs a little oilier.

The reason why whole-grain caviare is so expensive is that it requires fast and extremely careful processing. Once it has been vacuum-sealed in a container it will last at best for six months, assuming tightly-controlled temperature conditions.

Apart from being full of vitamins, low in calories and light, caviare is a meal in itself. It is often served in its own container in a deep dish of crushed ice with fresh toasted white or brown bread. Good-quality butter is handed separately; quarters of lemon and sometimes a small dish of finely-chopped onion and roughly-ground black pepper are additional accompaniments. The best and most 'correct' procedure for serving caviare is outlined below.

TABLE 9... AND KEEP YOUR BEAK OUT OF THE CAVIARE!

Strictly, caviare should be served with blinis, which are small buckwheat pancakes made with yeast, and a dish of soured cream. For total enjoyment, everything about the service of caviare should be 100 per cent fresh and the best liquid accompaniment is a good vodka!

Caviare House in London is one of the few suppliers in the world to make the real distinction between five types of caviare. These are:

- **Sevruga** The sevruga is the smallest of the snub-nosed sturgeons. Never longer than 1.5 metres, it rarely exceeds 25 kilograms. Sevruga caviare is dark grey with a fine grain and is appreciated in particular for its extremely fine flavour.
- **Oscietra** The oscietra is of a medium size with a retractile trunk below its slightly pointed nose. It can reach a length of two metres and weigh up to 200 kilograms, although the average is 1.2 metres and 80 kilograms. Oscietra caviare is dark brown to golden yellowish in colour and the flavour is generally described as nutty.
- **Beluga** The beluga is the largest of the sturgeons and the only one that is exclusively carnivorous. It is so rare that seldom more than one hundred are caught in one year. The beluga can reach four metres in length and weigh more then one tonne. Beluga caviare, light to dark grey, is valued above all for its large grain and the fineness of its skin.
- **Imperial** Imperial caviare originates from the oscietra sturgeon, consists of large gold-coloured grains and was previously reserved exclusively for the Shah of Iran's family. It is considered a truly exceptional caviare.
- **Royal Black** Royal Black caviare comes from a twenty-year-old Iranian oscietra sturgeon and consists of large black grains. Its flavour and texture are similar to those of Beluga caviare.

Serving caviare

Caviare can be served from a simple glass bowl using a plastic spoon; however, most people will give it more style, especially since caviare costs so much. Take the caviare from the refrigerator about fifteen minutes before serving, but do not open the jar or tin until the very last minute. Caviare does not favour air and heat.

Use either bone, gold-plated, mother-of-pearl or even plastic spoons. Never use stainless steel or silver or the caviare will rapidly lose its colour and flavour and will begin to oxidise in much the same way as wine oxidises. Plastic is better than metal because it does not carry a taste, is unaffected by acids, vinegar or oils and does not stain.

Special caviare dishes are made that hold crushed ice under a separate bowl. Keep this set of bowls chilled and add the caviare at the last minute. Another method is to fill a bowl with crushed ice and place the tin or jar on top. When scooping the caviare from the tin or jar, do so vertically from top to bottom—never horizontally, as this crushes the grains.

Allow 25 to 50 grams per person; it is best to have extra caviare on hand. The second tin can always be reserved for another occasion, but it can be embarrassing not to have enough.

Serve caviare with small blinis (buckwheat pancakes), finely-chopped red onion, chopped parsley, lemon slices and soured cream. Alternatively, serve it with scrambled eggs, with quails' eggs, or on canapés, small toasts or water biscuits, but only place the caviare on these toasts or biscuits at the last minute.

Smoked salmon

Smoked salmon is usually prepared by cold-smoking—a specialised process, varying from country to country, in which the fish undergoes salting and drying in smoke at 70 to 90 degrees Celsius for two to twenty days. European (especially Scottish) smoked salmon is regarded as the best. In the United States, smoked salmon is sometimes called Nova Scotia salmon—a reference to the fact that most American smoked salmon used to come from there. In Australia, the Tasmanian salmon is regarded as the best smoked variety. Other cold-smoked fish include eel and sturgeon, eel being a favourite in northern Europe.

Hot-smoking is a quicker process that cooks as well as flavours fish, but does not preserve it for very long.

A good-quality side of smoked salmon should have a bright, deep colour and be moist when lightly pressed with the fingertip at the thickest part of the flesh. A perfectly-smoked side of salmon will remain in good condition for no more than seven days when stored at a temperature of 18 degrees Celsius.

Smoked salmon is mostly bought sliced from good delicatessens. However, if a good salmon knife is available to cut the very thin slices at an angle, then a whole salmon is preferable. It should be moist because dryness may indicate saltiness. Allow about 50 to 75 grams per person (or more!) according to how lavish you wish to be.

Serving smoked salmon

The very thin slices of smoked salmon are served directly onto individual plates and accompanied with buttered wholemeal brown bread and horseradish cream sauce along with quartered lemon as a garnish. Freshly-ground pepper is often sufficient for smoked salmon, although capers, sliced onion and chopped hard-boiled egg can also feature as condiments.

Smoked salmon is so versatile that it can be served on its own, or with scrambled eggs for breakfast, in wafer-thin sandwiches as a first course, and so on. One of the most appropriate and enjoyable accompanying beverages you can recommend is, of course, champagne!

The art of the cigar

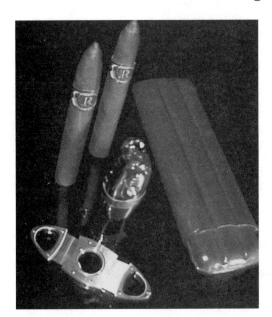

The requirements for the true enjoyment of a good cigar: cigars, cigar cutter and lighter.

The appreciation of fine cigars, like the appreciation of wines, is an exceptional art. First, what constitutes a fine cigar? A fine cigar is made by hand; it is 100 per cent tobacco. Machine-rolled cigars with a binder or wrapper of homogenised tobacco are generally not considered worth smoking.

It is worth understanding why people enjoy smoking cigars. It is a sophisticated pastime. The true connoisseurs are generally refined and enjoy their cigars without disturbing others in their immediate environment. Most cigar-smokers smoke not just because they can afford to, but because they genuinely appreciate the flavour and strength of cigars in comparison to cigarettes or pipes.

Most connoisseurs are able to select the cigar that coincides with the moment; the cigar that permits them to relax and grants them the most pleasure. Price is not a factor for experienced aficionados. The choice is based both on personal preference and on available time, since they want to be able to cherish all the qualities of the cigar at their leisure.

The following list gives some useful guidelines if you are in a position where you need to advise a guest. Cigars are named in all sorts of romantic ways and the names add some confusion to the grades and sizes of cigars. These represent a few of the names given to particular sized cigars:

- Panatellas: 5 to just over 6 inches, ring gauge 28-38
- Coronas: 5.5 to 6 inches, ring gauge 42-44
- Coronas Gordas: 5 to just over 6 inches, ring gauge 44-50
- Robustos: 5.5 inches, ring gauge 50
- Figurados: 6.5 inches, ring gauge 52-54
- Lonsdales: just under 7 inches, ring gauge 42
- Double Coronas: 7.5 to 8.5 inches, ring gauge 48-52
- Churchills: 7 inches, ring gauge 48.

The ring gauge is calculated in much the same way as a jeweller measures the size of a finger for a ring. The Figurados cigar is one of the few tapered varieties.

There are some special considerations you will need to take into account when recommending a cigar. These mostly concern the mood or current situation of the guest:

- Senoritas: the short break
- Panatellas: the day's first cigar
- Petit Coronas: the mid-morning cigar
- Coronas: extending a luxurious lunch
- Grand Coronas: an hour of leisure
- Double Coronas: crowning a regal dinner
- Giant Double Coronas: for the exceptional moment

Not only are cigars an acquired taste; there is also a definite art to lighting and smoking one. Smoking without haste appears to be the secret to enjoying a cigar. Most people, particularly gentlemen, who smoke cigars regularly seem to understand this; they usually smoke only one large cigar a day after dinner, when they have time to sit back and relax. Many cigar companies recommend that cigar-smokers smoke fewer but better. This is a point worth remembering when you are discussing cigars with a guest.

Cigar-smoking is very much on the increase. 'Cigar salons' are appearing in many top hotels around the world. There is a distinct trend towards providing cigar-smokers with the ultimate opportunity to indulge their pleasure without feeling that they may be ostracised by those who do not like being surrounded by the pungent smoke.

The cigar band?

The first question is whether to take off the advertising band around the bottom of the cigar. Cigar-smokers often wonder whether they should. Many cigar experts advise against this. Since cigar bands are put on most hand-made cigars manually, there is always a chance that the band will stick to the wrapper and damage it when it is removed. Therefore it is highly recommended that the band be left on for at least the first third of the cigar. However, there is another point of view: if the cigar is cheap it is unnecessary for others to know; if it is an expensive one, it is considered vulgar to show it off.

Cutting the cigar

An expensive cigar is hand-made. One end, called the cigar cap, is sealed to prevent the cigar from drying out in storage. How the sealed end of the cigar is cut ultimately determines the quality of the draw and the subtlety and intensity of the cigar's aroma. A correct cut will

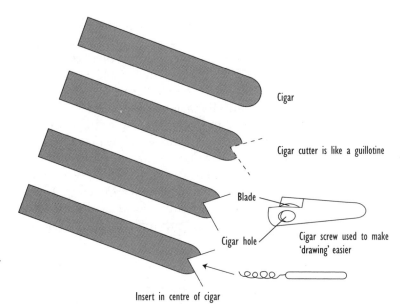

Cigar

Cigar cutter is like a guillotine

Blade

Cigar hole

Cigar screw used to make 'drawing' easier

Insert in centre of cigar

Cutting a cigar using a V-cut.

assure that the cigar remains evenly lit. The cut should be evenly and should be directly proportional to the thickness of the cigar—you would not make the same cut for all cigars. A properly cut cigar will permit a perfect draw.

There are many methods for cutting a cigar. The ultimate instrument is a special pair of scissors, a double-edged guillotine cutter or a round cutter. These tools have all been specifically designed to cut the cigar properly and yield a clear, neat, circular cut, regardless of the cigar's ring gauge. Some cigar-smokers also use a cigar skewer or a match to bore a small round channel through the centre of the cut end to ensure an even better draw.

Lighting a cigar

Always use a sulphur-free match to light a good cigar. A lighter will leave the taste of lighter fluid in the cigar afterwards and will completely spoil the fragrance. However, with the development of new lighter fluids, the use of lighters is becoming more acceptable. For best results, the cigar should be lit with a short flame. Hold the flame half an inch (one centimetre) under the open end of the cigar and rotate the cigar until the end is evenly lit. Then—and only then—is the cigar brought to the mouth for the first puff.

It never ceases to amaze experts that people who are knowledgeable enough to choose a fine cigar light their cigars with fluid lighters, candles or sulphur-tipped matches, all of which introduce noxious odours. To avoid spoiling a perfect cigar before the first puff is taken, use giant, slow-burning, sulphur-free matches or odourless gas lighters.

Storage

Since most cigars are expensive, they should be cared for properly. Like a fine wine, a fine cigar must be kept in an environment that protects it from changes in humidity and temperature, light and intrusive odours. A humidifier or humidor with built-in regulators that automatically maintain the interior of the case at a constant humidity of 70 to 72 per cent and a temperature of 68 to 72 degrees Fahrenheit (18 to 20 degrees Celsius) is advised. These humidors are available in a wide range of sizes, exotic woods and finishes. Each humidor is a classic example of the cabinetmaker's art and is crafted to last for countless years to come. It is a good investment, if many cigars are to be stored and smoked. The advantage of these devices is that they prevent the cigars from drying out and becoming bitter.

Offering and serving cigars

Traditionally, cigars are offered with style. Cigars, like champagne, deserve respect, so they are offered either from the box or from a tray with the attendant necessities such as the cigar cutter, cigar skewer, matches and ashtray.

When you offer a new box to a cigar-smoker, allow them to enjoy the aromas of the newly-opened box; this will show a real sensitivity to their passion for cigars. To a cigar-smoker it is like enjoying the bouquet of a fine wine.

If you intend to offer to cut the cigar, make sure you practise in advance, following the instructions already covered. Cigar-smokers will not appreciate a substandard result, as it will spoil their enjoyment. Before you attempt to light a cigar, allow the smoker to inspect the cigar chosen. A cigar in its prime will feel firm when it is rolled between the thumb and index finger, and slightly elastic when it is squeezed. Brittle cigars will not taste good and should be put aside.

A cigar should be smoked slowly, as this will make it draw. If the smoker puffs away at it like a train, it will burn quickly and the taste will be ruined. There will be a red glow on the end, even though it is in flames. If you watch a real cigar aficionado you will notice that the cigar is smoked so slowly that about half an inch of ash will hang from the end. A decent cigar will last anywhere from half to three-quarters of an hour.

A 'well cared for' cigar-smoker will appreciate your attentiveness and your appreciation of the serious business of cigar-smoking. After all, there is a lot at stake apart from the cost of the individual cigars.

Some of the top brands of cigars include:

- Romeo y Julieta (Cuba)
- Partagas (Cuba)
- Macanuda (Jamaica)
- Bolivar (Cuba)
- Arturo Fuente (Dominican Republic)
- Hoyo de Monterey (Cuba)
- Jose Marti (Nicaragua)
- Bahia Maduro (Costa Rica).

Training exercise: a cigar is a good smoke!

The above list gives you something to start with when you make a trip to a cigar shop or store to check out the brands of cigars available. Using the same methods you used when you were visiting the wine merchants (page 220), look at several brands and become familiar with the 'lingo' attached to cigars and cigar-smoking. The cigar merchant, who should be an expert in the field, will help you with extra information about storage and customer preferences.

Spirits

The history and the making

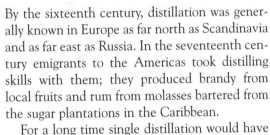

LEARNING TO APPRECIATE
SCOTCH WHISKY

By the sixteenth century, distillation was generally known in Europe as far north as Scandinavia and as far east as Russia. In the seventeenth century emigrants to the Americas took distilling skills with them; they produced brandy from local fruits and rum from molasses bartered from the sugar plantations in the Caribbean.

For a long time single distillation would have been the rule, until it occurred to someone to see what happened if the process were repeated. Credit for this innovation, at least in the context of cognac, is given to the Chevalier de la Croix Marron, who in the mid-sixteenth century had the idea of boiling and purifying his distillates for a second time, thus creating a more intense essence.

Whisky, vodka, genever, gin, some schnapps and akvavit derive mainly from grain, which is used to make a kind of beer or ale for distillation into spirit. Specific grains are sometimes important. Malt whisky (Scotch and Japanese) and genever are made from malted barley; the best vodka and certain Canadian blending whiskies from rye; Finnish vodka from wheat; German schnapps mostly from corn; and Japanese shochu from rice. Some Polish and Russian vodkas come from potatoes. The English styles of gin depend on the juniper and other botanicals that flavour it. Since these are macerated and then redistilled, all that is required initially is a clean, neutral spirit, irrespective of the base from which is has been made.

Most people regard the term 'brandy' to mean grape brandy distilled from wine, which is usually taken to be grape wine. Rum and cane spirit, including the Brazilian cachaca, are made mostly from sugar cane or beet molasses, and a small proportion of rum is produced direct from cane juice.

Proof and alcohol by volume

The term 'proof' as an indicator of alcoholic strength derives from the early use of gunpowder in testing spirits. With no prior knowledge of the possible strength of a given distillate, an operator would mix the spirit with the gunpowder and attempt to light it. If the mixture did not ignite, the spirit was underproof, if it lit and burned steadily this was 'proof' of a recognised level of alcoholic strength. However, if it exploded the operator (or his next-of-kin) could report the distillate as overproof, and recommend further dilution with water.

Both the USA and the UK have used 'proof' systems for expressing alcoholic strength, but it does not help that they are different from each other—100 per cent proof in the USA is only 87.7 per cent British proof. US proof was at least related to strength by volume, being exactly double the latter. But British proof was based on the relative volumes of alcohol and water at a temperature of 51 degrees Fahrenheit. The Gay-Lussac system expresses alcohol as a percentage of content in liquid; happily, this means of measurement is fast becoming universal. Note, however, that the Germans and Russians occasionally like to throw in the expression of percentage by weight.

Serving spirits

Refer to Chapter 8 (pages 167-8) for different ways in which the various types of spirits are served. You are also advised to read some specialised books on this subject, some of which are included in the bibliography at the end of this book.

Whisky and whiskey

'Whisky' (plural 'whiskies') is the correct spelling for whisky made in Scotland, Australia, Japan and Canada; 'whiskey' (plural 'whiskeys') is the spelling for whiskeys made in Ireland and the US.

In the world at large whisky tends to be associated with Scotland, although the spirit probably originated in Ireland and the first whiskey to have a presence in countries around the globe was Irish. However, when cognac succumbed to phylloxera in the 1870s and vanished from the world's tables and bars, Scotch was able to make a grand entrance and it has stayed centre-stage ever since. There are in fact other countries that make their own national styles of whisky (or whiskey) but allow for regional variation and individuality of house style by the manufacturers.

The original Scotch whisky is malt. It is produced from malted barley, which is dried over peat-fuelled fires, giving it a smoky, peaty finish. Quieter grain whisky is produced for blending with the malts to make famous brands like Ballantine's and Chivas Regal, which have become household names everywhere.

Whisky no longer needs to be Scotch or Scotch-styled to achieve credibility in consumers' eyes. Non-Scotch styles have been increasing their market share in numerous countries for some time now and look like continuing to do so in the future.

Scotch whisky

In Scotland, whisky had its origins in the heather ale brewed in prehistoric times. Heather is an evergreen plant or shrub with small purple, pinkish or white bell-shaped flowers, which grows on higher ground with peaty or sandy soils that are free of lime. The term 'peat' is often used in the descriptions of certain whiskies. Archaeologists on an island off the west coast of Scotland found some dregs in a pottery shard from 2000 BC; scientists, after analysing them, made a fresh brew. It was all a bit grassy, so when simple distillation techniques later came along, possibly from Ireland, a longterm flavour improvement program began.

In the 1870s phylloxera destroyed the cognac vineyards. As a result, demand for Scotch whisky boomed. The character of Scotch whisky has been determined historically by the aromas and flavours drawn from the barley that grew in the fields, the peat fuel used in the smoky fires to stop germination, and the yeasts that fermented the beer. It is only in the past 200 years that the study of still shapes and cask types has enabled finessing of the spirits. The merit, distinctiveness and renown of Scotch whisky today derive from its rich and varied pot-still malt spirit.

Malt whisky production in Scotland is divided into the following four geographic areas: Highland, Lowland, Islay and Campbelltown. Highland malts from the northern half of the country are mostly elegant and well flavoured, but this is a large category and there are a number of subgroups. The main ones are Speyside malts, which have an extra dimension of rich, sweeter complexity, and the smoky, spicy and concentrated Island malts.

Briefly, to make malt whisky, barley is soaked and left to germinate. At a critical point, when the starch has turned to sugar, the germination is stopped by drying the barley, traditionally with a peat-fuelled fire which imbues it with a smoky fragrance. Modern maltsters dry it with neutral heat and introduce measured amounts of peat smoke to aromatise the barley to the customer's requirements. Since the smokiness in the barley passes over in the distillation to the final spirit, the degree of peating—or peat reek—is an important stylistic decision.

The dried barley—peated or not—is called malt, and milled and mashed with hot water. The resulting sugary wort ferments to make a beer, which is distilled twice in copper pot stills.

Whisky must be aged in oak for at least three years, but most whiskies mature for much longer. Casks that have previously held bourbon whisky or oloroso sherry are widely used for ageing malts.

A good 'standard' blend has 30 to 40 per cent malt and grain whiskies in it and up to 40 per cent malt content; 45 per cent, such as is in Teachers, is a high malt count. Standard blends do not have an age statement, although in 1994 Bell's was upgraded to an eight-year-old. Most deluxe blends have an age statement—twelve years old is typical—but both unknown brands with blends too young to merit description as de luxe, and long-established brands with magnificently mellow blends, often do not. To distinguish between them, be guided by the names you know and the prices asked. As a rule of thumb, the more expensive the whisky, the better the quality.

Irish whiskey

Irish whiskey's origins can be traced back to the sixth century AD when it was introduced by missionary monks, probably from the Middle East. Peter the Great of Russia and Queen Elizabeth I of England liked it and Sir Walter Raleigh stopped off in Cork to pick up a cask of it on his way to Guyana in 1595. Irish whiskey is produced from one end of the Emerald Isle to the other, but unfortunately these days there is very little that gets made in between. Whereas once Ireland had more than 2000 distilleries there are now only three, although technology has enabled the survival of a score or more of different brands.

Irish whiskey is made from both malted and unmalted barley as well as grains but, with the exception of Cooley, the malts are not peated. The spirit is made in both pot and continuous stills but the former types, at Bushmills and Middleton, are triple-distilled, not double-distilled as in Scotland. Minimum maturation is three years by law, but in practice some premium whiskies are at least twelve years old.

Bourbon

Bourbon is minimum 40 per cent vol (80 per cent proof) whiskey made mainly in Kentucky in the USA, principally from corn, and aged for at least two years in new charred-oak barrels. The remaining content may be a mix of rye (which gives it a bitterish taste), barley malt and sometimes wheat. Better-quality bourbons have about 70 per cent corn, but good flavour is tied up with the grain mix rather than just the corn content; 90 per cent corn whiskey, for example, is one-dimensional, dull—and cheap.

One of the reasons why bourbon is not aged for very long is that new oak can make the whiskey over-woody. New wood gives the whiskey a pronounced oak (vanilla ice cream) aroma and flavour, and the char endows a toasted, caramel-like characteristic. These are signature features of bourbon whiskey. High strength is an indicator of quality in bourbon and US proof is twice the alcoholic strength by volume. Unlike Scotch, which loses strength during maturation in damp warehouses, bourbon gains strength in the hothouse phases of its maturation in Kentucky.

Tennessee whiskey

Tennessee whiskey is made in a similar manner to bourbon but a special filter process with charcoal and woollen blankets, introduced in the early nineteenth century and carried out before the spirit is matured, gives it a lighter, smoother texture and a touch more smokiness in the flavour. Tennessee whiskeys are now aged for at least four years by law.

Canadian whisky

Canadian whisky is made from a wide range of grains—rye, barley, wheat and, of course, corn. The mix for each brand decides the flavour profile and is a proprietary secret, as are details of the yeasts used. Canadian styles evolved out of a desire to combine good flavour with a softer spirit impact.

Japanese whisky

Two men are regarded as the 'fathers of Japanese whisky': Taketsuru, founder of Nikka, and Shinjiro Torii, founder of Suntory, who gave him the opportunity to make a prototype spirit when he returned to Japan. Taketsuru was the heir to a sake brewery, but he was more interested in whisky. He studied applied chemistry at Glasgow University, then worked in a distillery at Rothes. No one knows which distillery this was, because Taketsuru documented it only as 'Glenlivet' and three of Rothes' five distilleries (Glen Grant, Glenrothes and Speyburn) hyphenated their names with the word 'Glenlivet'. He also worked in Campbelltown before returning (with a Scottish bride, Rita) to Japan in 1920.

The Japanese could not afford the Scotch the Americans drank, so Suntory established the Tory whisky bars nationwide, with a facsimile American ambience and their own tariff-free local whiskies behind the counter. They became very successful.

A feature of today's bars is the 'owner's bottle'—a customer's personal pouring bottle kept for him or her, ticketed on a shelf in the same way as left luggage and untouched until the customer's next visit.

Luxury conclusions

All this luxury may seem over the top; however, knowledge about these products is invaluable, not just so that we can converse more confidently but also so that we can approach the handling and use of these products with greater ease. It is important not to be intimidated by these labels, but to admire the way in which so many companies strive for excellence.

11

Conclusion: a happy guest is our product!

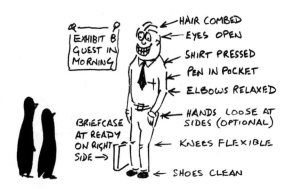

At the beginning of this book a number of questions were posed: What is service? How do we recognise great service? What is the true purpose of service? How can we achieve good service? How do we make our guests feel really special?

Now is probably a good time to reread Chapter 1. However, if you have read through this book and done the training exercises you should already be seeing the benefits in terms of your product—happy guests! However, there is just one more thing. The information and knowledge you have gained is to a certain extent passive while it remains in your head; its full value will not be realised till it becomes a part of your personality.

The relationship we have with our guests starts with the one we have with ourselves. The excitement we feel when we play a part in other people's lives should be infectious and exhilarating. This encourages guests to relax and enjoy themselves; they will feel comfortable and will most probably want to return. (Never forget that we are in the only business in the world whose assets continually walk out through the front door!) Whatever you do for guests, just remember: you will also feel a lot happier if you see it as a way of indulging yourself. In other words, enjoy your guests.

Each hotel or establishment has its own well-defined personality, which is determined by a number of things: the culture of its geographical location; the style of its cuisine; its choice of tastefully appointed rooms and suites; and its own philosophy of service. It is the way in which this service is delivered that can ensure a happy guest, and one who will return. Well-trained, kind, courteous, confident and willing guest service staff will create the right atmosphere. With a little extra flair they can also create a memorable experience for their guests.

It could be argued that service is the way guests feel after they have been served! Throughout this book there are many suggestions and instructions as to how this service can be given and improved on. In Chapter 1 (page 2) it was suggested that numerous dress rehearsals, re-runs and 'takes' were what made a stage show or movie really great. Practice is essential. Guest service staff should take every opportunity to make a difference to someone else's life, and to demonstrate that true and real service comes from the heart. And remember: this business is like show business. Have fun and show that you enjoy giving service!

Be innovative. If you see some aspect of the service in your establishment that needs updating, changing or improving, take the necessary steps to make it happen.

If you want to know what more you can do to make the guest happy, try the direct approach: ask them. When they give you an answer, write it down straight away. This way the guest will realise that you are serious about the question. And don't forget to thank them!

Great service can be recognised by what the service-giver does, not by what they say they will do. Some of the suggestions that guests make may be very worthwhile: follow them up. If you succeed in implementing any of these as new ideas, let the guest know. Thank them in writing for their feedback. They will be flattered to be acknowledged and will no doubt return to the establishment, perhaps out of curiosity, to experience this new service initiative.

When a guest leaves your hotel or establishment, not only smiling but also confirming that they enjoyed themselves, then you can feel proud of yourself and your fellow staff members for having met and excelled their expectations. This is not just your product; it is your goal—a happy guest who will return!

Appendix: Competency Standards

Australian Standards

Throughout this book reference has been made to Hospitality Industry National Competency Standards. Those skills that are covered are listed below:

Unit	Occupational area
Unit THHADFB01A	Provide Specialist Advice on Food
Unit THHADFB02A	Provide Specialist Wine Service
Unit THHADFB03A	Prepare and Serve Cocktails
Unit THHADFB07A	Provide Silver Service
Unit THHBFB02/3A	Provide Food and Beverage Service
Unit THHBFB040	Provide Table Service of Alcoholic Beverages
Unit THHBFB08A	Provide Room Service
Unit THHBFB09A	Provide Responsible Service of Alcohol
Unit THHBFB10A	Prepare and Serve Non-Alcoholic Beverages
Unit THHBFB11A	Develop and Update Food and Beverage Knowledge
Unit THHBFO01A	Receive and Process Reservations
Unit THHBFO02/3A	Provide Accommodation Reception Services
Unit THHBFO07A	Communicate on the Telephone (Front Office)
Unit THHBFO10A	Provide Porter Services
Unit THHBH01A	Provide Housekeeping Services to Guests
Unit THHBH03/4A	Prepare Rooms for Guests
Unit THHBH05A	Launder Linen and Guests' Clothes
Unit THHBH06A	Provide Valet Service
Unit THHBTHS03A	Maintain Safety of Premises and Personnel
Unit THHBTHS04A	Manage Intoxicated Persons
Unit THHBTHS16A	Provide Lost and Found Facility
Unit THHCOR01A	Work with Colleagues and Customers
Unit THHCOR02A	Work in a Socially Diverse Environment
Unit THHGCS01A	Develop and Update Local Knowledge
Unit THHGCS02A	Promote Products and Services to Customers
Unit THHGCS03A	Deal with Conflict Situations
Unit THHGCS08A	Establish and Conduct Business Relationships
Unit THHGGA01A	Communicate on the Telephone (General Administration)

City & Guilds (British and Scottish) Standards

NVQs (National Vocational Qualifications) and SVQs (Scottish Vocational Qualifications) are accepted in over 100 countries around the world. The ones that this book is relevant to are shown in the table below. They are available at four levels.

Occupational area	Level 1: Operative	Level 2: Craft	Level 3: Supervisory or Advanced Craft	Level 4: Management Specialist
Porter Service	NVQ/SVQ			
Preparing and Serving Food	NVQ/SVQ			
Guest Services	NVQ/SVQ			
Reception	NVQ/SVQ	NVQ/SVQ		
Housekeeping	NVQ/SVQ	NVQ/SVQ		
Food and Drink Service	NVQ/SVQ	NVQ/SVQ		
Residential Service		NVQ/SVQ		
Bar Service		NVQ/SVQ		
Hospitality Service		NVQ/SVQ		
Hospitality Quick Service		NVQ/SVQ		
Front Office Supervision			NVQ	
Accommodation Supervision			NVQ	
Drinks Service— Advanced Craft			NVQ	
Food Service— Advanced Craft			NVQ	
On-licensed Premises Supervision				NVQ
Restaurant Supervision			NVQ	
Multi-skilled Hospitality Supervision			NVQ	
On-licensed Premises Management				NVQ

Occupational area	Level 1: Operative	Level 2: Craft	Level 3: Supervisory or Advanced Craft	Level 4: Management Specialist
Kitchen Management				NVQ
Restaurant Management				NVQ
Multi-skilled Hospitality Management				NVQ
Front Office Management				NVQ
Accommodation Management				NVQ

Glossary I: the language of champagne

The following glossary contains many of the words referred to in this book plus others that are frequently used in the hospitality industry.

AC See **Appellation Contrôlée**.

appellation Legal designation guaranteeing a wine by geographical origin, grape variety and production method. Champagne is the only *appellation* wine that does not state the AC formula on its label.

Appellation Contrôlée A government certification of a French wine guaranteeing that it originates from the particular geographical area specified on the bottle label and that it meets with government standards of production.

assemblage Blending of still wines from different villages. It often takes years to create a **cuvée** or blend ready for bottling and **second fermentation**. Also, one of two methods used to colour rosé champagne; still red wine is blended with white to produce the desired colour.

autolysis Enzymatic breakdown of dead yeast cells. This takes place in the wine after the **second fermentation**. It gives complexity of flavour.

balthazar Large bottle containing 12 litres, equivalent to 16 standard bottles.

blanc de blancs Champagne made only from the juice of white grapes.

blanc de noirs Champagne made only from the juice of black grapes.

brut Dry champagne, containing not more than 15 grams per litre of residual sugar.

CIVC Comité Interprofessional du Vin de Champagne: co-ordinating body that regulates grape growing and wine production in Champagne.

crémant Style of sparkling wine with a less vigorous sparkle than normal. Up till September 1994 this term was available only to champagne, but it is now used for sparkling wines from other parts of France.

cru Literally 'growth': the vineyards of a village.

cuvée The first 2050 litres of juice pressed from every 4000 kilograms of grapes— the highest-quality juice. Also a finished blend, usually a combination of many *crus*.

cuvée de prestige Top-of-the-range wine, usually vintage-dated, always expensive.

dégorgement Removal from the bottle of yeast sediment, left after the **second fermentation**. It is usually now done *à la glace*—by freezing the neck of the upended bottle so that the sediment forms an icy plug, which can then be easily ejected.

demi-sec Sweet champagne, containing between 33 and 50 grams of residual sugar per litre.

deuxième taille The final 206 litres of juice that may be pressed from every 4000 kilograms of grapes. Less fine in quality than the **cuvée** and the *première taille*, it is used for cheaper and sweeter champagnes.

dosage Amount of sugar added to finished champagne in the *liqueur d'expèdition*; it governs final sweetness.

dry/*sec* Medium-sweet champagne, containing between 17 and 35 grams of residual sugar per litre.

extra dry/*extra-sec* Medium-dry champagne, containing between 12 and 20 grams of residual sugar per litre.

grand cru Village rated at 100 per cent on the 'ladder of growths'; champagne made entirely from grapes grown in these villages may be labelled a *grand cru*.

grande marque Term describing the largest and most important champagne houses.

jeroboam Large bottle containing three litres, equivalent to four standard bottles; also known as a double magnum.

lattes Wooden slats used to separate layers of bottles during and after the **second fermentation**. During '*sur lattes*' ageing the wines acquire depth and complexity from contact with the **lees** from the second fermentation.

lees Coarse sediment, such as dead yeasts, deposited by a wine after **fermentation** (first and second).

liqueur d'expèdition Solution of sugar and wine added to champagne after **dégorgement**.

liqueur de tirage Solution of sugar, wine and yeast added to the finished blend when it is bottled, in order to provoke a **second fermentation**.

macération One of two techniques used to colour rosé champagne. It involves steeping a part of the pinot noir or meunier juice with the skins to leach out colour.

magnum Double-sized bottle containing 1.5 litres. The best size for champagne that is to be aged for a long period.

mare The capacity of a champagne press, equivalent to 4000 kilograms of grapes. Also the debris of pips, skins and stalks left after pressing and the spirit distilled from this debris.

methusalem Large bottle containing six litres. Equivalent to eight standard bottles.

millésime See **vintage champagne**.

mousse Froth of bubbles that results from the **second fermentation** in the bottle.

must Newly-pressed grape juice which is ready for **fermentation** in the bottle.

nebuchadnezzar Large bottle containing 15 litres, equivalent to 20 standard bottles.

non-vintage Champagne blended from several years and sold without a vintage date.

own label A common English term for champagne—one labelled with the name of the seller rather than that of the producer.

premier cru Village rated at between 90 and 99 per cent on the 'ladder of growths'; champagne made entirely from grapes grown in such villages may be labelled *premier cru*.

première taille The second pressing of the Champagne grapes.

prise de mousse Process whereby champagne acquires its sparkle; it takes place slowly inside the bottle during the **second fermentation**.

pupitre Two hinged boards containing 60 angled holes each, used for holding the bottles during ***remuage***.

racking Transferring wine from one container to another to separate it from its **lees**.

rehoboam Large bottle containing 4.5 litres, equivalent to six standard bottles; also known as a triple magnum.

remuage Riddling. The twisting, jolting and gradual inversion of the bottle in ***pupitres***. The aim is to gather the **second fermentation** deposits in the neck, ready for ***dégorgement***.

reserve wines Still wines of a particular vintage set aside and stored. They are used for blending in subsequent years.

salmanazar Large bottle containing nine litres, equivalent to 12 standard bottles.

sec See **dry/sec**.

second fermentation **Fermentation**, provoked by the sugar and yeast in the *liqueur de tirage*, which takes place inside the bottle. It causes the wine to acquire a sparkle.

vintage champagne Champagne made from the wine of a single, good-quality year. Also known as *millésime*.

Glossary 2: menu terms

This list has been compiled to help you understand some of the culinary terms used in restaurants. The definitions are based on international standards, both classical and modern. You may find that some chefs, managers and restaurateurs have a slightly different interpretation. However, the basics are very often the same, albeit with slight variations. The following list offers plenty of information plus some provoking definitions.

abalone 1. Large mollusc used in soups, **chowders** and Chinese/American dishes. 2. Large white mushroom with a slightly seafood taste.

accompaniment Condiment or extra dish offered by waiters or butlers with specific dishes. These accompaniments are usually traditional: e.g. mint sauce or jelly with roast lamb; mango chutney with curry; Parmesan cheese with pasta.

adrak (Ind.) Ginger.

agneau (Fr.) Lamb.

ail (Fr.) Garlic.

al dente (It.) Texture of food, such as pasta or vegetables, cooked so as to be firm and not soft when bitten.

à la carte (Fr.) A style of **menu** that prices each item separately.

à la crème (Fr.) With cream, added either before or after cooking.

allemande (Fr.) 'In the German style': usually with a garnishing of **sauerkraut**, mashed potato or smoked sausage.

aloo (Ind.) Potatoes.

amande (Fr.) Almond.

amandine (Fr.) With almonds.

amatriciana (It.) Hot and spicy.

amrood (Ind.) Guava.

anchovy Small, very salty fish.

anglaise (Fr.) Name given to simply-cooked dishes.

anguille fumé (Fr.) Smoked eel.

antipasto (It.) Mixed **hors d'oeuvres** comprising salami, **anchovies**, ham, small artichokes in oil, raw vegetables etc.

arborio (It.) Type of Italian rice used for **risotto**.

argenteuil (Fr.) Term applied to dishes featuring asparagus; named after a district in France.

aroma Fragrance or smell.

assiette (Fr.) Plate; the usual term used for seafoods, cold meats etc.

au bleu (Fr.) Very underdone (soft to the touch); applied to meat or to a specific fish dish, **truite** au bleu.

au four (Fr.) Cooked or baked in the oven.

au gratin (Fr.) Sprinkled with breadcrumbs and/or cheese and melted butter and browned under the grill.

au jus (Fr.) Usually refers to meat served in its own cooking juices, e.g. roast meat.

baak faahn (Ch.) Boiled rice.

baba (Fr.) A rich yeast-leavened cake, usually soaked in rum and sugar syrup and served with cream.

back of house The parts of the establishment not normally seen by guests, including the kitchens, administrative offices, housekeeping etc.

bagna cauda (It.) Hot **anchovy** dip served with **crudités** or raw vegetables.

baguette (Fr.) French breadstick.

bahmie (Indon) Fried **noodles**.

baklava (Gr.) Greek thin layered pastry made with honey and nuts.

ballotine (Fr.) 1. Small rolls or balls of meat or poultry. 2. A type of **galantine** served hot.

balsamic vinegar Matured, fragrant, sweeter wine vinegar used for more intense flavourings of dressings for fruit and salads.

basmati rice Long-grained rice used for Indian cooking.

bati (Ind.) Deep-fried pastries with spicy potato filling.

bavarois (Fr.) A rich custard of egg yolks, milk and whipped cream set with gelatine; various flavours.

bean curd Very bland curd made from soya beans, also called **tofu**; looks like soft cheese and used for protein instead of meat, chicken or fish. Popular for its level of flavour absorption.

béarnaise (Fr.) Rich butter sauce. A derivative of **hollandaise** sauce, with the addition of tarragon.

béchamel (Fr.) Basic white sauce made by the **roux** method with herb or onion flavoured milk.

beignets (Fr.) Deep-fried, puffed-up balls of **choux** pastry.

belle heléne (Fr.) Dessert with poached pears, ice-cream and hot chocolate sauce.

bercy (Fr.) Style of fish dish usually cooked in shallots, parsley, white wine and fish stock; sauce is reduced and butter added to coat the cooked fish.

beurre meunière (Fr.) **Beurre noisette** with lemon juice added.

beurre noisette (Fr.) Butter heated until brown and served very hot.

bhaji (Ind.) Any kind of vegetables cooked with hot spices.

bhajjias (Ind.) Small spiced batter fritters, usually vegetable, deep-fried.

bien cuit (Fr.) Term used for over-cooked steak.

bill of fare See **menu**.

biriani (Ind.) Saffron rice served with meat or fish (marinated in lemon juice and yoghurt) or lentil curry sauce.

bisque (Fr.) Thick creamy soup usually made with seafood.

black pepper Pungent dried berry, ground and used for flavouring.

bleu (Fr.) or **blue** Extremely rare (steak).

blini (Rus.) A type of traditional Russian pancake made with buckwheat flour and yeast.

blue vein Blue mould in blue or green cheese.

bocconcini (It.) Small balls of fresh white **mozzarella** preserved in whey to retain moisture. Bocconcini are served as part of an **antipasto** or in salads.

bockwurst (Ger.) Sausage resembling a large frankfurter.

bolognese (It.) Refers to rich meaty tomato sauce served with pasta.

bombe (Fr.) Frozen dessert, usually made with ice-cream, moulded in a rounded shape.

Bon appetit! (Fr.) Enjoy your meal! Good appetite!

botrytis Mould that affects grapes, producing 'noble rot'; dishes with this style of wine added will be sweeter in flavour.

bouillabaisse (Fr.) A fish stew made with a variety of fish, flavoured with herbs.

bouquet (Fr.) Term used to describe a distinctive and characteristic fragrance and usually referring to wine.

Brie (Fr.) Soft, creamy cow's-milk cheese with a soft, edible crust.

brioche (Fr.) Light, sweet bread dough baked in small, deep-fluted moulds.

brochettes (Fr.) Food grilled and served on a skewer.

bruschetta (It.) Baked or toasted slices of bread that have been brushed with oil and sprinkled with chopped herbs, usually basil, and served as an appetiser.

brunoise (Fr.) Mixed vegetable garnish, cut in tiny dice.

burghul (Mid-E.) Cracked wheat whose grains have been hulled, removed from their husks, steamed and cracked.

cacciatora (It.) Usually chicken in a tomato and wine sauce with chopped shallots and sliced mushrooms.

Caesar salad Salad consisting of cos lettuce, dressing, almost-raw eggs, Parmesan cheese, diced crisp bacon, **anchovy** fillets and **croûtons**, often served as a very substantial first course or a light main course.

café (Fr.) 1. Coffee. 2. Coffee-flavoured.

calamari (It.) Squid.

Camembert (Fr.) Soft cheese made from cow's milk with a soft, downy skin.

cannelloni (It.) Stuffed tubes of pasta.

carafe (Fr.) Glass bottle or jug used for serving water or wine.

carbonara (It.) Bacon, egg yolks and cream combined with **black pepper** and served with pasta.

carne (Sp.) Meat.

carpaccio (It.) Air-dried beef.

cassoulet (Fr.) A mixed stew of haricot beans and meats.

caviare Salted sturgeon's eggs, often served with **blinis** and vodka.

champignons (Fr.) Mushrooms.

chanterelle (Fr.) Edible mushroom with a rich yellow colour and a pleasant smell.

Chantilly cream Slightly sweetened, **vanilla**-flavoured whipped cream.

chapati (Ind.) Whole-wheat bread, which is puffy with air pockets when hot but flattens as it cools.

charlotte (Fr.) This can be a hot dessert consisting of layers of fruit and bread or sponge, or a cold dessert comprising a rich custard, whipped cream, fruit and sponge fingers.

Châteaubriand (Fr.) Thick cut from the whole fillet of beef.

chatni (Ind.) Chutney.

chaudfroid (Fr.) A creamy sauce containing aspic, which sets to form a jellied coating or glaze.

cheung gyun (Ch.) Fried **noodles**.

chilli con carne (Sp.) Spicy dish with minced beef.

chipolata Very small sausage.

chirinabe (Jap.) A dish of boiled fish and vegetables eaten with a soy dip sauce.

choron sauce A **béarnaise** sauce with fresh tomato **purée** added.

choux (Fr.) A light pastry made with an egg-enriched dough of piping consistency, used for **profiteroles** and éclairs. The hollow is filled with a sweet or savoury filling.

chow choi (Ch.) Stir-fried vegetables.

chowder Stew or very thick soup, usually milk-based, made with seafood and thickened with potatoes.

chow mein (Ch.) Fried **noodles**.

churros (Sp.) Small, crisp doughnuts fried in oil.

commis (Fr.) Assistant or trainee.

commis waiter Ordinary assistant waiter or trainee waiter.

compote (Fr.) Fresh or dried fruits cooked in a syrup and served hot or cold.

concassé (Fr.) Skinned and de-seeded tomatoes chopped in fine dice.

consommé (Fr.) Thin, clear meat soup.

corkage Charge made by establishments for opening bottles bought by customers.

coulibiac (Rus.) Salmon or fish pie.

coulis (Fr.) Meat juices or **puréed** vegetables or fruit served over, around or under the main ingredient.

coupe (Fr.) Shallow glass dish for serving cold desserts and sometimes seafood cocktails.

cover Term used for a place setting for one guest.

crème caramel (Fr.) Dessert made with eggs, sugar and milk, cooked in a caramel-lined mould, turned out and served cold.

crème fraîche (Fr.) Mixture of soured and whipped thick cream to which has been added lemon juice or vinegar to give a characteristic flavour to certain dishes.

créole (Fr.) A style of dish prepared with rice, peppers (sweet), spices and tomatoes with either chicken or fish.

crêpe (Fr.) Wafer-thin pancake, usually rolled or folded round a sweet or savoury filling.

crevettes (Fr.) Shrimps.

croissant (Fr.) Usually flaky, rich, crescent-shaped roll of bread or yeast-leavened pastry.

croustade (Fr.) A hollowed-out 'box' of fried bread filled with a savoury mixture.

croûte (Fr.) A round or slice of fried, baked or toasted bread on which savouries may be served.

croûtons (Fr.) Small cubes of toasted or crisply-fried bread served scattered over soup or used as a garnish, such as on **Caesar salad**.

crudités (Fr.) Raw vegetables.

crustacean Any of a group of mostly aquatic creatures including crabs, crayfish, **lobsters** etc.

dahi (Ind.) Yoghurt.

dal (Ind.) See **dhal**.

damper (Austral.) Bread dough made from flour and water and traditionally baked in the ashes of an outdoor camp fire.

dashi (Jap.) Broth.

dauh gu gai (Ch.) Stir-fried chicken pieces.

decant Pour liquor, usually wine, carefully without disturbing the sediment from a bottle into a **decanter**.

decanter Narrow-necked jug or stoppered bottle to contain **decanted** wine or port.

dégustation (Fr.) From *déguster*, which means to taste, to sip, to enjoy, to appreciate. So a **menu** dégustation could be interpreted as a series of many courses, perhaps with smaller portions, to provide an opportunity to taste or sample from the larger main **menu**.

demi-glace (Fr.) **Espagnole** sauce (brown), reduced by boiling fast to half the quantity for maximum flavour.

dhal (Ind.) Split pulses; a **purée** of split pulses.

diable (Fr.) Devilled; highly seasoned.

dijonnaise (Fr.) Usually refers to the inclusion of French mustard in the dish.

dim sum (Ch.) Small tea-house snack.

dolmades (Gr.) Stuffed vine leaves.

duchesse (Fr.) Name given to piped, creamed potatoes served either in individual portions or as a border around a dish.

dumpling Ball of dough, either baked or simmered in a casserole; it may be sweet or savoury and flavoured with sugar or herbs.

eggs benedict Poached eggs with grilled ham served on a toasted muffin with **hollandaise** sauce.

enchiladas (Mex.) Mexican dish consisting of a tortilla (maize pancake) spread with meat filling and served with spicy chilli and tomato sauce.

ensalada (Sp.) Salad.

entrecôte (Fr.) Steak cut from the boned sirloin; a true entrecôte is taken from between the ribs.

entrée (Fr.) Although in French this word literally just means 'beginning', it does not in the culinary sense mean the first course as some people seem to believe. The entrée originally signalled the first of the meat dishes, usually in the form of a heavier dish; therefore a great entrance was made—whence the use of this word internationally to signify the main course of the meal.

escalope (Fr.) Thin, boneless slice of meat, usually pork or veal, sometimes coated with egg and breadcrumbs, shallow fried.

espagnole (Fr.) Rich, thick brown sauce made with a **mirepoix**, forming the basis for many other sauces.

eye fillet Thick slice cut from the fillet of beef.

falafel (Mid-E.) An Israeli snack made from chick peas and spices.

farci (Fr.) Stuffed.

feta (Gr.) Greek cheese made from goat's milk.

fettuccini (It.) A type of ribbon-like pasta.

filet mignon (Fr.) Slice cut from the fillet of beef.

filo pastry (Gr.) A very thin type of pastry from Greece.

fine dining room High-class dining room with formal service, usually found in five-star hotels.

flambé (Fr.) To sprinkle food with brandy or rum and ignite it.

fleurons (Fr.) Small crescents of puff pastry used to garnish sauced fish dishes.

florentine (Fr.) Term that usually means the dish is garnished with spinach.

fondue (Fr./Swiss) A dish that consists of hot oil or a thick sweet or savoury sauce into which small pieces of bread are dipped for cooking or coating.

formaggio (It.) Cheese.

fragole (It.) Strawberries.

framboises (Fr.) Raspberries.

française (Fr.) In the French style.

frangipane (Fr.) Custard type of confection usually flavoured with almonds.

frappé (Fr.) Iced.

fritto (It.) Fried.

fritto misto (It.) Mixed vegetables or meat pieces deep-fried in batter.

fromage (Fr.) Cheese.

fumé (Fr.) Smoked.

funghi (It.) Mushrooms.

gado gado (Indon.) Vegetables cooked in peanut sauce with hard-boiled egg.

gai si tong mein (Ch.) Chicken **noodle** soup.

galantine (Fr.) Cold dish consisting of boned, stuffed, cooked meat usually glazed with aspic jelly.

galette (Fr.) Thin flat pastry cake or thin fried cake of mashed potato.

gambero (It.) Crayfish.

garam (Ind.) Descriptive term meaning 'hot and spicy'.

garam masala (Ind.) Aromatic mixture of ground spices.

gastronome An expert on good eating and drinking.

gâteau (Fr.) Rich, elaborate cake, usually having a sponge or pastry base with any type of cream and decorated with fruit and nuts.

gazpacho (Sp.) Cold soup made with tomatoes, garlic and peppers, thickened with breadcrumbs.

gelato (It.) Ice-cream.

génoise (Fr.) or **genoese** (Fr.) Type of sponge cake made by whisking the eggs and sugar and adding the flour and melted butter.

génoise sauce Mayonnaise flavoured with herbs and pistachio nuts.

ghee (Ind.) Soft clarified butter used extensively in Indian cooking.
glacé (Fr.) Glazed or iced.
gnocchi (It.) Little pasta **dumplings**.
gohan (Jap.) 1. Steamed rice. 2. Japanese name for meal.
goreng (Indon.) Rice dish.
gougère (Fr.) Cheese-flavoured **choux** puff served warm.
goujon (Fr.) Small strips of fish cooked in various ways, usually fried with bread
    crumbs.
goulash Thick meat stew of veal or beef, highly seasoned with paprika.
gourmand (Fr.) Lover of food; a glutton.
gourmet (Fr.) Expert in food and wine; an epicure.
gratinated As for **au gratin**.
grillé (Fr.) Grilled.
guacamole (Mex.) A dip made with avocado, lemon juice and garlic.
guéridon (Fr.) Trolley or table on which food is prepared and cooked in front of
    the customer in the dining room.
gulab jamun (Ind.) Sweet made of milk and flour, fried and served with syrup.

halva (Gr.) Sweet confection made from crushed sesame seeds and honey.
hashi (Jap.) Wooden chopsticks.
haute cuisine (Fr.) French cooking and service of a very high standard.
hoi sin sauce (Ch.) Sweet and spicy sauce made of soya beans, garlic and spices.
hollandaise (Fr.) Dutch style; name given to a rich sauce made with butter, egg
    yolks, peppercorns and vinegar, served with poached fish or
    vegetables.
hors d'oeuvres (Fr.) Any of the various savoury foods served as an appetiser.
hoummos or **humus** (Gr.) Thick paste made from crushed sesame seeds, chick
    peas, garlic and lemon juice.
huîtres (Fr.) Oysters.
hung siu paaih gwat (Ch.) Red cooked spare ribs.

ikra (Rus.) Caviare.
insalata (It.) Salad.
italienne (Fr.) In the Italian style.

jalapeños (Mex.) Sweet peppers.
jalebi (Ind.) Crisp-fried pastry twirls, soaked in heavy syrup and served hot or cold
    as a sweetmeat.
julienne (Fr.) Cut into long thin strips; usually vegetables or ham.
jus (Fr.) Juice.
jus-lié (Fr.) Thickened gravy.

kaeng phet kai (Thai) Chicken curry.
kaeng phet nua (Thai) Beef curry.
kai tom kah (Thai) Chicken soup.
kai tord (Thai) Fried chicken.
kaki (Jap.) Oysters.
kao pad (Thai) Fried.
kapi (Thai) Shrimp paste.
kartoffel (Ger.) Potato.
karui (Jap.) Salty, hot (taste).
kebabs Cubed meat and vegetables grilled on a skewer.
kheema (Ind.) Minced lamb or beef with onions, garlic, tomatoes, ginger and
    spices.

kilpatrick Sauce usually served with oysters made from bacon, tomatoes and Worcestershire sauce.

kofta (Ind.) Small balls of minced meat or vegetables, fried.

kohlrabi A cabbage with a turnip-shaped stem.

korma (Ind.) Meat in a rich but mildly spiced yoghurt sauce.

kulfi (Ind.) Ice-cream.

kulibyaka (Rus.) See **coulibiac**.

kung tord (Thai) Grilled king prawns.

langue de chat (Fr.) 1. A long, thin, finger-shaped crisp biscuit. 2. A chocolate.

lardons (Fr.) Strips of fat, either threaded into meat or added to certain dishes and garnishes.

lasagne (It.) Flat sheets of pasta layered with meat and cheese sauce.

lasun (Ind.) Garlic.

lié (Fr.) Thickened; applies to sauce.

lobster Large salt-water shellfish with flesh and taste like that of crayfish. Real lobsters are not found in the waters of the southern hemisphere.

lu chin nua (Thai) Spicy meat balls.

lyonnaise (Fr.) Usually describes dishes featuring onions.

macaroons Small almond cakes composed mainly of egg whites, sugar and ground almonds.

macédoine (Fr.) Mixture of diced fruits or vegetables.

Madras curry (Ind.) Very hot curry.

maître d'hôtel (Fr.) Steward, head waiter.

marengo (Fr.) Usually a chicken dish with crayfish, fried eggs, mushrooms and tomatoes.

marinade A blended liquid, usually wine, oil or vinegar, used to soak food before cooking.

marinara (It.) Usually denotes a dish that includes an ingredient from the sea.

marinate To soak in a **marinade**.

Marsala Sweet fortified wine from Italy, used in desserts.

masak lemak (Malay) A spicy vegetable dish.

masala (Ind.) Combination of spices.

mayonnaise Emulsified dressing of egg yolks and oil flavoured with vinegar, salt, pepper and mustard.

medallion A small round piece of meat, often veal.

medium rare Term used to describe degree of doneness of grilled steak. The steak should appear well browned, juices should be pink, and inside the meat should be red to rose pink. Just firm to the touch.

medium well Term for steak that is well browned on the outside with crisp fat, no juices; inside flesh should be faintly pink. Firm to the touch.

melba, pêche Term used for a dish with ice-cream, peaches and raspberry sauce.

melba toast Very thin toast made by splitting toasted bread and grilling the untoasted cut sides.

menu (Fr.) The range of items served in an establishment, usually printed on a card or written on a blackboard.

meringue A mixture of stiffly-beaten egg whites and sugar.

mesclun (Fr.) Mixed salad greens of varying types, textures and colours. Usually served with **vinaigrette** or French dressing.

meunière (Fr.) Term for fish that is lightly floured and shallow-fried.

milanese (It.) Term for **escalopes** of veal or lamb cutlets that have been coated in egg and breadcrumbs.

mille-feuille (Fr.) Thin puff pastry layered with cream or other filling.

minestrone (It.) Rich, thick vegetable soup containing some pasta.

mint sauce Thin sauce made from chopped fresh mint, sugar and vinegar.

mirepoix (Fr.) A mixture of diced vegetables (e.g. carrots, celery, onions) sautéed and used as a base for brown sauces or as a bed on which to braise meat.

miso (Jap.) Soya bean paste with delicate Japanese seasoning.

misoshiru (Jap.) Soup made with **miso**.

misto (It.) Mixed.

mornay (Fr.) Cheese sauce.

moules (Fr.) Mussels.

moussaka (Gr.) Layered meat (usually lamb) and eggplant with tomatoes and mushrooms, finished with a cheese sauce and baked.

mousse (Fr.) Light, frothy, sweet or savoury cold dish set in a mould with cream, gelatine and/or whipped egg whites (optional).

mousseline sauce (Fr.) Light savoury sauce made by adding stiffly-whipped cream to **hollandaise** sauce.

mozzarella (It.) Italian cheese, waxy in texture, which becomes stringy when cooked; it is a classic topping for **pizza**.

murgh (Ind.) Chicken.

naan (Ind.) Shaped unleavened bread, usually baked in a **tandoor** oven.

nachos (Mex.) Corn chips.

nam prik (Thai) Very hot chilli sauce used as a dip.

napolitaine (Fr.) Method of preparing **spaghetti** with a tomato and cheese sauce to which tomato **concassé** has been added.

nasi goreng (Indon.) Fried rice.

Neufchatel (Swiss) A soft white creamy cheese, low in fat with a sharp taste.

Newburg Sauce for shellfish containing cream, butter, sherry and egg yolks.

niçoise (Fr.) Usually describes a dish containing tomato, **anchovies**, olives, green beans and garlic.

niku (Jap.) Meat.

noisette (Fr.) Small, round, tender piece from a loin of lamb (bone and fat removed).

noodles Similar to pasta, usually cut into thin strips or rolled in thin sheets, sometimes used as wrappers in Chinese cooking. Most European noodles are made from wheat flour, potatoes or rice and mixed with eggs. Asian noodles seldom include eggs.

nuoc nam (Viet.) Salty, pungent fish sauce used in cooking. *Nuoc cham* is nuoc nam with chilli, garlic, sugar and lime juice added, used as a dipping sauce.

omelette (Fr.) Eggs beaten with seasonings and fried in hot butter until just set.

omelette espagnole (Fr.) **Omelette** containing pimentos, **anchovies**, tomato **concassé**, onions and olives.

osso buco (It.) Slices of veal shank braised in rich sauce with tomato and white wine and traditionally served with rice.

paella (Sp.) Dish of rice, vegetables, meat and fish (usually chicken, prawns, mussels etc.) flavoured with saffron.

pain (Fr.) Bread.

pain au chocolat (Fr.) **Croissant** containing chocolate.

pakhoras (Ind.) Small deep-fried chick pea fritters served with chutney.

palate 1. Word used to describe the sense of taste. 2. The upper part of the mouth.

panettone (It.) Northern Italian Christmas cake made from yeast and containing dried fruit, nuts and spices.

panna (It.) Cream.

papillote (Fr.) Greased paper wrapper or bag in which food is cooked.

pappadam (Ind.) See **poppadom**.

paratha (Ind.) Thick wheat bread, griddle fried in **ghee**.

parfait (Fr.) Rich frozen flavoured dessert.

Parmesan Originating from Parma in Italy this is a very hard, dry, strongly-flavoured cheese that is often used and served grated (Italian *parmigiano*).

pasto (It.) Meal.

pastrami (USA) Spiced, cured roast beef silverside rubbed in spices and black peppercorns. Sliced very thin, it is usually served on rye bread sandwiches with dill pickle.

pâté de foie (Fr.) Liver pâté.

pâté maison (Fr.) Pâté in the style of the house or restaurant.

paupiette (Fr.) Thin slice of meat or poultry that is stuffed, rolled and tied with string before cooking.

pavlova (Austral.) Soft, light **meringue** cake made from whipped egg whites and topped with fruit and cream.

pecorino (It.) Hard, pungent cheese made from sheep's milk.

Peking duck Mandarin duck with crisp crackling, rolled in a pancake and eaten with spring onion, cucumber and **hoi sin sauce**.

penne (It.) Type of pasta.

pepperoni (It.) Hard, spicy beef and pork salami (not to be confused with peperonie-preserved sweet peppers).

pesto (It.) Paste made by blending fresh basil, Parmesan cheese, pine nuts, garlic and olive oil.

petits fours (Fr.) Name given to all kinds of small fancy cakes or baked biscuits.

phulgobi (Ind.) Cauliflower.

pilau, pilaff, pilaw Seasoned rice cooked in stock or water.

piquant (Fr.) Sharp tasting.

pizza (It.) Plate-like base of dough covered with a topping which usually includes cheese, tomato and herbs. Often cooked in a wood-fired oven.

pla prio wan (Thai) Fish fried in sour sauce.

poisson (Fr.) Fish.

poivre (Fr.) Pepper.

polenta (It.) Type of porridge made with maize or semolina, cut into shapes, sprinkled with cheese and melted butter and baked.

pomme (Fr.) Apple.

pomme de terre (Fr.) Potato.

pomodoro (It.) Tomato.

poppadom/poppadum (Ind.) Light, wafer-thin, plain or spiced pancake, made from lentil flour, cooked in oil, usually deep fried and served as an appetiser or with curries.

porterhouse Large beef steak cut from the fillet end of the sirloin.

portugaise (Fr.) Term that indicates that tomatoes, oil and onions are featured in a dish.

poulet (Fr.) Chicken.

profiteroles (Fr.) Small hollow balls of cooked choux pastry usually filled with a sweet mixture.

prosciutto (It.) Smoked spiced Italian ham, usually served very thinly sliced.

provençale (Fr.) Dish characterised by the use of tomatoes, garlic, onions and olive oil.

purée (Fr.) Smooth pulp.

quennelles (Fr.) Small ball shapes of seasoned meat or fish mixture poached in stock or fried and either used as a garnish or served in a sauce.

quiche (Fr.) Open flan or pie filled with ingredients such as cheese, onions, tomato and bacon, covered with a savoury custard and baked in the oven.

raan (Ind.) Leg of lamb.
rack Joint of lamb cutlets from the rib loin, usually four to six chops in the rack.
ragoût (Fr.) Well-seasoned stew of meat and vegetables.
ramekin Individual dish used with savoury or sweet foods.
rare Light degree of doneness; brown outer appearance, no visible shrinkage, juices red and meat still soft to the touch.
rasam (Ind.) **Dhal** soup with tomatoes and green chillies.
ratatouille (Fr.) Cooked vegetable dish of onions, tomatoes, zucchini, eggplant and garlic.
ravioli (It.) A stuffed, square variety of pasta.
rendang (Indon.) Very hot spicy beef.
risotto (It.) Rice cooked with vegetables, and sometimes meat or fish, in wine or stock until all the stock or liquid is absorbed.
Roquefort (Fr.) Cylinder-shaped French cheese with greenish-blue marbling.
roti (Ind.) Type of flat bread served with curry.
rôti (Fr.) Roast.
roulade (Fr.) Stuffed roll of food. A light wrapper rolled around chopped ingredients in thick sauce; can also be sweet, e.g. chocolate or plain sponge filled with cream or sweet filling before rolling.
roulé (Fr.) Much the same as **roulade**.
roux (Fr.) Fat and flour mixture used as a basis for thickening sauces.

sabayon (Fr.) Consists of egg yolks beaten with liquor (wine or liqueur) and sugar.
salsa (It./Sp.) Sauce or combination of chopped and usually raw vegetables.
saltimbocca (It.) Thin rolled slices of veal and ham cooked in butter.
sambal (Indon.) Spicy side dish.
sambol (Ind.) Side dish or salad of vegetables or fruit served cold with spicy dressing.
samosa (Ind.) Crisp deep-fried pastries with savoury meat or vegetable filling.
sashimai (Jap.) Raw fish.
satay (Indon.) Cubes of meat grilled and served with a spicy peanut sauce.
sauerkraut (Ger.) Pickled white cabbage.
saumon (Fr.) Salmon.
sauté (Fr.) To fry quickly in a small amount of fat.
schnitzel (Ger.) Thin slice of veal or chicken flattened into a thin slice.
seekh kabab (Ind.) Same as **shish kebab**.
set menu A **menu** that allows no choice to the guests; all items are pre-selected. Usually used for functions.
shashlik (Mid-E.) **Kebab**.
shish kebab (Mid-E.) **Kebab** cooked on skewers.
shoyu (Jap.) Japanese-style soy sauce.
si ju kuo ha (Ch.) Stir-fried crab meat with black beans.
silver service Style of service in restaurants whereby the waiter apportions food and places it on to the guests' plates at the table.
sindhi gosht (Ind.) **Marinated** spicy casserole of lamb.
sorbet (Fr.) Water ice (flavoured).
soufflé (Fr.) Light fluffy savoury or sweet dish incorporating stiffly-beaten egg whites into a thick sauce before cooking.
soup du jour (Fr.) Soup of the day.
sous-chef (Fr) Deputy chef.
souvlaki (Gr.) Pieces of meat grilled on a pole or skewer and served with yoghurt or sharp-tasting sauce.

spaghetti (It.) Thin strips or strings of pasta.

spare ribs The rib bones of beef or pork, often **marinated** and baked.

spoom Water ice to which a double quantity of Italian **meringue** has been added.

steak tartare Minced raw fillet beef garnished with capers, minced onions and parsley and served in a mound with raw egg yolk in the centre.

Stilton Rich, creamy, blue-veined cheese. Traditionally served as a whole cheese, the cheese being scooped out with a specially-shaped spoon. Port is spooned into the hole created, thus improving the flavour and preserving the cheese at the same time. Usually served on cheese boards, but is preferred, because of its strong flavour, on a separate board. Named after its village of origin in England.

stroganoff (Rus.) Rich dish of beef or veal strips, flamed in brandy and cooked in a sour cream sauce.

suprême (Fr.) Breast of chicken, best cut of veal, chicken or fish; term used to describe the best or most delicate.

sukiyaki (Jap.) Dish of thin slices of meat, soya beans and vegetables cooked in soy sauce, sake and sugar.

sushi (Jap.) Cooked rice flavoured with vinegar and sugar.

table d'hôte (Fr.) Meal at a fixed price for three or four courses.

taco (Mex.) Crisp-fried corn shell.

tai (Jap.) Sea bream.

tandoori (Ind.) Style of cooking meat in a special oven.

tapas (Sp.) Snacks, canapés.

taramasalata (Gr.) Pinkish paste made from smoked cod roe, seasoned with garlic and lemon juice and served as an appetiser.

tarte (Fr.) Tart or pie.

tempura (Jap.) Pieces of fish or vegetables deep-fried in batter.

teppanyaki (Jap.) Meat, fish and vegetables traditionally fried or grilled at the table.

teriyaki (Jap.) Meat or fish marinated in teriyaki sauce and grilled.

terrine (Fr.) Food, e.g. pâté, cooked and served in a loaf-shaped mould and then sliced.

thermidor (Fr.) Style of cooking **lobster** using white wine and **mornay** sauce.

tiède (Fr.) Lukewarm.

tikka (Ind.) Small pieces of meat **marinated** in yoghurt and spices and then grilled on a wood or charcoal burning stove.

timbale (Fr.) Creamy mixture, usually meat and vegetables, baked in a cup or shaped mould.

tofu (Jap.) **Bean curd.**

tohng chou gu lou tunhk (Ch.) Sweet-and-sour pork.

tom yam (Thai) Spicy, clear soup flavoured with lemon grass.

tom yam kung (Thai) Spicy prawn soup.

tonno (It.) Tuna.

tortellini (It.) Stuffed rings of pasta.

tournedos (Fr.) Small steak cut from the centre of the beef fillet.

tronçon (Fr.) Slice from flat fish including the bone.

truffle 1. Edible dark and wrinkled fungus regarded as a delicacy. 2. Rich, creamy, soft sweet made with chocolate.

truite (Fr.) Trout.

tuiles (Fr.) Wafer-thin biscuits, usually containing almonds.

udon noodles Thick **noodles** made of wheat flour, popular in China and Japan. These noodles are often boiled in stock for flavour and served as a snack.

vacherin (Fr.) Layered **meringue** cake or **gâteau** filled with fruit and whipped cream.

vanilla Sweet, fragrant flavouring from the bean of the vanilla orchid.
velouté (Fr.) Basic white sauce made with fish or chicken stock.
vichyssoise (Fr.) Thick leek and potato cream soup usually served cold.
vinaigrette (Fr.) Oil and vinegar dressing for salads.
vindaloo (Ind.) Heavily-spiced sauce with vinegar.
vitello (It.) Veal.
vol-au-vent (Fr.) Small, round puff pastry case that is filled with a savoury or sweet filling and topped with a lid. Tiny ones are called **vongole**.
vongole (It.) 1. Clams. 2. Miniature vols-au-vent.

Waldorf (USA) Salad consisting of apples, walnuts and celery chopped and mixed with **mayonnaise**.
wasabi (Jap.) Japanese green horseradish.
watercress Green leafy vegetable grown on a freshwater bed, with small round leaves and a strong pungent flavour, high in iron.
wiener schnitzel (Austrian) **Escalope** of veal, cooked with egg and breadcrumbs.

yam (Thai) 1. Roast vegetable. 2. Tossed salad.
yang chow (Ch.) Special fried rice.
yu tsi tang (Ch.) Shark's fin soup.

zabaglione (It.) Beaten mixture of egg yolks, sugar and **Marsala** served warm or cold as a dessert.
zakuski (Rus.) Starter, **hors d'oeuvres**.
zest Thin, outer peel of a citrus fruit used as a flavouring.
zuppa (It.) Soup.
zuppa inglese (It.) English-style trifle.

Glossary 3: sporting jargon

Golf

ace A **hole-in-one**.

address To prepare to hit (the ball).

approach shot A shot made from the **fairway** towards the **green**.

birdie A score of one shot under **par**.

blind hole A **green** that the golfer cannot see when making an **approach shot** or driving a shot.

bogey A score of one shot over **par**.

bunker A sand trap, usually placed at the side of a **green**.

caddie A person who carries a golfer's clubs.

carry The distance a ball stays in the air after being hit.

chip A short, low **approach shot**.

cup The name given to the hole that the golf ball is intended to finally rest in.

divot A piece of turf dislodged by the player's stroke.

double bogey A score of two over **par**.

drive The first shot towards the **green**, generally from a **tee**.

eagle A score of two under **par**.

fairway The area of well-mown, hazard-free grass between the teeing-off area and the **green**.

flagstick The marker on the **green** indicating the location of the **cup** and the number of the hole.

green The area of short, well-tended grass surrounding the **cup**.

handicap The number of strokes that are deducted from the score of a weak player when they compete against a more skilful opponent.

hole-in-one The act of hitting a ball from the **tee** into the hole in one shot. Also called an **ace**.

hook A shot in which the ball veers in midflight to the left for a right-handed golfer, or to the right for a left-handed golfer.

iron A club with an angled, blade-like metal head.

links A golf course (derived from the Scottish word for the undulating land by the sea where the early courses were built).

nineteenth hole The clubhouse bar.

par The score an expert player in good weather is expected to make on a particular hole.

putter The flat-faced iron club used for making short, accurate shots on the **green**.

slice The opposite of a **hook**.

tee The wooden or plastic peg used to raise the golf ball off the ground before it is driven, or teed off.

wood A club with a hardwood head, used for long shots.

Horse-racing

birdcage The area where horses are paraded before a race begins.

colt A male horse that is younger than four years.

correct weight Confirmation, following weighing of the jockey and the saddle, that the horse did carry its allocated **handicap** weight. Bets can then be paid.

dead Term used to describe a track that will neither aid nor slow down a horse.

double A bet on two horses in different races in which the winnings and stake from the first race are placed on the horse in the second.

favourite The horse that has been most heavily backed to win a race.

filly A female horse that is younger than four years.

firm A shortening of odds being placed on a horse, indicating that **punters** are confident of its ability to win.

gelding A castrated male horse.

handicap The weight a horse is required to carry in a race, usually based on its previous performances.

horse A male horse that is more than four years old.

mare A female horse that is more than four years old.

mudlark A horse that performs well in wet conditions.

on the nod To bet on credit with a bookmaker.

outsider A horse that is given little chance of winning or gaining a place in the race.

parley Picking four winners and/or other place-getters in four races at the same race meeting.

punter A person who places bets on horses (or cards).

quadrella Picking the winners of four selected races.

quinella Picking the first two place-getters in a race but not necessarily in the correct order.

ring The betting ring, an area where the bookmakers take bets.

TAB Australian government-run betting system—initials for Totalisator Agency Board.

tote (short for 'totalisator') The form of betting in which the total amount that is bet on a race (less overheads and taxes) is divided among those betting on a winner.

trifecta Picking the first three place-getters in a race in correct order.

weight-for-age race A race in which all horses are given **handicaps** according to age and type.

yearling A horse, male or female, that is between one and two years old.

Sailing

aft Rear or **stern**.

anchor A metal structure (sometimes heavy) used to moor a ship to the sea bottom.

astern Rearwards or in reverse.

beacon A signal station, such as a lighthouse.

beam A ship's breadth at the widest part.

berth A bunk or sleeping-place on a ship or boat.

boom The long pole used to keep the bottom of a sail stretched.

buoy An anchored, floating object marking a navigable channel, showing the position of submerged rocks, etc.

cast anchor Lower the **anchor** overboard.

compass A device for determining direction, with a needle that points to magnetic north.

deck Any of the horizontal floors in a ship.

dinghy A small open boat driven by **oars** or **sails**, or a small inflatable rubber boat.

drop anchor Release the **anchor** overboard.

fore Front of a ship or boat

fore-and-aft sail A **sail** that is aligned **fore** and aft.

gps Global Positioning System, used to identify the location of a vessel.

head 1.Prominent outcrop of land into the sea. 2. Nautical term for toilet.

helm The tiller or wheel by which a ship's **rudder** is controlled.

keel The timber or steel structure along the base of a ship on which the ship's framework is built.

ketch A small sailing-boat with two **masts**.

knot Unit of speed used in ships and boats. One knot = one nautical mile per hour.

luff The forward edge of a **fore sail** or an **aft sail**.

mast A tall **spar** or hollow metal structure rising vertically from the **keel** or **deck** of a vessel and used to support the **sails**.

motor boat A boat, usually without **sails**, driven by a motor.

oar A pole with a flat blade at one end, used to row or steer a boat.

port The left side of a ship when facing forward.

rigging The ropes, etc. used to support **masts** and control the **sails** on a ship.

rudder A vertical piece of wood or metal hinged to the **stern** of the boat and used for steering.

sail A piece of fabric spread on **rigging** to catch the wind and drive a ship or boat along.

sheet Rope or chain attached to the lower corner of a **sail**.

sloop A sailing ship with one **mast**.

spar Any pole that supports the **sails** on a boat.

speedboat A fast **motor boat**.

spinnaker Large triangular extra **sail** on a racing **yacht**.

starboard The right side of a ship when facing forward.

stem Front of a boat or ship.

stern The rear end of a boat or ship.

steward A passengers' attendant on board ship.

tack The direction of a ship's course as determined by the position of its **sails** (**port** tack), or an oblique course towards but not directly into the wind.

trim the sails Adjust the **sails** to suit the wind.

winch Machine for hoisting by means of a cable that winds around a revolving drum.

yacht A light sailing vessel for racing.

Tennis

advantage The first point scored after **deuce**.

backhand A shot played with the back of the hand towards the tennis ball.

backspin The effect on the ball when a stroke makes it rotate in the direction opposite to its flight, causing it to bounce backwards or to stop after bouncing.

break point When the receiver needs only one point to win the game, and so break the opponent's serve.

deuce The score in a game when both players have won three points (in effect a score of 40-40). To win a game from a deuce, a player must win two consecutive points.

double fault A point lost by a server for serving two consecutive **faults**.

down-the-line shot A ball hit along the sideline deep into the corner of the opposing player's court.

drop shot A shot that is hit softly just over the net, usually played when an opponent is back near the baseline.

fault A service that is not valid because it fails to clear the net, lands outside the proper **service court**, or is adjudged a **foot fault** by the umpire.

fifteen The first point scored by a player in the game.

foot fault A **fault** caused when the service foot touches or crosses the baseline while the player is serving.

forecourt The section of the court nearest the net.

forehand A shot played with the palm of the hand towards the ball.

forty The third point scored by a player in a game.

game The basic scoring unit in a match. A player must win at least four points with a margin of at least two points to win a game.

lob A ball that is hit high above an opponent's head.

love Zero.

match point The point that, if won, will give a player the match.

rally When the players hit the ball back and forth several times before a point is decided.

service court The two subdivisions of each **forecourt**; a server must place the ball within the opponent's cross-court service court.

set A unit of a match; to win a set, a player must win at least six games with a margin of at least two games.

set point The point that, if won, will give a player the **set**.

singles A match played between two individual players.

thirty The second point scored by a player in a game.

tie-break The game played to decide a **set**, which is tied at six games all. The first player to score seven points with a margin of a least two points wins the tie-break and the **set**.

volley Return of the ball before it has bounced.

Bibliography

Australian Women's Weekly, 1990. *Household Manual*, Sydney.

Berlitz, Charles, 1995. *Passport to the World*, Signet Books, New York.

Boeckmann, Susia, 1995. *A Passion for Caviar*, Mitchell Beazley, London.

Braham, Bruce, 1985. *Hotel Front Office*, Virtue & Co., Coulsdon, Surrey.

Bremner, Moyra, 1989. *Modern Etiquette*, Random Century, London.

Brown, Graham and Hepner, Karon, 2000. *The Waiter's Handbook*, 2nd edn, Hospitality Press, Elsternwick, Victoria.

Carmichael, Sheena, 1989. *Good Business*, Hutchinson Business Books, London.

Carpenter, Sue, 1992. *Courvoisier's Book of the Best*, Random House/Vermilion, London.

Craddock, Harry, 1983. *The Savoy Cocktail Book*, Chancellor Press, London.

Dictionary of Food and Drink, 1983. Longman, Harlow, UK.

Fitzgerald, Helen, 1998. *Cross-Cultural Communication for the Tourism and Hospitality Industry*, Hospitality Press, Elsternwick, Victoria.

Ive, Josephine, 1992. *By Jeeves! The Essential Guide to Clothing Care, Valeting & Packing your Suitcase*, Josephine Ive, Melbourne.

Ive, Josephine, 1983. *Table Napkin Folding: An Elegant Art ...*, Josephine Ive, Winchester, Hampshire, UK.

Jefford, Andrew, 1991. *The Magic of Champagne*, Sainsburys, London.

Johnson, Hugh, 1997. *Pocket Wine Book*, Mitchell Beazley, London.

Kinton, Ronald, Ceserani, Victor and Foskett, Prof. David, 1992. *The Theory of Catering*, Hodder & Stoughton, London.

Mackay, Harvey, 1988. *Swim with the Sharks*, Little, Brown, Boston.

Mayle, Peter, 1986. *An Acquired Taste*, Bantam Books, London.

Montague-Smith, Patrick, 1970. *Debrett's Correct Form*, Headline, London.

Morgan, John, 1996. *Debrett's Guide to Etiquette and Modern Manners*, Headline, London.

Pease, Allan, 1982. *Body Language: How to Read Others' Thoughts by their Gestures*, Camel Publishing Company, North Sydney.

Phillips, Mary-Louise, 1988. *Food Service*, Polly Book Publishing Co., Balmain NSW.

Robinson, Jeffrey, 1996. *The Hotel*, Pocket Books, an imprint of Simon & Schuster, London.

Steabben, Russell, 1999. *The Australian Bartender's Guide to Cocktails*, 4th edn, Hospitality Press, Elsternwick, Victoria.

Sullivan, Jim, 1991. *Service that Sells!*, Pencom International, Denver, Colorado.

Willingham, Ron, 1992. *Hey! I'm the Customer!*, Prentice Hall, New Jersey.

Wise, Brian, 1991. *The Business of Hotel and Restaurant Management*, Hospitality Press, Elsternwick, Victoria.

Index